THE BLUE and GRAY in BLACK and WHITE

THE BLUE and GRAY in BLACK and WHITE

A History of Civil War Photography

BOB ZELLER

PRAEGER

**Westport, Connecticut
London**

Library of Congress Cataloging-in-Publication Data

Zeller, Bob, 1952–
    The blue and gray in black and white : a history of Civil War photography / Bob Zeller.
       p. cm.
    Includes bibliographical references and index.
    ISBN 0–275–98243–2 (alk. paper)
    1. United States—History—Civil War, 1861–1865—Photography.   2. United States—History—Civil War, 1861–1865—Art and the war.   3. War photographers—United States—History—19th century.   4. War photographers—United States—Biography.   5. Daguerreotype—United States—History—19th century.   6. Photography—United States—History—19th century.   I. Title.
    E468.9.Z45 2005
    779'.99737—dc22   2005017483

British Library Cataloguing in Publication Data is available.

Library of Congress Catalog Card Number: 2005017483
ISBN: 0–275–98243–2

First published in 2005

Praeger Publishers, 88 Post Road West, Westport, CT 06881
An imprint of Greenwood Publishing Group, Inc.
www.praeger.com

Printed in the United States of America

The paper used in this book complies with the
Permanent Paper Standard issued by the National
Information Standards Organization (Z39.48–1984).

10 9 8 7 6 5 4 3 2 1

The image on the title page is a portable developing box on a tripod created and used during the Civil War by Chicago photographer John Carbutt, who photographed Illinois troops in Kentucky in 1864. (Courtesy of Scully & Osterman)

*This book is dedicated to William A. Frassanito
and all of the other photo historians, enthusiasts, and collectors
who have advanced the field of Civil War photography in modern times.*

CONTENTS

ACKNOWLEDGMENTS

So many people have been so generous with their time and their images that this book seemed to come together as much from a group effort as from individual initiative. First and foremost, my heartfelt thanks go to John Beshears, my colleague in writing and personal editor, who added immeasurably to the text, and to John J. Richter, my chief photographic consultant, who worked computer magic on many illustrations. I am indebted to William A. Frassanito, who provided images, information, and a meticulous review of the narrative, as did Harvey S. Teal and Michael J. McAfee. Thanks to Stephen H. Sears for reviewing the narrative, and to Mark H. Dunkelman not only for his assistance but also for being the catalyst who brought this book into being. Jack Thomson was a gracious and enterprising Charleston host and guide, and he also lent images. John Kelley provided valuable information and the term "embedded with the troops" in connection with Andrew J. Russell's 1863 photography at Fredericksburg. Garry E. Adelman contributed an exhaustive review of the narrative, providing dozens of suggestions and pointing out more than a few errors and omissions. Harris J. Andrews and the late Brian C.

Pohanka became experts on Civil War photography while producing the Time-Life book series *The Civil War*, and I am in their debt for all they have shared with me over the years, particularly in connection with Russell's accomplishments. Michael O'Connor, project manager at Greenwood Publishing, contributed his keen visual talents to the photographic presentation and volunteered many hours of his own time to restore photographs to their original conditions. Larry and Jean Kasperek hosted me in Cleveland, and Larry provided research at the Western Reserve Historical Society. With partner Al Fuchs at Fuchs & Kasperek Photography in Cleveland, Larry also contributed original photography. My mother, Ruth W. Zeller, sponsored my research trips to Washington, D.C., and has always been an inspiring spirit. And a special thanks to Beth Bilderback at the South Caroliniana Library at the University of South Carolina for last minute help with images, as well as my wife, Ann G. Bailie, for her patience with the demands of this project, and for coming up with the title.

Of the thirty-seven collectors and institutions that contributed photographs, those who went beyond the call in providing unpublished or ultra-rare gems deserve special citation. They are Wes Cowan, the Huntington Library, Matthew Isenburg, the New York Public Library, Jeffrey Kraus, John J. Richter, Robin Stanford, David Wynn Vaughan, the Valentine Richmond History Center, Larry J. West, and George S. Whiteley IV.

Also, thanks to Sam Alston, Dan Beaman, Wm. B. Becker, Walt Bogdanich and Stephanie Saul, Keith Brady, Jim Burgess, John S. Craig and his invaluable Craig's Daguerreian Registry, Chris Fonville, Andy Fulks, Rob Gibson, William A. Gladstone, Mike Gorman, Nick Graver, Mike Griffith, Paula Fleming, John Hannavy, John Hennessy, Harold Holzer, Brooks Johnson, Lawrence T. Jones III, Lee Joyner, Bob Kalasky, Richard Kyle, Fuchs & Kasperek Photography, Ross J. Kelbaugh, David Humiston Kelley, Lee Kennett, Jennifer L. Kon, Howard Looney, Thomas and Beverly Lowry and The Index Project, Dennis McDougal, John McWilliams, Marie Melchiori, Wilbur E. Meneray, Chuck Morrongiello, Heather Milne, Mark Osterman and France Scully Osterman of Scully & Osterman, Mary Panzer, Dr. Ronald Rietveld, Charles Rhoden, John Ross, David Ruth, Tim Smith, Gary and Jimmie Stuckey, Bill Turner, Chet Urban, J. R. Wickersty, Susan E. Williams, and Mark Zimmerman.

I am grateful as well to Kim Bauer at the Abraham Lincoln Presidential Library, Randy Hackenburg and Richard Sommers at the Army Heritage and Education Center, Carlisle, Pennsylvania; Jane McGraw at Capital City Press;

Asterisk Typographics, Inc., Joe Struble and Barbara Galasso at the George Eastman House in Rochester, NY; Keith F. Davis and Sarah Wood-Clark at Hallmark Cards, Rebecca Ebert and Mary Ellen Hassler at the Handley Regional Library in Winchester, Virginia; Jennifer Watts and Erin Chase at The Huntington Library, San Marino, California; Carol Johnson, Mary Ison, Paul Hogrorian, and Eva Shade at the Library of Congress; Heather Milne at the Museum of the Confederacy; Michael Musick and Jill Abraham at the National Archives and Records Administration; Thomas Lisanti at the New York Public Library; Heather Staines and Lisa Pierce at Praeger/Greenwood; Pat Johnson at the Sacramento Archives and Museum Collection Center, Shire Publications; Mike Coker, Pat Kruger, Nic Butler, and Lisa Reaves at the South Carolina Historical Society; Meghan Glass, Teresa Roane, and Billy King at Valentine Richmond History Center, the West Point Museum; Anne Salsich, Ann Sindelar, Sarah Starr, George Cooper, and Jon Logue at the Western Reserve Historical Society; and Naomi Saito at the Beinecke Rare Book and Manuscript Library at Yale University.

Photographs that are uncredited are from the author's collection. Some images have been electronically restored to more closely resemble their original appearance.

Bob Zeller
Trinity, North Carolina
July 19, 2005

INTRODUCTION

In the autumn of 1862, a *New York Times* writer ducked under a placard above the door of the Mathew B. Brady photographic studio that read "The Dead of Antietam" and followed the crowd up the stairs in search of photographs that were the talk of Broadway. No larger than today's snapshot prints, the albumen prints from the Antietam battlefield portrayed a sepia-toned surfeit of death and gore, demanding both revulsion and awe from the viewer. They forever changed the unidentified reporter's perception of war. "These weird copies of carnage" left viewers hushed and reverent, he wrote. "Mr. Brady has done something to bring home to us the terrible reality and earnestness of war. If he has not brought bodies and laid them in our dooryards and along the streets, he has done something very like it."

The Antietam photographs were the first images of American dead on the battlefield, and their "terrible distinctness" altered at once the vision of the conflict for those on the home front. If no other artifact of the Civil War existed, if nothing had ever been said or written about the conflict, the Antietam photographs would be enough. Today, more than 140 years later, their impact is still visceral.

When Alexander Gardner, the Brady photographer who actually took the photographs, set up his camera amidst the carnage of Antietam, he surely was aware that he had achieved the photographic coup of the war. Gardner was at the right place at the right time, but his accomplishment was more than a serendipitous accident. It was built upon like-minded efforts by other professional photographers—men like Brady, Gardner, George Barnard, A. J. Russell, and Jacob F. Coonley from the North, and George S. Cook, J. D. Edwards, and Richard Wearn in the South. They had learned from one another how to overcome a welter of difficulties when they took to the field, in effect building on each other's work as they endeavored to capture the most dramatic and compelling scenes of the conflict.

The images from Antietam marked a pinnacle in the photography of the Civil War, but Gardner's accomplishment was by no means the only peak of achievement. In a steady series of triumphs from the beginning to the end of the war, photographers on both sides of the Mason-Dixon line attained new levels of photographic success. Some of these moments received considerable press attention, such as Southern pho-

The photographs of the dead of Antietam, including these Louisiana Confederates piled along Hagerstown Pike, gave Americans their first good look at the horror of war. A *New York Times* reporter wrote: "The living that throng Broadway care little perhaps for the Dead at Antietam, but we fancy they would jostle less carelessly down the great thoroughfare, saunter less at their ease, were a few dripping bodies, fresh from the field, laid along the pavement." (Library of Congress)

tographer George S. Cook's images of Maj. Robert Anderson and his officers holed up in Fort Sumter in 1861 and Cook's combat action photos of Union ironclads in action in 1863. Other moments, seemingly unforgettable in retrospect, such as the Haas and Peale battle image of the *New Ironsides* belching cannon smoke in Charleston Harbor in 1863, would become lost in time's passing and overlooked until rediscovered by modern researchers. Only in recent years have we come to understand the scope and immediacy of the remarkable series of photographs taken on May 3, 1863, by Capt. A. J. Russell, who was all but embedded with the troops during and after the second battle of Fredericksburg.

Graced with almost limitless opportunities, the photographers of the Civil War more than fulfilled the promise of their craft, producing thousands of images from the battlefields and camps,

including millions of portraits of soldiers taken in small town galleries and tent studios on muddy sutlers' rows. For every prominent photographer named in this work, dozens of unknown cameramen, mostly simple camp photographers, will remain unnamed, though their contributions of countless numbers of soldier portraits must be acknowledged.

No matter who the photographer was, following the army was no easy task. It was a great adventure, yes, but it was one that was fraught with hardship and danger, frustration and doubt. They were bedeviled by the same flies and gnawed by the same mosquitoes that plagued the soldiers in the trenches. They were hardened by the same soaking rains and baking sun that tormented the long lines of men trudging beside their wagons. In Charleston in 1863 and 1864, George S. Cook not only had to wage a daily battle

Connecticut militiamen engage in a "sham battle" in this rare, previously unpublished, damaged albumen print that probably dates from after the war. This was the first image pasted on the first page of the Civil War scrapbook assembled in the 1880s by Union veteran and sketch artist James E. Taylor, an avid Civil War photograph collector in the late nineteenth century. (This item is reproduced by permission of The Huntington Library, San Marino, California)

More than 600 of the most badly wounded soldiers from the battle of Antietam were cared for at Smoketown Hospital, a tent facility established
just north of the battlefield about two weeks after the fighting on September 17, 1862. The existence of six photographs of the hospital, including this image, was largely unknown until 1994.

In a hollow near Union Mills, Virginia, on the Orange and Alexandria Railroad, work crews of two U.S. Military Railroad trains posed for the camera of Capt. A. J. Russell. Just below the center of the image is Russell's photographic assistant, who stands by the developing tent, stereoscopic camera, and other equipment. (This item is reproduced by permission of The Huntington Library, San Marino, California)

GARDNER, Photographer.   M. B. BRADY, Publisher.

This previously unpublished Alexander Gardner photograph shows the headquarters tent of the U.S. Secret Service near the Antietam battlefield in October 1862. Lincoln posed for Gardner's camera in front of this tent, probably on the same day. The identities of the two sitting men are unknown, but lounging on the grass reading a newspaper is John C. Babcock, a Union spy (known then as a "scout"), who managed to appear in a half-dozen other Gardner photographs.

against Confederate inflation, he had to endure the daily bombardment of the city. Still, his customers came, and he was there to greet them.

As a whole, the photographic achievements of the Civil War far exceeded those of any other war in the nineteenth century. Despite the limitations of the wet-plate collodion technology of their time, the photographers established a level of sophistication and breadth of coverage that would not be surpassed until World War I, long after the era of the glass negative.

Photography worked its way into the fabric of American life in a relatively short time after its introduction in 1839, but at no time before the war did it reach the poignancy of understanding and illumination of tragedy as it did during the conflict. As the war began, card photographs and stereo views were being mass marketed for the first time, and photography came to serve as American home entertainment, satisfying the desire to collect both keepsakes of loved ones and mementos of celebrated people, places, and events.

Photographs not only bore witness to mankind's great and small moments, they also satis-

Twenty miles northeast of Nashville, at a military railroad bridge over the Holston River at Strawberry Plain, Tennessee, George Barnard used his stereoscopic camera in March 1864 to capture this image of the bridge that included his large-plate camera, manned by Barnard or an assistant. (Library of Congress)

fied its baser instincts. Inevitably, the camera went to places it wasn't supposed to go and took pictures it wasn't supposed to take, such as the Union fort on Alcatraz Island and Lincoln in his casket. The images were ordered to be confiscated, banned, and destroyed, but somehow prints would survive.

The story of the photography of the Civil War is recounted to some degree in every work on the Civil War that is illustrated with photographs. Yet, no single volume has existed, until now, where a coherent narrative replete with photographs serves to explore why the war came to be photo-graphed as extensively as it was, who took the photographs, how they did it, and what it meant.

The study and presentation of Civil War photography from after the Civil War until the past thirty years were haphazard at best, generally eschewing solid scholarship and characterized more by preservation and accumulation of images. The first books of Civil War photographs, exemplified in the ten-volume *Photographic History of the Civil War* published in 1911, sought mostly to present an abundance of images, and they succeeded grandly in doing so, despite many flaws in the textual information. The next phase came in the mid-twentieth century, when a new generation of Americans learned of Civil War photography through photo-rich, but flawed, biographies of its most famous figure, Mathew B. Brady, that gave him credit for far more than he actually did.

The modern era of Civil War photographic study started in 1975 with the publication of William A. Frassanito's groundbreaking *Gettysburg: A Journey in Time*, which redefined the study of Civil War photography and put Brady's considerable accomplishments in their proper perspective with those of the other notable war photographers. Frassanito's landmark work on Gettysburg and his subsequent studies were interspersed with other works, including the massive, six-volume *Image of War* series in the 1980s, biographies of nearly all the notable war photographers, and an abundance of smaller works and articles, many of which are cited in this book. Of no small consequence have been the dozens upon dozens of discoveries of previously unknown Civil War images that have surfaced in recent years and continue to show up with startling frequency—each exciting new find providing another unique window into our nation's greatest conflict.

The time has now come for a comprehensive study anchored by an appraisal of all that has been learned in the past thirty years—a time that has been distinguished by more specialized and intense study of the various aspects of American photography during the war. *The Blue and Gray in Black and White* marks the first attempt to synthesize all of the new information with the known facts from the past. Coupled with new scholarship, this work presents in a single volume, for the first time, a comprehensive verbal and pictorial narrative history of Civil War photography, both North and South.

The Blue and Gray in Black and White is not meant to close the door on the subject of Civil War photography but to open it even wider, presenting to future scholars a less cluttered landscape for continued exploration. As my friend and editor John Beshears has noted, "A photo-graph is like a dinosaur footprint. It is not a complete history itself, but a moment in time." These moments of time from the war are so numerous and so visually rich, a vast amount of historical information remains to be gleaned from them.

The images herein are not designed merely to supplement the text but to add their own dimension to the work. Some show the wide use and application of photography; others are examples of the most notable photographic accomplishments. More than a few are exciting new finds and are identified in captions as previously unpublished or "published for the first time." This notation is to indicate that the image has never been published in a book or magazine. It is not meant to discount the fact that the photographs were "published" at the time they were made and sold in the form of albumen prints pasted onto cardboard mounts.

After the war ended, Alexander Gardner wrote in a preface to his masterwork *Gardner's Photographic Sketch Book of the Civil War*, "Verbal representations of such places, or scenes, may or may not have the merit of accuracy; but photographic presentments of them will be accepted by posterity with an undoubting faith." Gardner was reiterating an oft-repeated theme in the writings of early American photography: a photograph was an incontrovertible form of reality that presented a level of truth and accuracy unattainable by any other means. No sketch or written account could match its veracity. The irony is that few fields of Civil War study have been so infected over the years by so much misinformation and myth as Civil War photography. The pervasiveness of misinformation is underscored by the fact that Brady has been credited in some works as having taken nearly every Civil War photograph and discredited in other works as having taken none at all. As this narrative explains, the truth lies somewhere in the middle. Most of the myths and misconceptions have been corrected in recent years, particularly in Frassanito's works, but the niche that remained to be filled was that of a single, basic overview that attempted to sort fact from fiction over the broader story of Civil War photography.

The modern viewer of Civil War photographs cannot help but be moved by the expressions of raw humanity staring back through time. It is all there, the entire tapestry of what it meant to be a society at war. There is the defiant glare of the youthful Rebel, the doleful look of the armless veteran, and the grizzled look of the bewhiskered general, brow furrowed and pinched by the grim slaughter over which he knows he must soon preside.

From its awe-inspiring introduction a brief twenty-two years before the Civil War, photography matured with such amazing speed that it became a tool powerful enough to take on the daunting task of chronicling one of the most consequential wars of modern times. Some of the men who became the war's greatest photographers are the same men who nurtured photography through its infancy and brought it, broad-shouldered and vigorous, to the doorstep of the conflict. These men could trace their roots back to the very dawn of American photography. This is where we begin their story.

1

THE ERA OF THE AMERICAN DAGUERREOTYPE

As New Yorkers settled into the Christmas season of 1839, an exhibition opened on December 20 in the Granite Building at Broadway and Chambers Street that changed the life of a twenty-year-old civil engineer named Edward Anthony. On the wintry day of his visit, Anthony could scarcely have known where the spark of excitement caused by that exhibition would lead him. Soon, he and a handful of others found themselves on a path of technological and entrepreneurial innovation that not only changed forever the way mankind viewed the world but also fundamentally altered the way individuals saw themselves.

What Anthony saw was a modest display of only about thirty items—each a simple, silvered plate of copper that from a distance had the appearance of a small, rectangular mirror, but up close revealed a sight so astonishing that the journals of the day struggled to find words to fully articulate their awe.

"Wonderful wonder of wonders!!" exclaimed *The New Yorker*.[1]

Each plate held a scene that shimmered elusively through the mirrored reflection beaming from the silver surface. These were among the first photographic images, although they were known as daguerreotypes rather than photographs. Some showed street scenes in Paris; others captured still life arrangements. Several of the daguerreotypes had just been made in New York and showed images of the city that were nothing short of perfect, with every building, each window, and every cornice, every last detail, in precise, exact perspective. It was as if the reality reflected on the surface of a mirror had somehow been captured and preserved forever. "Their exquisite perfection almost transcends the bounds of sober belief," reported *The Knickerbocker*.[2]

To a world that had known only paintings and drawings, photography provided exact, unvarnished images from life. Artists worried that it foreshadowed the end of painting. To the less educated, it invoked suspicions of black magic. Almost everyone had trouble saying "daguerreotype" (dag-ear-oh-type). To a learned young man such as Anthony, who had graduated from Columbia University in 1838, the object was so captivating that it sparked an immediate desire to learn how to make one. Late in his life, long after Anthony had built the largest photographic supply house in the United States and almost twenty years after he had published Civil War photographs by the thousands, he recalled in 1883 how that first sight of a daguerreotype had affected him:[3] "I immediately became an enthusiastic amateur, and set about manufacturing an apparatus to take daguerreotypes. This I did at large expense—the camera, lens and all costing a sum total of twenty-five cents. With this crude instrument I amused myself by taking pictures out of the back windows."[4]

Anthony was not the only Civil War photographic entrepreneur who began his career at the very dawn of photography. Other young and spirited Americans were drawn to the new art as well. An intense, red-haired, teenaged artist with thick glasses named Mathew B. Brady would soon become the best-known daguerreian artist in the United States. Brady's name would also become synonymous with Civil War photography, and he would receive credit not only for his own work but also for the images taken by nearly every other Civil War photographer.[5]

In late 1839 or early 1840, a thirty-one-year-old German immigrant named Philip Haas may have set aside his profession as a skilled lithographer and print publisher in Washington, D.C., to travel directly to Paris to learn the new art. Haas was one of the earliest resident daguerreian artists in the nation's capital and was probably the first to produce a lithograph from a daguerreotype, which he did in 1843. Twenty years later, as the Union Navy unleashed a thunderous bombardment on Confederate-held Forts Sumter and Moultrie in 1863, Haas and his wartime partner, Washington Peale, captured an actual scene of battle as the smoke from the booming cannons of the U.S.S. *New Ironsides* spread across the water and drifted hundreds of feet into the salty coastal air.[6]

Just as the daguerreotype captivated Brady and Anthony in New York, and Haas in Washington, in New Orleans it became the passion of a young Connecticut orphan named George S. Cook. Cook had left home at fourteen to explore the world, making his way southward through

New Jersey, eventually grabbing itinerant jobs on riverboats of the Mississippi and Ohio rivers before settling in New Orleans and becoming a daguerreian artist by 1843. Two decades later, at the height of the Civil War, Cook was one of the few Southern photographers still in business, enduring almost daily bombardment in Charleston, South Carolina, to keep the doors open to his thriving studio. On an early September day in 1863, Cook took time away from his King Street gallery to make his way out to Fort Sumter, where by happenstance he became history's first combat photographer—the first photographer to capture an image of enemy operations while himself under fire.[7]

Anthony, Brady, Haas, Cook—all were young, ambitious men caught up in the fervor of American capitalism on the eve of a glorious new era of progress and invention. The daguerreotype was not only an intriguing new art form, but it was also a new way to make a living. These men and thousands of other Americans, including several dozen African Americans and almost 250 women, embraced the new invention with an unbridled passion. These early photographic pioneers blazed a trail marked by rapid improvements and innovations that put America at the forefront of the development of photography. The photographers themselves would develop a fraternal bond on a national scale, linked by common goals, interests, and controversies. They kept in touch through correspondence, exhibitions, and competitions and, beginning in 1851, by reading photographic trade periodicals that included gossip columns filled with news and notes about their contemporaries.[8]

From the beginning, Anthony, Brady, and other leading photographers viewed their craft as being more than a mantelpiece nicety. They recognized that photography represented a new and powerful tool to be placed in the service of history. They purposefully began arranging sittings for the great statesmen and celebrities of the day, capturing portraits with their cameras. They also began to make daguerreotypes of the momentous scenes and events of their times.

The invention of practical photography was, by all reckoning, a miraculous achievement. It was closely seconded, however, by the speed with which photography progressed from a parlor room curiosity to a powerful and indispensable medium that illuminated, as never before, the human experience. It is doubtful that Anthony, as awed as he was by what he saw, could have realized that the seeds of wonder that he carried from that 1839 New York exhibition would find such fertile ground in which to grow. But grow they did, and, in a phenomenally short period of time, photographers, their gear, and studios became as familiar on the American landscape as blacksmiths or a team of mules.

By the eve of the Civil War, only twenty years after Anthony's epiphany, photography had undergone so many rapid changes and developments that the daguerreotype was relegated to the curio cabinet of quaint obsolescence. By 1861, America's leading photographers, spurred by the dual motive of preserving history and making money, were not only equipped with the latest cameras and equipment but now had the means to mass market their images and offer them for sale nationwide through mail-order catalogs and other dealers. Whether the war was to be long or short, the conflict promised to be the greatest spectacle of their lives, and they resolved to chronicle it with their cameras.

Thirty years after the war, in his only extensive published interview, an elderly Brady explained, "My wife and my most conservative friends had looked unfavorably upon this departure from commercial business to pictorial war correspondence, and I can only describe the destiny that overruled me by saying that, like Euphorion, I felt that I had to go. A spirit in my feet said 'Go' and I went."[9]

Between 1840 and the end of the Civil War, Anthony and kindred spirits were probably too busy innovating and making money to reflect on how profoundly photography tapped into one of the deepest wellsprings of human longing: the desire to chronicle the human experience and the world around us. This fundamental trait is rooted in the earliest annals of intelligent man, stretching back more than thirty thousand years to the ancient cave paintings of France and Italy. In this light, it is not surprising that the antecedents of modern photography extend far back into time as well.[10]

For centuries, man had known and worked with the essential elements of photography—the camera obscura and light-sensitive materials such as silver. The camera obscura, which was the forerunner of the photographic camera, had existed for several hundred years before the invention of photography. Its underlying principle had been known since the fifth century BC, when the Chinese philosopher Mo-Ti wrote of a "locked treasure room" and its display of an inverted image that came from the outside and through a tiny opening. The camera obscura is that "treasure room"—a dark box or enclosed area with a small hole on one side that takes in light from the outside. The light beams through the hole and projects, on the opposite wall, a view of the outside scene that is inverted and laterally reversed.[11]

The camera obscura remained an obscure plaything of artists and scientists until a wealthy Frenchman, Joseph Nicéphore Niépce (pronounced *knee-yeps*) entered the scene. Niépce, as had countless artists, inventors, and scientists before him, became intrigued by the notion that the picture produced in the camera obscura could somehow be captured and then permanently fixed on some form of light-sensitive material. In 1826, after years of trial and error, Niépce's efforts paid off when he created a barely visible image on a polished pewter plate coated with a mildly light-sensitive bitumen of Judea. It is considered the world's first photographic image, the exposure having taken eight hours. Niépce called his image a "heliograph," and it dimly displays the scene from a second-floor window at Gras, the Niépce family estate in Burgundy.[12]

In 1835, nine years after Niépce's initial success, an inventive and inquisitive Englishman of landed gentry, William Henry Fox Talbot, created a rudimentary form of the photographic negative, which Talbot called a photogenic drawing. Though mostly overlooked during the early years of the art, Talbot's invention was the first form of photography accomplished in the United States. In the spring of 1839, John Locke, a professor of the Medical College of Ohio, successfully duplicated Talbot's method and displayed a "few small specimens" of his photogenic drawings in a Cincinnati bookstore.[13]

Talbot's invention, however, would have to wait its turn because of the achievements of a Frenchman, Louis Jacques Mande Daguerre, who had also become obsessed by the idea of permanently fixing the image reflected in the camera obscura. The beauty, clarity, and detail of the eponymous daguerreotype would set Daguerre's process apart and establish him as the inventor of the first fully realized form of photography.

Daguerre knew of Niépce's work, and, in 1829, the two men entered into a wary partnership. By then, Niépce was experimenting with two essential keys to the daguerreotype—copper plates coated with a highly polished silver plating, and fumes of iodine to create a highly light-sensitive coating on the silver plating. But he remained unable to permanently fix the image. In 1833, at age sixty-eight, Niépce died suddenly of a stroke, and his name and accomplishments were all but forgotten by history until photo historian Helmut Gernsheimre discovered his earliest heliographs in 1952.[14]

By 1835, Daguerre had discovered that fumes of mercury would bring out the latent image on the silver plate. He could take pictures, but still could not preserve them. After two more years of work, he solved that final problem in 1837 with the salt from his dinner table. When Daguerre bathed the exposed plate in a solution of hot salt water, the silver iodide on the surface stopped reacting to light. After centuries of dreaming, more than two decades of serious experimenta-

tion, and no small measure of frustration, a practical, repeatable, and marketable form of photography came into being.[15]

In early 1840, Edward Anthony sought out the painter and inventor Samuel F. B. Morse, who is considered the father of the American daguerreotype, and arranged to take daguerreotype lessons. Morse charged from $25 to $50 for the course of instruction (about $450 to $900 in 2005 dollars). M. B. Brady was probably among Morse's students in 1840 and may have become acquainted with Anthony at that time. Morse likely was happy to receive the teaching income because his other experiments had left him strapped for cash, and he needed more money to continue perfecting his own premier invention, the electromagnetic telegraph.[16]

Morse probably told Anthony, Brady, and his other students about how he became personally acquainted with Daguerre. Morse was in Paris during the winter of 1838–1839 to demonstrate his electromagnetic telegraph to the French Academy of Sciences and to seek foreign patents. When Daguerre's remarkable invention was revealed in newspapers in January 1839, Morse was caught up in the excitement that spread through the city and sought an audience with his fellow inventor. Morse wrote his brother that the "two great wonders of Paris just now" were his telegraph and Daguerre's daguerreotypes.[17]

On March 7, 1839, just before Morse returned to New York, he met with Daguerre and saw a daguerreotype for the first time. "It is one of the most beautiful discoveries of the age," he wrote in a letter published in the *New York Observer*. "The exquisite minuteness of the delineation cannot be conceived. No painting or engraving ever approached it."[18]

Thanks to Morse and a smattering of others, the genie was out of the bottle. The Frenchman's process flourished around the world, particularly in the United States, and the first fifteen years or so of American photography was the era of the daguerreotype. Talbot's invention was overshadowed by Daguerre's and would remain so through the 1840s, even though Talbot developed a new and better way of making negatives and positives in 1841 that he called the calotype process. By the late 1850s, however, improvements in photographic negatives and positive prints put Talbot's invention at the forefront of a new era of photography and made the daguerreotype all but extinct. One of the obvious advantages of Talbot's process was that photographs could be mass duplicated and mass marketed, which occurred just in time for the Civil War. The daguerreotype may have vanished by that time, but the roots of Civil War photography came out of the daguerreian era and coursed through the lives of the men who made the pictures.

The first newspaper documentation of an American daguerreotype appears in the September 30, 1839, edition of the *New York Morning Herald*, which reported that "a very curious specimen of the new mode, recently invented by Daguerre in Paris," was on display at James Chilton's pharmacy at 263 Broadway. The daguerreotype, which showed a part of St. Paul's Church, had been made three days earlier by one D. W. Seager, who played a key role in the introduction of the daguerreotype in America. No one knows how Seager mastered the art so quickly, but he dropped out of the scene almost as quickly and mysteriously as he appeared.[19]

The details of Daguerre's process soon spread, and in Philadelphia on October 16, 1839, Joseph Saxton, a curator at the U.S. Mint, used a converted cigar box to make a small daguerreotype of the Philadelphia Arsenal and the Central High School. This image survives as the earliest extant American photograph.[20]

When the daguerreotype was introduced, portraiture was considered all but impossible because it took up to fifteen minutes to expose a plate, and it was thought that no one could hold still for the length of the exposure. In the fall of 1839, however, several American daguerreian experimenters succeeded, almost simultaneously, in making portraits; who took the first is still a matter of debate. For portraiture to become truly practical, the exposure time had to be reduced, and in early 1840, experimenters in Philadelphia discovered that bromine could be used to accelerate the exposure time. In March of that year, the first commercial daguerreotype studio opened in New York, and before year's end, studios opened in Boston, Philadelphia, and Charleston, South Carolina. They advertised the exposure time as being a mere thirty seconds. Family portraits, which had been the domain of the wealthy in the form of paintings and artwork, were now accessible to nearly everyone.[21]

A new industry was born in the 1840s as daguerreian studios opened throughout the United States. American business geared up to provide the necessary chemicals, ever-improving cameras, silver-clad copper plates by the thousands, the glass and metal mats used to cover the image, and the small leather and wood cases that were used to house the images. Beginning as early as 1840, traveling daguerreian artists visited smaller communities not large enough to support their own studio. By the hundreds and soon by the thousands, families and people from all walks of life would visit the gallery in their town, or the traveling artist's studio, to have their likenesses taken. By 1853, it was estimated that 3 million daguerreotypes were being taken annually, the vast majority of those being personal portraits taken of the sitter, for the sitter.[22]

Reproduction of an existing daguerreotype was a challenge, but as early as 1840, daguerreotypes of famous people and notable scenes were either being copied onto other daguerreotype plates or converted into more reproducible forms of communication—lithographs and engravings. The latter were sold individually as prints or reproduced in books and periodicals. The use of photography in the mass media had thus begun, mostly as portrait engravings of daguerreotypes published in illustrated periodicals, but it would be 1873 before a photograph itself could be printed as a halftone reproduction in a newspaper.[23]

Edward Anthony gained his greatest fame for building E. & H. T. Anthony & Company, a photographic print and supply house that was the Kodak of its day, but he was a daguerreotype artist before he was a supplier. Anthony was the first to successfully take daguerreotypes on a wilderness expedition and the first to use a daguerreotype camera to visually document a part of the United States.

During the summer of 1840, the federal government asked Anthony's former professor, James Renwick, to survey the Maine wilderness to establish the boundaries between the United States and Canada. Renwick hired Anthony to join the 1841 expedition with his camera. Anthony wrote more than forty years later:

> Professor Renwick requested me to take a daguerreotype apparatus on the survey, and take views of the highlands, which would place their existence beyond dispute. I did so, and though the facilities for making views in the wilderness were very poor at that time, yet I succeeded in taking a number of the objects required, which were copied in water colors, and deposited in the archives of the State Department at Washington.

In 1844, a year before M. B. Brady began exhibiting the daguerreotype portraits of "illustrious" Americans that would bring him fame and fleeting fortune, Edward Anthony and his partners led the way in this Gem business directory advertisement with the first comprehensive list of photographic portraits of prominent Americans.

Today, Anthony's work survives at the National Archives and Records Administration in the form of five pen and ink drawings, although the daguerreotypes themselves are not known to exist.[24]

Although M. B. Brady's pre-war fame was largely built on his promotion of a gallery filled with the portraits of famous Americans, it was Anthony who pioneered that concept, too. In 1842, two years before Brady opened his first gallery, Anthony co-founded Anthony, Edwards & Company in Washington, D.C., and began taking daguerreotypes of members of Congress and other famous people. In 1844, as Brady was just getting started with his "Daguerreian Miniature Gallery" at 205–207 Broadway, Anthony, Edwards & Company already had its own "National Miniature Gallery" at 247 Broadway featuring daguerreotype portraits of some 300 American notables and celebrities on display, with copy daguerreotypes available for purchase.[25]

But the business of selling actual copy daguerreotypes of celebrities paled in comparison to the business of selling celebrity engravings based on daguerreotypes, which were far easier and less expensive to mass produce. In Washington, Philip Haas pioneered that business, and Anthony, Edwards & Company soon followed, along with other leading daguerreian artists. In March 1843, Haas took daguerreotypes of former president John Quincy Adams and then created lithographs from those images, thus becoming the first publisher in the United States known to produce a lithograph directly from a daguerreotype. Haas produced lithographs of his daguerreotypes of John C. Calhoun, Henry Clay, James K. Polk, and others before moving to New York and establishing a daguerreian gallery there in 1844, where he continued making and selling celebrity lithographs.[26]

In 1843 or 1844, Anthony's company also began making engravings from daguerreotypes. Anthony's most popular engraving was an 1845 rendering of Henry Clay's farewell address to the U.S. Senate in 1842. It showed visages of every member on the floor of the Senate, and a

In their quest for celebrity portraits, Edward Anthony, possibly M. B. Brady, and other daguerreian artists journeyed to Tennessee in the spring of 1845 to capture the likeness of Gen. Andrew Jackson before his death on June 8. This profile of the seventy-eight-year-old former president probably was taken by Anthony or either Frederick or William Langenheim. (Library of Congress)

number of dignitaries in the gallery; individual daguerreotype portraits were used to reproduce the faces of almost 100 people. Anthony was also one of several daguerreians who traveled to Tennessee and took daguerreotypes of former president Andrew Jackson at his Hermitage plantation several months before his death in June 1845.[27]

By then, Anthony was winding down his brief career behind the camera and branching into daguerreotype materials. In 1847, Anthony severed all ties with his previous partners and moved into the same building as Brady at 205 Broadway to sell engravings and daguerreotype supplies. As Brady's growing collection of national and international awards and celebrity portraits further enhanced his reputation as

New York's leading daguerreian artist, Anthony devoted his energies to managing what soon became the country's largest photographic supply house. He also became the leading spokesman and advocate of the new trade.[28]

Brady had established himself as one of the leading daguerreians almost as soon as he went into business. In 1844, the same year he opened his New York gallery, Brady won the top prize for a daguerreotype portrait at the annual fair of the American Institute. In 1845, taking a cue from Anthony, Brady "formed the project of collecting all the portraits of distinguished individuals he could induce to sit for the purpose, with the intention . . . of making in the end a more complete collection than had ever before been made of the distinguished men of the nation," the *Photographic Art-Journal* reported. In 1891, Brady himself recalled, "From the first I regarded myself as under obligation to my country to preserve the faces of the historic men and mothers."[29]

The Brady National Daguerreian Gallery soon became the premier studio in New York. It was more than a place to go to have one's portrait made; it was a lavishly appointed portrait museum that showcased the new art of the daguerreotype. In exchange for a free daguerreotype, most celebrities accommodated the engaging and purposeful young daguerreian artist with a sitting. Brady's gallery was far removed from the simple studios of most daguerreian artists, who, like the town blacksmith or dry goods merchant, served a local clientele.

A world apart from Brady was George S. Cook, who spent his early photographic career as an itinerant daguerreian artist. Cook had begun his daguerreian career sometime between 1840 and 1843 in New Orleans. In October 1845, Cook returned to Newark, New Jersey, where he had been raised by his maternal grandmother a decade earlier after the deaths of his parents. In Newark, Cook made seventy-five daguerreotypes and took in $137 between October 4 and October 31, then packed up and headed back to the South. Always a meticulous recordkeeper, Cook kept a detailed account book that showed he made $174.75 in Vicksburg, Mississippi, in November and December 1845, then moved down the Mississippi River to Port Gibson, Mississippi, where he grossed $391.50 during the first three months of 1846, making daguerreotypes of the wealthy planters and slaveowners of the region. Cook also charged $75 to give daguerreotype lessons in Port Gibson to a man named Robrock. Then he was off to Grand Gulf, Mississippi, for a month, Gallatin, Tennessee, for three weeks, and back to Vicksburg for the hot summer of 1846.[30]

Portraiture was the bread and butter of every daguerreian artist, but when great events occurred within range of the eye of the camera, artists could not resist expending the time and materials to preserve those moments. The first photograph of a newsworthy event in the United States may have been made in Philadelphia on May 9, 1844, when artists William and Frederick Langenheim made a daguerreotype during a military occupation of the city after riots in which Protestants fought Catholics.[31]

The Mexican War from 1846 to 1848 was the first war to be photographed. About thirty-five outdoor daguerreotype scenes from the Mexican War have survived, including at least thirteen images of American soldiers in Mexico and other military-related subjects. Nearly all of these images are in two separate groups—each group having probably been commissioned by American officers and privately held by them. Thus, the daguerreotypes taken in the field during the Mexican War were seen by almost no one and had no apparent impact on the general public. These two groups of war images were eventually forgotten and were not rediscovered until the twentieth century.

The Mexican War was the first American war that was extensively covered by American newspapers. The "scoop" came into being, and with it a huge new demand for scenes of the conflict based on eyewitness accounts. This in turn produced a tremendous demand for prints and en-

Abner Doubleday, a tall, young, first lieutenant of artillery, stands with a group of unidentified Mexicans in this sixth-plate Mexican War daguerreotype taken around 1847, probably near Saltillo. Some fourteen years later, in 1861, Doubleday would pose for another camera while holed up with the small Union garrison holding Fort Sumter in defiance of the new Confederate States of America. (Courtesy of the Beinecke Rare Book and Manuscript Library, Yale University)

gravings of war scenes. More than thirty artists created hundreds of Mexican War lithographs and engravings. Although the business of converting daguerreotypes into lithographs was now well established by Anthony, Haas, Washington daguerreian artist John Plumbe Jr., and others, there is only a single extant example of a Mexican War lithograph made from a daguerreotype. It shows General (and soon-to-be President) Zachary Taylor in the field, with his arms crossed, wearing a wide-brimmed planter's hat. Photography played a role in the first American war to

come along after its invention, but it was a small one. As historians Martha A. Sandweiss and Rick Stewart have written, "Though daguerreotypists joined printmakers for the first time in chronicling an event, the Mexican War did not mark the emergence of photography as an important recording medium."[32]

A year after the Mexican War ended, the California Gold Rush began. This massive social upheaval was far more thoroughly documented by the daguerreotype camera. At daguerreian studios all over the country, artists preserved the

The California Gold Rush was the first great social movement extensively documented by the camera. As this half-plate daguerreotype taken at "Timbucktoo" on the Yuba River shows, the forty-niners who flocked to the gold fields were not immune from coarsely playing for the camera, even in the Victorian era. (From the collection of Matthew R. Isenburg)

likenesses of thousands of men and women before they embarked on their arduous land or sea journeys to California. In San Francisco, Sacramento, and other California cities, daguerreian artists took pictures by the hundreds of newly outfitted gold miners headed to the fields or coming back from them, some with huge golden nuggets, others with the gaunt look wrought by the hardships of their adventures.

More than ever before, photographers ventured into the wilderness, searching out the gold fields to focus and record on their silver plates views of small, ramshackle towns with the smell of fresh-cut pine and names such as Grizzly Flat, Volcano, Rough and Ready, and Yreka. They made multi-plate panoramas of burgeoning San Francisco and captured events as they happened or shortly thereafter, such as a flood in Marysville,

a squatter's riot in Sacramento, and the aftermath of an 1851 fire in San Francisco. The daguerreotype of the scene of the Sacramento riot was later modified into a woodcut engraving and published in the *Illustrated California News*.[33]

Sadly, the work of Robert H. Vance, a young daguerreian artist who migrated West, opened several galleries in northern California, and systematically recorded many aspects of the Gold Rush, has been lost to history. Vance assembled a massive collection of more than 300 plates depicting miners at work, dancing American Indians in their native garb, portraits of notable individuals including pioneer John A. Sutter, and landscapes and panoramas of mining towns throughout gold country. Today, all that remains of Vance's collection is an 1851 catalog from an exhibition of his work in New York City. Modern daguerreotype collectors regard the lost images, said to be some of the best ever taken, as the craft's "Holy Grail."[34]

By the early 1850s, daguerreian artists were firmly woven into the fabric of American society. They flourished not only in American towns but also at vacation spots such as Niagara Falls. Artist Platt D. Babbitt controlled the daguerreotype concession at the American falls and was legendary for his aggressive tactics to discourage competitors. Babbitt and his allies would stand between a competitor's camera and the falls, "swinging large-sized umbrellas to and fro" to prevent the interloper from getting a picture.[35]

On July 19, 1853, one of the most dramatic and poignant rescue attempts in the legend and lore of antebellum America unfolded in an agonizing, daylong drama near the precipice of the American falls. When Babbitt arrived at his daguerreian pavilion that morning, he could see a man stranded in the middle of the rapids, sitting on a log wedged between rocks, not more than 500 feet from the deadly drop. He was Joseph Avery, a seventeen-year-old German immigrant. After having a few drinks the previous evening, he and one or two friends decided to cross from Goat Island to the mainland. Their small boat was swept into the rapids and dashed against the rock outcropping. Avery's friend or friends were swept over the falls to their deaths, but the young German immigrant managed to grab onto the log, where he remained perched throughout the night.[36]

After dawn, thousands gathered to watch one failed rescue attempt after another. On a building, someone attached a huge handwritten sign: "We Will Save You." A visiting Southern planter offered $1,000 to anyone who could do it. Babbitt turned his camera toward the stranded man and exposed at least one daguerreotype of Avery perched on the log. In Manhattan, the *New York Daily Times* churned out extra editions with the latest news by telegraph:

On July 19, 1853, daguerreian artist Platt Babbitt made a daguerreotype image of the doomed Joseph Avery clinging to a log wedged in rocks in the Niagara Rapids just above the American falls. Babbitt's image is an early example of an American daguerreotype serving as a news photograph. This quarter-plate daguerreotype was one of a number of copies Babbitt made from the original and sold to the public. (Library of Congress)

9 a.m.: The excitement here is intense. We have no life-boat, and the common boats are swamped as soon as they touch the rapids. A life-boat has been sent for from Buffalo. Parties on shore have succeeded in floating a box of refreshments to the poor fellow, who can be plainly seen from the shore.

Second Dispatch—Noon: The man is still in the rapids, apparently drooping.[37]

After two unsuccessful rescue attempts, an unmanned boat reached Avery, but the rope became stuck in the rocks. For hours, Avery worked to free it, as did citizens on shore, until the life-line finally broke. In the meantime, volunteers built a sturdy raft. It was let out into the rapids from upstream. It reached Avery, and he managed to get on. Hopes rose among the great

From a rooftop in Oswego, New York, photographer George N. Barnard made this dramatic daguerreotype of the fire-ravaged city after flames had swept through a large portion of the business and industrial district, burning some forty-five acres of mills, warehouses, and homes. Barnard, like Babbitt, sold copies of his images as keepsakes of the conflagration. Barnard's "maker mark" is stamped in the lower left corner of the metal frame, or mat. (Courtesy of the George Eastman House)

throng of onlookers as Avery was pulled closer to safety—until the rope was caught in rocks. Avery was again stuck in the current, riding the lurching raft. Another boat was launched. It reached the raft. Exhausted, soaked, and freezing, an unsteady Avery grabbed for the boat but failed to hold on. He plunged into the roiling water.[38]

Third Dispatch—6:30 p.m.: The man went over the falls at 6 o'clock. . . . He attempted to swim to a small island, but failed to reach it. He raised himself up to his full height, gave a shriek, waved his arms wildly, and disappeared.[39]

The "small island" was Chapin's Island, a tiny rock outcropping that during the nineteenth century sat in the rapids at the very edge of the American falls. Avery came so close to the island in water so shallow that he was actually able to regain his feet for an instant before falling back into the rapids. The piercing scream that came from Avery's lungs as he plunged over the falls to his death haunted those who heard it for the rest of their lives. Babbitt immediately began making copy daguerreotypes of "Avery Stranded" and selling them as poignant souvenirs of the tragic but memorable episode. At least four copies of "Avery Stranded" survive today; many more probably were sold.[40]

Earlier during that same month of July 1853, less than 200 miles east, another daguerreian, George N. Barnard, took dramatic photographs of a news event and, like Babbitt, marketed them as keepsakes. Barnard had been a hotel manager, in Oswego, New York, before he learned how to make daguerreotypes at age twenty-six. Opening a studio there in the summer of 1846, Barnard quickly put his hotelier days behind him and established himself as one of the finest artists in the state. On a windy July 5, 1853, Barnard took several images of a massive fire that, like Babbitt's daguerreotype of the doomed Joseph Avery, are considered among the first American news photographs. The conflagration broke out in a large flour mill on the east side of the Oswego River; wind-whipped flames burned forty-

five acres of the city, leaving 2,000 people homeless. Barnard took at least one daguerreotype from directly across the river before moving to a higher vantage point to get a wider view of the destruction, where he took a shot showing smoke streaming east at the head of a stiff breeze. A third image showed ruins. A week after the fire and for two months afterward, Barnard ran an advertisement in the *Oswego Daily Times* offering:

PICTURES OF THE LATE FIRE
DAGUERREOTYPE PICTURES of the late fire taken while burning, may be obtained at Barnard's Daguerrean [sic] Rooms. These pictures are copied from large pictures and are faithful representations of the different stages of the fire as it appeared on the 5th. Also views of the Ruins as they now appear.[41]

This whole-plate, gold-toned daguerreotype of the famed Swedish singer Jenny Lind, one of the most popular celebrities of the 1850s, was taken at M. B. Brady's New York studio in September 1850 at the time of her American debut. Protected in its sealed case, a daguerreotype is a remarkably durable and lasting photographic image. But the bare plate alone, without protection, can be easily scratched, as happened to this image. (Library of Congress)

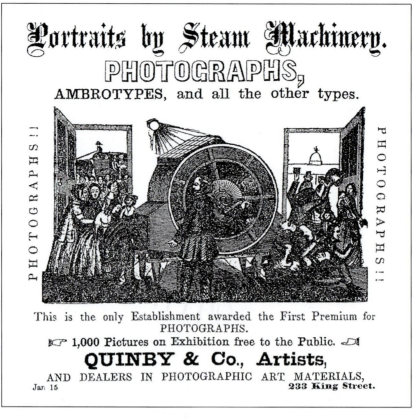

In the hyper competitive world of the Charleston daguerreian artists, where "fifty cent daguerreotypes" dominated the business, C. J. Quinby focused instead on technology in this 1858 ad. Another version that also featured this strange contraption boasted: "The Celebrated Portrait Factory in Full Blast This Day." (Courtesy of Harvey S. Teal)

We do not know how many pictures Barnard sold, although copy daguerreotypes of two of the images still exist. Barnard's fire images, and Babbitt's daguerreotype of Avery stranded, came relatively early in their long careers as photographers. Babbitt chose to remain at Niagara Falls, using the falls as a backdrop, until at least 1870, taking countless photographs of visitors as well as the daredevil wirewalkers who plied their trade across Niagara Gorge. Barnard, however, would move to Syracuse and then to New York City by 1860, where he would begin shooting stereo photographs for Edward Anthony's ever-growing catalog of views. During the Civil War, Barnard would join the ranks of those few war photographers who concentrated on documen-

tary photography. Before the war was over, Barnard would carry his cameras on one of the epochal campaigns in military history, and he would establish himself as one of the greatest photographers of the conflict.[42]

Most copy daguerreotypes made in the 1850s were of celebrities, and no celebrity was more popular than the "Swedish nightingale," Jenny Lind, the most renowned singer of the age. When Lind appeared in Baltimore, daguerreotypists there battled for the privilege of a sitting. Artist Jesse Whitehurst paid $100 at auction for a front row center theater seat and earned an exclusive sitting from Lind as well. Whitehurst aggressively advertised his Jenny Lind image as the only one taken in Baltimore, but his competi-

Published here for the first time, this circa 1855 quarter-plate daguerreo-type shows Charleston photographer George S. Cook, standing, and two acquaintances, possibly his gallery assistants. By 1856, the business was changing, and Cook was advertising "good pictures, either in daguerreotype, ambrotype or colored photographs." The era of the daguerreotype was coming to an end. (From the collection of George S. Whiteley IV)

tors nonetheless marketed other copy images of Lind, igniting a feud among the city's artists.[43]

The early 1850s were the golden years of the daguerreotype. In 1850, there were seventy-one daguerreian rooms in New York City, staffed by 127 operators and assisted by eleven ladies and forty-six boys. Daguerreian artists had succeeded in taking daguerreotypes of the moon and stars through telescopes and of a fly's foot through a microscope. Daguerreotypes were made of surgery on human beings, of a lightning bolt in the sky, and of ever more news events. In August 1853, just weeks after the Oswego fire and Avery's plunge, a Rhode Island daguerreian artist captured the aftermath of a train crash on the local railroad.[44]

The daguerreotype was a manifestation of the progressive, lively years before the Civil War. A daguerreotype projected absolute truth and veracity and thus seemed to perfectly fit the ethos of the time, which was individual improvement and social progress through hard work, honesty, and faith.

"This is a 'wonderful age,' truly; and he who lives in the nineteenth century may esteem himself fortunate in having fallen upon such auspicious times," wrote essayist H. E. Insley in 1851. Insley's prose was inspired by the apparent discovery in 1850 of color photography by Levi L. Hill, an eccentric, former Baptist preacher who took up the art of making daguerreotypes because he believed the chemicals improved his bronchitis.[45]

When Hill announced that he could make daguerreotypes in natural colors, which he called "hillotypes," he was at first widely hailed as Daguerre's own equal. Pressed to display his work, Hill was reluctant to comply. He stalled for months. Eventually, most of the daguerreian fraternity turned against him, and he came under increasingly harsh attacks in the photographic journals. In 1853, the controversy was debated on the floor of the U.S. Senate, as Hill unsuccessfully sought a patent and government aid. The controversy never fully died until after Hill's own death in 1865, and the mystery of whether Hill actually succeeded in making the first color photographic images was not answered until 1977, when photo historian Wm. B. Becker found Hill's original experimental hillotypes, still retaining their original subtle colors, buried in a dusty storage area at the Smithsonian Institution. In 1984, modern photographic experimenter Joseph Boudreau successfully created modern "hillotype" daguerreotypes in natural colors after untangling the arcane language of Hill's published formula (the "fuming liquid of Libavius" was actually tin chloride).[46]

In 1850, the daguerreian community in the United States was a rapidly maturing fraternity, linked by local and state associations and by the national trade journals that were first published that year. Although working on opposite sides of New York State, Barnard and Haas got to know each other while serving together on a state daguerreian association committee in 1851. By 1849, Cook had a young family, so he abandoned the life of an itinerant daguerreian and settled in Charleston, South Carolina, where his gallery soon began to receive frequent mention in the photographic journals. Cook formed alliances with Brady, Anthony, and others when he came to New York City for an extended stay in 1851. He ran Brady's gallery for some months, when Brady sailed for Europe, and briefly opened his own gallery. Cook headed back to Charleston after Brady returned to the States with a World's Fair grand prize medal.[47]

Even as the daguerreotype reached its peak in the United States, its death knell had been sounded. As Brady and other American daguerreian artists swept the daguerreotype awards at the World's Fair at London's new Crystal Palace in 1851, articles were appearing in the scientific and photographic journals hailing a new form of photography—the wet collodion glass plate negative. This process, which was a variation of Talbot's, was developed by English sculptor Frederick Scott Archer. Archer freely gave it to the world, thus earning no royalties from the invention, and died penniless in 1857.[48]

Archer's wet collodion process was easier and less expensive than the daguerreotype process. It reduced typical exposure times to a few seconds and allowed for the limitless duplication of prints on the improved photographic paper developed during that decade. The daguerreotype's magic was wearing thin by the late 1850s and, given the glass plate negative, became regarded as an old-fashioned process that produced an effect difficult to see and impractical to reproduce. In the rush of new technology, the magical mirror image invented by Daguerre was assigned to history's dustbin.

2

THE ROOTS OF CELEBRITY

On the clear and cool evening of February 27, 1860, in New York City, a country lawyer and politician from the far reaches of Illinois named Abraham Lincoln delivered a speech at the Cooper Union Institute that captivated his audience, galvanized feelings in the North, and vaulted him toward the presidency of a bitterly divided nation.

Lincoln was a stranger to the city, and that afternoon he did what nearly all tourists did in New York in the nineteenth century—he took a stroll down Broadway. Lincoln was clearly out of place in the metropolis, appearing ungainly and self-conscious in a black suit that showed wrinkles from being packed in a valise during his four-day train trip from Illinois. Beyond his disheveled appearance, his height made him stand out, looking even taller in his top hat. Lincoln was nonetheless not quite the country bumpkin he appeared to be. More than a decade earlier, he had resided in Washington during a single, undistinguished term in Congress. He emerged as a leading politician in the newly formed, antislavery Republican Party on the strength of his brilliant speeches, which first caught the country's attention in 1858 during debates with Stephen Douglas in Lincoln's unsuccessful Sen-

ate campaign. Lincoln spoke a dozen times in the Midwest in the last half of 1859, drawing large crowds from Council Bluffs to Columbus. But this was New York. A political speaker could face no sterner test. Lincoln's appearance at the Cooper Union Institute would be nothing less than an audition for president, and he would respond with one of his greatest orations: a masterful anti-slavery message that became a rallying cry across the North, and a provocation in the South. Three months later, Lincoln would win the Republican Party's nomination for president at the national convention in Chicago.[1]

Lincoln was well accustomed to the "sun pictures" in the photographic galleries that proliferated on Broadway. In 1846, the year before he went to Congress, he and his wife Mary had posed for companion daguerreotype portraits. Since then, he had sat for at least fifteen different portraits, most of them in 1858 and 1859 as his political career blossomed. Several of those sittings had come at epochal moments in his life, and February 27, 1860, was no exception. Though he had a politician's eye for self-promotion, Lincoln could not have divined the enormous impact of the photograph that M. B. Brady took of him that

The softening of Abraham Lincoln's appearance in M. B. Brady's "Cooper Union" photograph in February 1860 becomes apparent when contrasted with Samuel G. Alschuler's photograph of the president elect taken in Chicago ten months later, just after Lincoln had begun to grow his famous beard. (Library of Congress)

day. In the months to come, Brady's "Cooper Union" photograph, and to a lesser extent the other photographs of Lincoln, would spread his visage across the nation in the form of prints, engravings, and thousands of copies of the photographs themselves. It would be so influential that years later Brady would recall Lincoln saying, "Brady and the Cooper Institute made me president."[2]

Lincoln's portrait was unmatched in popularity after his Cooper Union speech, and particularly after his nomination. Copies of Brady's image sold by the thousands. Lincoln was often described as homely, sometimes downright ugly,

but Brady sought to make the gangly, Western lawyer look as dignified and statesmanlike as possible. Brady saw promise in Lincoln's rugged dignity, and he was capable of creating a muted elegance from the roughest of forms. Lincoln had no facial hair at Cooper Union; he grew his famous beard later. Taking note of that, Brady said, "I had to pull up his shirt and coat collar." This had the effect of shortening Lincoln's long neck. Brady also posed Lincoln in a standing position, which emphasized his height.[3]

Lincoln's Cooper Union photograph reached the height of its popularity during his campaign for the presidency. It was reproduced in a myriad

Brady's Cooper Union photograph of Lincoln received its greatest exposure on the cover of *Harper's Weekly* when this woodcut engraving of the image was published on November 10, 1860, four days after Lincoln's election as president. More than 150 other Brady photographs, mostly portraits, were converted to *Harper's Weekly* engravings from 1861 to 1865. (Library of Congress)

of formats, including prints, engravings, book pages, buttons, badges, medallions, and banners. The Cooper Union photograph, argues historian Harold Holzer, was

the most important single visual record of Lincoln's, or perhaps any American presidential campaign; an image-transfiguring Mathew Brady photograph. Its later proliferation and reproduction in prints, medallions, broadsides and banners perhaps did as much to create a "new" Abraham Lincoln as did the Cooper Union speech itself.[4]

It is not known whether Brady convinced Lincoln's hosts to bring him to his gallery at 643 Broadway, or whether Lincoln himself selected Brady's establishment. Given Brady's insatiable appetite for collecting images of leading politicians, it seems most plausible that Brady took the initiative to secure an appointment to photograph the Cooper Union's featured speaker of the evening. Had Lincoln made the decision on his own, he would have been bewildered by the choices.

"What a wonderful place New York is for photographic galleries! Their number is legion and their size is mammoth," English writer and photographer, John Werge, exclaimed after visiting Broadway in April 1860. New York's newest, most lavish gallery was the "New Photographic and Fine Art Gallery" at 707 Broadway, a bit farther up the busy thoroughfare than Brady's Gallery. It was owned by Brady's keenest competitor, Jeremiah Gurney, who, like Brady, had won national and international awards. In 1853, Gurney had captured the Anthony Prize, a massive, silver pitcher awarded a single time by Edward Anthony for what were judged to be the four best daguerreotypes in the country.[5]

Gurney had opened his new gallery in November 1858 amidst "joy and gladness, wine and wassail," a photographic journal reported. The city was growing northward, and Gurney's move "uptown" allowed him to separate his establishment from the dozens of galleries further downtown (New York had about 200 galleries in 1858). Gurney's spacious, modern facility was built for photography. The new studio was on the second floor. Delicately attired ladies would no longer have to climb three or four flights of stairs in their hoop skirts to reach his skylight-illuminated studio.[6]

Brady had moved uptown, too, but was in a temporary gallery at 643 Broadway (while also operating his "downtown" studio) until a new facility—the grandest, most elaborate Brady gallery yet—opened in the fall of 1860 at 785 Broadway. Even if Brady, as one journal reported, did not have "quite such elegant or commodious rooms in his uptown quarters as Gurney [had] in his," it was still lavishly appointed. Elegance became the industry standard for a leading New York photograph gallery of the mid-nineteenth century. Extravagances included satin and gold wallpaper, colorful velvet tapestry carpeting, lace curtains, rosewood furniture, marble-top tables, ceiling-to-floor mirrors, frescoed ceilings, and a six-light gilt and enameled chandelier with prismatic drops.[7]

Brady himself dressed the part. A silk scarf usually accented his black diagonal coat. He wore muslin shirts, black doeskin pants, and a merino vest tailored for him at Bellantoni's. He used linen handkerchiefs and carried a cane, as well as several pairs of eyeglasses and spectacles. His toiletries included Lubin's soap, lavender water, and Atwood's cologne. He was fond of old Renault brandy.[8]

Brady was infected with a cavalier extravagance that spread, unfortunately, to his attitude about business. By 1856, he had begun to overextend his credit by not paying off long-standing debts. Ambition exceeded good sense, however, and in January 1858, Brady expanded to Washington, opening a gallery on Pennsylvania Avenue. In 1859, Brady was forced to mortgage property in Brooklyn to pay other debts. Almost immediately upon opening his new uptown gallery in 1860, Brady had to mortgage its contents.[9]

Not all of Brady's decisions were poor; one of his best was the appointment of Scotsman Alexander Gardner as manager of the Washington gallery. Gardner had immigrated to the United States with his family in 1856. The burly, moon-faced Gardner had been a man for all seasons in Scotland. He had worked as a jeweler, a silversmith, a proponent of the rights of the working man, organizer of a cooperative community of Scottish farmers who immigrated to Iowa in 1850, a newspaper publisher, and finally, just before his own emigration, a photographer who specialized in Talbot's process, apparently with little success.[10]

It is unknown how Gardner and Brady got together, but their affiliation and the decision to open a gallery in the nation's capital enhanced Brady's ability to expand his portrait gallery of famous Americans. "Mr. Brady seems determined to secure the largest collection of portraits of American celebrities in the country," reported the *Photographic and Fine Art Journal* in 1858. Brady himself said, "In those days, a photographer ran his career upon the celebrities who came to him."[11]

The typical gallery of 1860 offered a far different range of images than it had just a few years earlier. Gone were the old-fashioned daguerreotypes, their beauty and magic having devolved into a state of archaic obsolescence. The latest innovation in portraiture was to have a photographic negative made and then purchase multiple copies in the form of a small card photograph known as a *carte de visite*. Lincoln's Cooper Union photograph was primarily reproduced as a *carte de visite*, and Anthony printed and sold them by the thousands.

Sitters who wanted a traditional "cased" image, which came in a folding case like a daguerreotype, purchased either an ambrotype or a tintype (also known as a ferrotype or melainotype). The ambrotype and the tintype, like a daguerreotype or today's "instant" Polaroid photograph, were one-of-a-kind, positive images, except that both were created through the use of Frederick Scott Archer's wet collodion process. The ambrotype was a collodion image on glass; the negative was made positive by coating the reverse side with black lacquer. The tintype was a collodion image on a thin sheet of iron (not tin). The cases they came in, however, did not change from those used in the daguerreian era. Thus, it was impossible to tell what type of image was housed in the case until it was opened. To this day, tintypes and ambrotypes are often confused with daguerreotypes.

The ambrotype and tintype processes were introduced around 1855. The growth of the ambrotype process was hobbled, however, when one photographer, James A. Cutting, filed patent infringement lawsuits against other photographers and triggered a bitter legal dispute. Many in the American photographic community banded together to fight Cutting's efforts to monopolize the process. The tintype soon became the most popular type of cased image, not only because of the patent dispute but also because it was less expensive to make, cheaper to buy, more durable, and easier to create than an ambrotype, particularly for an itinerant artist. The tintype was the photograph for the masses, and in the war to come, the total number of soldiers, from both the North and South, who had their tintypes made in tent studios would figure into the millions.[12]

Ambrotypes and tintypes were fine as far as they went, but for many customers, and for the photographer in a permanent gallery, the *carte de visite* was far more desirable. "Cartes de Visite are the rage now-a-days, and the photographer who is not prepared to make them may consider himself behind the times," *Humphrey's Journal* declared in 1861. The *carte de visite* was an albumen paper print made from a glass negative and pasted onto an approximately two-by-four-inch card. The *carte de visite* instantly popularized the photograph album, which soon became a staple in American parlors. Albums could easily hold several dozen *cartes de visite*, with tintypes fitting in almost as easily. Owners filled their albums with family photos, often including images of statesmen, military leaders, and celebrities as well.[13]

The development of photography on glass, both as the glass plate negative and the ambrotype, had transformed Talbot's inferior method of making photographic negatives. Talbot had been marketing his "calotype" process since the 1840s with limited success. He used a paper negative to make a positive image on another sheet of paper that was treated with light-sensitive salts; the positive became known as a "salt print." Archer's wet collodion glass negative and the introduction of egg white–based, albumenized

photographic paper, developed by French photographer Louis-Désiré Blanquart-Évrard in about 1850, were vast improvements over Talbot's materials. Using a glass plate negative and albumen paper, photographers now had a high-quality, reliable photographic process that readily allowed the creation of multiple copies. This development opened the door for the mass production of individual photographic images, which, on the eve of the Civil War, created a vast new market among average Americans, not only for portraits of themselves and celebrity portrait photographs but for images of notable places and scenes.

At the same time Americans fell in love with the *carte de visite*, they became enthralled by another type of paper photograph: the stereoscopic view card. This type of card photograph, most commonly known as a stereo view, was also popularized by the development of the collodion wet plate negative. The stereo view, also known as a "stereograph" (and sometimes misidentified as "stereogram" or "stereopticon") was a pair of three-by-three-inch, albumen photographs. They were pasted side by side on a three and one-quarter by six and three-quarter-inch card that was slightly thicker than the card stock used for the *carte de visite*.

The discovery of stereoscopic vision occurred at about the same time as the introduction of practical photography. English physicist and inventor Sir Charles Wheatstone first outlined the principles of stereoscopy and made a reflecting stereoscope in 1838, the year before the introduction of the daguerreotype. Wheatstone discovered that humans see objects in three dimensions because each eye views those objects from a slightly different angle. The practical use of stereoscopic vision in photography, however, did not occur until 1850, when another Englishman, Sir William Brewster, invented the lenticular stereoscope. Brewster's viewer opened a market for stereoscopic photographs, which were taken with a camera with two lenses affixed side by side, an eye-width apart. When the viewer looks at the two slightly different images

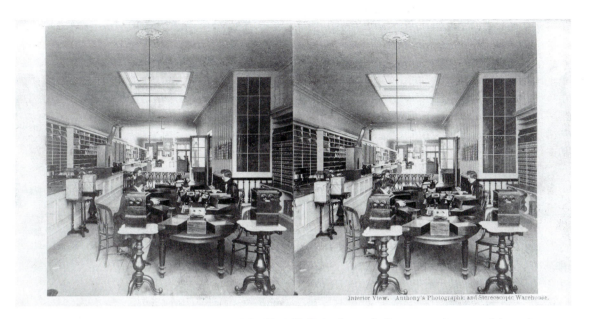

A circa 1860 stereo view of the interior of the E. & H. T. Anthony & Company photographic and stereo-scopic depot at 501 Broadway shows an array of table-top stereo viewers and dozens of built-in cabinet nooks to hold views and photographs. (From the collection of Jeffrey Kraus)

through the binocular lenses of a stereoscope, they come together into one eye-popping image filled with the illusion of depth.[14]

"The mind feels its way into the very depths of the picture," wrote Oliver Wendell Holmes, the essayist, poet, and inventor who is credited with developing in 1859 the first practical, inexpensive, handheld viewer for viewing stereo view cards. The stereoscopic view served a different purpose than the *carte de visite*. The card portrait was a photographic keepsake; the stereo view was a photographic viewing experience. The latter invited the eye to wander through its 3-D scenes, lingering to study the spatial relationships and the lay of the land. It was almost like being there and seeing the scene with one's own eyes. In that sense, it was the closest thing Civil War–era Americans had to movies or tele-

vision, and it would remain so throughout the rest of the nineteenth century until the advent, in 1896, of actual motion pictures.[15]

Stereo images immediately became popular when they were introduced in Europe in the early 1850s as daguerreotypes and salt prints. They were slower to catch on in the United States, although the sale of stereo daguerreotypes was enhanced considerably in 1853 with John F. Mascher's invention of a daguerreotype case with a fold-up viewer. In 1854, the Langenheim brothers, Frederick and William, who were based in Philadelphia, began marketing their own views on glass and paper, including scenes of Philadelphia, Baltimore, Washington, Pittsburgh, and the "beauties of the Hudson River."[16]

Edward Anthony arrived rather late to the stereoscopic business, but it was not long before

Facing page: From factory to home, the fledgling but booming stereo photograph business is depicted in these three circa 1860 stereo views. The top view was taken inside a French stereo view production shop, the middle view shows the D. Appleton Stereoscopic Emporium at 346–348 Broadway, and the bottom view depicts an evening in the parlor of a proper British home, with the patriarch studying stereo views being handed to him by the young woman at right. (From the collection of Jeffrey Kraus)

he dominated it. In the 1840s, he had been a daguerreotypist, gallery operator, merchant, engraver, and lithographer before devoting his career, around 1847, to selling photographic materials. Four years later, Edward formed a partnership with his brother, Henry, and together they built E. & H. T. Anthony & Company, a photographic supply house that in the 1850s dwarfed all others with its array of "photographic, ambrotype & daguerreotype materials of every description."[17]

By 1857 or 1858, when the Anthony company issued its first stereoscopic photographs—a boxed set of a dozen views of the Fulton Street Prayer Meeting—other Broadway merchants had been in the business for years. The D. Appleton Company had been selling stereo views, their own and others, since 1852. By mid-1859, the Anthony company was ready to become a serious competitor in the stereo view business, and it launched its own line of views with an extensive advertising campaign. Edward Anthony had hired former painter and ambrotypist Jacob F. Coonley in 1858 to manage his new stereoscopic print shop, and the twenty-six-year-old Coonley had embarked on photographic expeditions to secure new and different stereo views of scenic places. In a few short years, war would come, and Coonley would turn his camera toward the camps and battlefronts.[18]

At about the same time that the Anthony company entered the stereo business, it also began aggressively to market celebrity and scenic *cartes de visite*, as well as the photograph albums to hold them. It was probably inevitable that with the rise of the personal, *carte de visite* portrait there would also be a boom in the business of selling commercial card photographs, particularly those of statesmen, military leaders, luminaries of the stage, and other notable people. By 1862, the Anthony company was issuing separate stereo view and card photograph catalogs, each offering hundreds of different images for sale.[19]

The timing could not have been better, particularly for the Anthony company's entry into the stereo business. In 1859, Oliver Wendell Holmes, with help from Boston photograph dealer Joseph L. Bates, developed an inexpensive, hand-held stereo viewer. Holmes did not attempt to patent his viewer, and like Archer's freely given collodion process, the hand-held stereoscope flourished in many different forms. The simple, inexpensive Holmes-Bates stereo viewer was to stereoscopic photography what the Ford Model T was to the automobile; it created a vast new market among middle class, nineteenth-century Americans and popularized the first media-driven form of American home entertainment. The Holmes-Bates stereoscope "not only met with immediate enthusiastic success but it shifted the center of stereo activity to America, where it remained unchallenged for eighty years," writes historian William C. Darrah. The stereo viewer and a stack of view cards would soon become commonplace in American dwellings, including a home in Springfield, Illinois, where one sat, and still sits, on a side table in Abraham Lincoln's formal parlor.[20]

When the Anthony company launched its stereo view business in earnest during the summer of 1859, it immediately captured a significant share of the market by offering a type of stereo view unlike anything anyone had ever seen. The company's first major series of about 175 stereo views depicted scenes in and around New York. Known as "Anthony's Instantaneous Views," they were nothing less than stop-action photographs. Anthony's Instantaneous Views, together with the Holmes-Bates viewer, took American photography to another level.[21]

Edward Anthony had been fascinated with "instantaneous" photography since around 1849, when experimental daguerreotypists had managed to make the first approximations of stop-action photographs by using faster-acting chemicals to reduce exposure times and crude forms of mechanical shutters. In 1852, the first article on the subject appeared in an American photographic journal, reprinted from a British article by none other than Henry Fox Talbot. By 1857,

The worst fire to hit New York City in fifteen years destroyed the Cyrus Field warehouse and other buildings in downtown New York on December 29, 1859. This detail from an Anthony Instantaneous stereo view of the blaze is probably the first photo ever made of the New York Fire Department in action. The original label on the reverse reads: "Photographers will appreciate the merits of this picture when informed it was taken on a dark day just previous to a heavy snow storm with the thermometer below 20 degrees."

photographers in France and England were issuing instantaneous views that appear to have had an exposure of less than a second.[22]

Anthony was among the first to issue such views in America. Their clarity and sharpness, particularly the many scenes looking up and down Broadway, set them apart and gave them an obscure but important niche in American photographic history. As far as Oliver Wendell Holmes was concerned, they were miraculous. Holmes said that if a stranger from another planet had asked mankind, at that point in time, "to hand him the most remarkable material product of human skill," he would offer without hesi-

tation one of Anthony's instantaneous stereo views of Broadway.[23]

Anthony's own advertisements boasted:

Anthony's Instantaneous Stereoscopic views are the latest photographic wonder. They are taken in the fortieth part of a second, and everything, no matter how rapidly it may be moving, is depicted as sharply and distinctly as if it had been perfectly at rest. . . . These views have surprised everybody who has seen them. No visitor should leave New York without some of them to astonish friends at home.

Perhaps the most popular of the dozens of views taken of Broadway were several titled "Broadway on a Rainy Day." Anthony was able to overcome the most unfavorable lighting conditions to produce clear, vivid stereo views, a testament to Yankee photographic skill and ingenuity.[24] Most of the instantaneous views were scenic or landscape views. Some, however, were more indicative of photojournalism, showing events such as the visit from the Prince of Wales or the Independence Day parade in 1860.

On the frigid morning of December 29, 1859, a large fire spread through several blocks of downtown New York, destroying six warehouses, including the paper warehouse of Cyrus W. Field. The image taken of this fire may be the first stop-action news photograph taken in the United States, and it is almost certainly the first photograph of the venerable New York Fire Department in action. No sales figures have survived for the instantaneous views, but they were unquestionably best-sellers, because they still abound today. Every dealer of antique photographs will have at least a few of them in their New York City section of stereo views.[25]

The existence of mass marketed, stop-action photographs *before* the Civil War prompts obvious questions. Why did Civil War photographers generally not use the instantaneous camera in the field? Why were the vast majority of Civil War outdoor scenes, stereoscopic and otherwise, taken with traditional, wet plate equipment that required exposures of three to twenty seconds? The greatest obstacle apparently was the collodion. The various mixtures and recipes for the instantaneous photograph were too sensitive for the rugged conditions in the field. Modern wet plate photographer Rob Gibson explains:

> The chemicals are more inconsistent, and there's a very good probability that the chemistry for instantaneous views wouldn't last as long. That's not good if you're gone for a week or two, and because it is less stable, your collodion might be bad by the time you reached the battlefield. They just couldn't afford for that to happen.[26]

The difficulties of shooting in the field made instantaneous photography next to impossible,

U. S. Revenue Cutter Agassiz firing a Salute.

Although the instantaneous camera was rarely if ever used in the field during the Civil War until 1865, the stop-action technology was more than capable of freezing the smoke of a naval broadside. When the U.S. Revenue Cutter *Agassiz* fired a salute in the harbor at New Bedford, Massachusetts, sometime between 1863 and 1865, the instantaneous camera of the Bierstadt Brothers stopped the action.

During the Crimean War in 1855, English photographer Roger Fenton took an image of his photographic wagon with assistant Marcus Sparling on the front seat. "The carriage, which has already had an existence chequered with many adventures by field and flood, began its career . . . in the service of a wine merchant at Canterbury," Fenton wrote. (Library of Congress)

but it didn't stop the photographers from loading their wagons and sallying forth to seek the action, because there was still plenty of opportunity to make a buck. The financial incentive had already been fueled by the burgeoning demand for *cartes de visite* and, even more significantly, stereo views. The impact of these developments on Civil War photography cannot be understated. By the eve of the war, Americans had experienced not only collectable card photographs but also the magic of the 3-D photograph. They hungered for more. The American appetite for the stereo view would last long beyond the war, extending well into the twentieth century and transmuting itself into a passion for the View Master and eventually, in our time, of the IMAX 3-D Theater and many other applications.[27]

Stereoscopic photography and other innovations aside, the vast majority of American photographers in the late 1850s confined their efforts to what had been the lucrative business of personal portraiture. The good times for photographers ended with the financial Panic of 1857. The popular rise of the *carte de visite*, beginning around 1860, would help many photographers recover, but until then, the business of personal portraiture dried up. Parlor room treasures suddenly became unaffordable vanities. Many of the New York photographers "have plenty of leisure," the *American Journal of Photography* reported in December 1860, and "there are very few galleries in the south which pay their working expenses."[28]

In Charleston, South Carolina, George S. Cook was no exception. Day after day, through the fall of 1860, he wrote "nothing done" in his account book. In September alone, he had no customers for fourteen of twenty-five business days at his gallery on King Street. From September 10 through 18, with relatively good weather, Cook had only a single customer and recorded $2 in gross receipts.

War brings death and destruction, but to some it brings prosperity. Photographers were among the more fortunate, and so it was for Cook. In a matter of months, his business would be brisk; if a half-dozen customers did not come through the door, it would not be considered a particularly good day. With the impending separation

Roger Fenton was frequently under artillery fire in the Crimea and saw firsthand the horrors of war. He wrote: "I had a man killed at my side while looking on at a lookout near the mortar battery." He chose, however, to photograph none of the gruesome scenes he wrote of, though his camera did capture images of the imposing enemy works and possibly distant battle smoke. This Fenton panorama from in front of the mortar batteries features the Russian fortifications, the Mamelon and the Malakof, on the flat hilltops at center and left center. (Library of Congress)

from family and home and the threat of injury and death, the most personal of mementoes—a photograph—became an essential keepsake, not only for the soldiers and officers marching off to war, but for those staying at home.[29]

"Let us try to think that the good time coming is near at hand, and that we should prepare for it!" the *American Journal of Photography* proclaimed, with notable prescience, in December 1860. "If the hot-headed politicians will cry havoc! and let loose the dogs of war, let us not be distracted from our duties and our pleasures. We are told: In time of peace prepare for war, but a far more Christian maxim is: In time of adversity prepare for prosperity."[30]

By 1860, it had been more than a decade since the daguerreian artists of the Mexican War took the first photographs of war. Much had

happened since then. A number of European photographers had managed to make photographs of various conflicts in the 1850s, including the Second Burma War of 1852–1853, the Crimean War of 1854–1855, the Sepoy Mutiny in India in 1857–1859, and the Franco-Austrian War in 1859.[31]

Of these efforts, the most notable work was done by Englishman Roger Fenton, a professional photographer who took a series of 360 glass plate negatives on the Crimean Peninsula from March 8 to June 26, 1855 (these were taken during the siege of Sebastopol, but months after most of the key battles). Most of Fenton's images are outdoor portraits and group photographs of officers. He also took several images of the harbor at Balaclava, a memorable shot of a road littered with Russian cannonballs, and a number of wide landscape views from the British-held prominence of Cathcart's Hill looking down on Sebastopol. Some of Fenton's views from Cathcart's Hill can be placed side, by side, by side to form panoramas, a technique that first gained popularity during the daguerreian era and one that Civil War photographers used time and again.[32]

Fenton was also possibly the first photographer to expose a plate showing distant combat. An 1855 account claims that "many of these admirable photographs were executed under a fire from the Russian batteries," adding that Fenton's large photographic wagon sometimes became an especially tempting target for the gunners who mistook it for a huge ammunition wagon. Unlike most of the photographers of the Civil War, Fenton left a narrative about his exploits in the Crimea—a unique, 5,000-word contribution to history from one of the earliest practitioners of war photography. Fenton described all manner of hardships and gave a gripping account of watching a battle: "[We were] scarcely conscious of the shot and shell which were hissing over our heads, except on one occasion, when a spent ball, which everybody saw coming, passed through the thickest of the throng, killing one man who got confused in his effort to avoid it."[33]

One would think Fenton would have alluded to taking photographs while under fire had he done so, but he is silent on that subject. Still, at least one of his broad landscapes from Cathcart's Hill may show distant artillery smoke, and another is labeled "French attack left." Two others, titled "Officers on the lookout," show military men peering into the distance. Fenton's images included a variety of landscapes, group photographs, and portraits but did not show corpses or any of the human toll of war, though he vividly wrote about such scenes in his correspondence. Whatever the shortcomings of Fenton's work, he was the most ambitious and prolific of all war photographers before the Civil War, and his images became the first war photographs to be widely seen when they were exhibited in the fall of 1855 upon his return to England. Articles about the images were published in British journals and reprinted in American photographic periodicals. Several images were reproduced as woodcut engravings in the *London Illustrated News.* All of the photographs were taken with a non-stereo, single-lens camera and reproduced as salt prints. They were sold to the public, but sales waned when peace came in 1856; the enterprise was a financial failure.[34]

The difference between Fenton's venture and the vast and successful sales of Civil War photographs can be traced to the stereo view, the availability of new technology to a mass audience, and the renewed demand for photography as war brought an end to the economic downturn. For the first time, images and simple viewers were both readily available and inexpensive. The photographers who ventured into the field took stereo views by the hundreds because they could sell hundreds of copies of each. They were well aware of their role as photographic historians, but their primary motive remained grounded in the American ethic of making money. The roots of Civil War photography in the field had taken hold.

3

THE REBELS SHOOT FIRST

A hopelessly divided Democratic Party offered two presidential candidates in the 1860 election, Stephen A. Douglas for Northern Democrats and pro-slavery John C. Breckenridge for the South. On November 6, Republican candidate Abraham Lincoln easily defeated them both. Four days later, as if to underscore the Cooper Union photograph's significance in popularizing Lincoln, the image was featured as an engraving on the cover of *Harper's Weekly*, complete with Brady's modifications to make Lincoln more attractive.

Nothing Brady could do would have made Lincoln acceptable in the South. His election hastened secession, and on December 20, South Carolina led the way by removing itself from the United States. Less than a week later, on the day after Christmas and under the cover of darkness, U.S. Army Major Robert Anderson moved his small garrison of 85 Union officers, sailors, and soldiers from Fort Moultrie to Fort Sumter to secure, for the Union, the massive masonry fort on a tiny island at the entrance of Charleston Harbor.

The South regarded Anderson's move as blatant provocation, and as more Southern states seceded, rebel militia units rushed to secure other Federal forts and garrisons in their areas. Regardless of these aggressive gambits, Fort Sumter remained a kind of ground zero, as both halves of a divided nation were consumed by the drama of Anderson and his small band of holdouts refusing all Confederate demands to give up the fort. The threat of war did not stop commerce or the mail, and in Charleston, George S. Cook carried on a lively correspondence with his friends in the North, all of whom expressed concern for his well-being. Some also added their own commentary on the state of affairs. A. W. McCormick, a former Cook assistant, managed to do both at once in a letter from Oxford, Pennsylvania, dated January 2, 1861:

> You have toiled long and hard to establish your Gallery and you certainly deserved to be sustained under every difficulty for establishing such a Gallery as you have. And I hope you may be, although no doubt you will have to take your share of the burden which must necessarily fall upon the whole people of your state under the present state of affairs.[1]

If Cook was concerned, he didn't show it. He obtained a deed of property for a lot on the

Five recently freed slave women hold their new babies, the first generation to be born into freedom, as they stand by their quarters on the T. J. Fripp plantation at St. Helena Island, South Carolina. This circa 1864–1865 stereo view, published here for the first time, was probably taken by Beaufort photographer Erastus Hubbard. (From the collection of Robin Stanford)

battery in mid-January and began building a new, three-story house facing Charleston Harbor and the very fort that consumed the country's attention. Business was good and getting better, and Cook was in high spirits. Another former assistant, J. B. Van der Weyde, who had recently returned North, replied, on January 19, to an obviously upbeat letter from his old boss:

> I must confess that although you do not seem to be at all alarmed at the present state of affairs, I cannot share so hopeful a sentiment. The prospects of a quiet settlement are daily growing smaller; the condition of the country is alarming. Even should everything go on smooth for a month or so, Lincoln's inauguration will upset all. Like the witches in Macbeth I say, "Beware the Ides of March!" With all our troubles I am glad you do feel sanguine for with you it is not (as with me) a matter of mere inconvenience but a question of safety or ruin.[2]

Far more significant to Cook and his prosperity that January was the correspondence he re-

ceived from three Northern photographic firms, each with the same request. One letter was written on January 11—less than three weeks after Anderson occupied Fort Sumter—by Philadelphia photographer Walter Dinmore:

> A Major Anderson is quite popular [in the] North. I think that we might make considerable money if we had his picture. If you can procure us a ½ plate ambrotype of him, we will copy it into photographs and divide the profits accruing from the sale. Answer soon, delays are dangerous, the furor may wear off.[3]

There is no record of how Cook responded to Dinmore, but by the end of the month, he had received similar requests from New York photographer Thomas Faris and from Edward Anthony. Faris, however, had also taken the trouble to write to Anderson, sending his first letter on January 2, only one week after Anderson occupied the fort. "Impossible," Anderson had replied on January 31, almost a month later. "I feel compli-

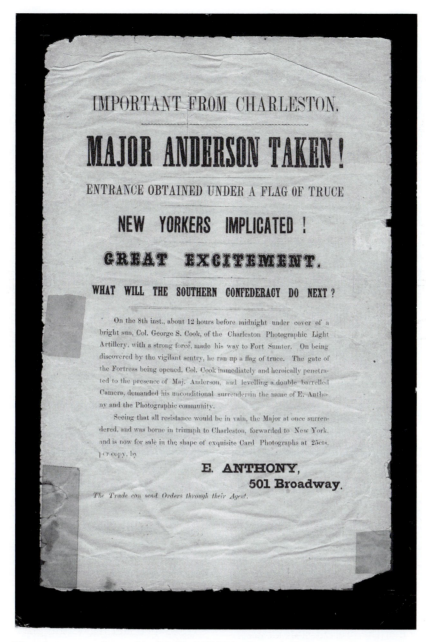

The play on words used in this E. & H. T. Anthony & Company advertisement offering *carte de visite* photographs of Major Robert Anderson appears to have originated from the photographer himself, George S. Cook. After taking the images, Cook wrote to Anthony: "The Castle or Fort is taken, or rather its commander and officers. . . ." (Courtesy of Valentine Richmond History Center)

mented by the request you made me, but I cannot get to Mr. Cook, and he cannot get to me."[4]

Cook, however, appealed to South Carolina Governor Francis W. Pickens through his young wife, Lucy Holcombe Pickens, whose large blue eyes and reddish gold hair accentuated an attractiveness that held sway over most men, including her husband. What had been an impossibility suddenly became possible, and in fine weather on February 8, Cook paid the relatively high price of $5 to rent a boat to ferry him, his camera, and his supplies to Fort Sumter.[5]

In one of the only first-hand accounts written by a Civil War photographer, Cook described the visit in a letter to Anthony. Inscribing his letter as being from the "Confederate States of North America," Cook wrote:

> Friend Anthony: The Castle, or Fort, is taken, or rather its commander and officers, yesterday 8th inst. at two o'clock. I took the Major an hour after the other officers. I had some difficulty in getting them and much in getting the permit to go. Mrs. Pickens kindly interceded in my behalf. I was restricted to one assistant. We had a delightful time; the officers were very kind. Major Anderson is all and more than has been said of him. He is a conscientious, honest, kind and noble man. You are drawn towards him with feelings of love the moment you see him. All his officers seem to adore him; he was most kind to us and treated us handsomely.

In a separate letter to Faris, Cook said that "explicit orders had been given that no one should go to the Fort," and that he had obtained the privilege "only by great perseverance" and, of course, the help of the beautiful Mrs. Pickens.[6]

Almost immediately upon returning to his gallery, possibly even the same day, Cook made copy negatives and shipped them to Faris and Anthony, charging them each $25. "Mr. Anthony's chief object was the preparation of card photographs of which he has been printing about 1,000 daily," the *American Journal of Photography* reported.[7]

On February 11, the *Charleston Courier* carried a brief story about Cook's accomplishment, with a headline that read "Major Anderson Taken," the play on words that Cook had used in his letter to Anthony. That same day, Cook recorded in his account book the first sale of Anderson's photograph to a walk-in customer (though he told Faris he had refused to sell any until February 14, despite great demand). In the days to come, Anderson's photograph became Cook's best-selling image in the South and Anthony's best-seller in the North.[8]

No one was more eager to obtain copies than Anderson himself. On February 14, six days after Cook's visit, Anderson's assistant, Capt. Samuel Wylie Crawford, M.D., penned a letter to the photographer on behalf of his commander. Cook had sent proof photographs back out to the fort for Anderson's review, as if the embattled Union commander was just another customer who had come into his gallery at 235 King Street. Crawford's response and critique of Cook's work was typical of what the photographer heard from his customers each day in the studio.

Major Anderson "desires me to say that he considered the one of himself with the cloak over the shoulder and the hand <u>just below</u> the hilt of the sword as the best of the single ones," Crawford wrote. He described the other group photographs and single images that had been deemed to be the best, and placed a preliminary order. As for his own image, Crawford was disappointed. "I would like you to retouch the eyes of mine, as they show badly," he wrote.[9]

Crawford, a slim, thirty-two-year-old Pennsylvanian with bushy sideburns, was a surgeon with ten years of experience in Indian country. He aspired to be a combat commander, which prompted Anderson to give him command of several guns at Fort Sumter. Cook had offered to return to the fort to provide another sitting, but Crawford told him that Anderson said it wasn't necessary "at present." Cook apparently had also asked whether it would be acceptable to give a copy of Anderson's image to the "artist of the *London News.*" Anderson had no objection, Crawford said, but the matter of whether Cook could sell the image to the public was another issue altogether. "It has been reported to us that our likenesses are exposed <u>for sale</u> in Charleston," Crawford wrote. "I hope this is not the case as I understood from yourself that no such thing would be done or any copy furnished to anyone. Please let us know."[10]

How Cook reacted is unknown, since his letters no longer exist. It may have sent a chill up his spine, though, because the deed had already

Cook's photograph of Major Robert Anderson and his staff in Fort Sumter on February 8, 1860 (*above*), was converted into a woodcut engraving and featured on the cover of *Harper's Weekly* (*right*) six weeks later. To Anderson's right sits Capt. Abner Doubleday, holding his sword. At the commander's left is Union surgeon Dr. Samuel Wylie Crawford, who acted as Anderson's representative in placing photo orders with Cook before the bombardment. (*Top*: Photography Collection, Miriam and Ira D. Wallach Division of Art, Prints and Photographs, The New York Public Library, Aster, Lenox and Tilden Foundations; *right*: Library of Congress)

been done. Not only had Cook begun to sell copies at his own gallery, but he had guaranteed national, mass distribution with his sale of copy negatives to Anthony and Faris. Despite this apparent breach of trust, the veteran photographer must have handled the matter smoothly. Crawford's second letter to Cook, dated February 26, acknowledged the receipt of additional photographs, also possibly proof images, and said, "Please let me know the price of the photographs as some of the officers desire copies, some two, others three, should the price be moderate." Crawford, backing away from making public sale of the photos an issue, added this postscript: "There is no objection to any friend of the officers having a copy of the photographs should they desire it."[11]

Twice in his letter of February 26, Crawford urged Cook to reply "at once," underlining those words both times for emphasis. No one knew how long Anderson would be ordered to hold out, when he might receive an order to withdraw, or whether the South would lose patience and attack. The tension was increasing day by day as Southern states took possession of one Federal fort after another, and Anderson and his small group hunkered down at Fort Sumter in staunch defiance. Despite the remarkable circumstances of the siege, Crawford's business-as-usual correspondence with Cook continued. The nation might be on the cusp of civil war, but there was little to do in Fort Sumter except wait, and the men had plenty of time to mull over their images, suggest changes, make choices, and negotiate with Cook,

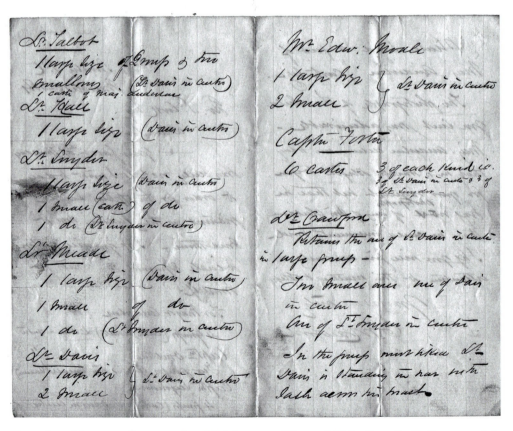

Reproduced here are the second and third pages of Samuel Wylie Crawford's four-page letter to Cook of March 12, 1861, where he orders photos from Cook on behalf of the entire command staff. On the first page of this letter, Crawford ordered four copies each of the group photograph for Anderson, Doubleday, and another captain. (Courtesy of the Valentine Richmond History Center)

using all the stubborn Yankee skill they could muster.[12]

Crawford wrote on March 3, 1861:

We do not understand whether or not the price of the originals is to be charged to us. They think that as impressions of them have been sold to others, that it cannot be your intention to charge the original price to them. Please let us know in reference to this as the officers are only awaiting your answer before ordering several copies for each. If it should be your intention to charge the original price, some other conclusion will probably be arrived at.[13]

By this time, Anderson and his officers were well aware of their celebrity status. Crawford's eight letters underscore that regular mail service existed to and from the besieged fort and was undoubtedly carried by boats flying white flags of truce. Anderson's second-in-command, Capt. Abner Doubleday, who had been daguerreotyped in Saltillo during the Mexican War, wrote:

We saw advertisements now in the Northern papers showing that dramas founded on our occupation of Fort Sumter, and confinement, were being acted both in Boston and New York. It was quite amusing to see our names in the play-bills, and to find that persons were acting our parts and spouting mock heroics on the state.[14]

Cook diplomatically handled the question about his prices, because Crawford's next letter, dated March 12, placed an order on behalf of Anderson, Doubleday, himself, and eight others for a total of thirty-eight photographs. Anderson wanted four *cartes de visite* of the group photograph; Doubleday wanted four images, two large and two small; Captain Truman Seymour wanted four cartes. . . . On it went, for three more pages. The total cost, in the end, was a bargain at $13.50; Cook had extended his generosity beyond expectations.[15]

On March 26, Crawford wrote:

I was not aware nor were the other officers that the large size photographs were intended to be free to them. They desire me to express to you their sincere thanks. I have read your letter to Maj. Anderson who desires me to thank you especially for your kind attention and liberality in this matter as regards himself, and I add again with my own the thanks of all of us. I was glad to know that your visit was a source of profit and pleasure, a combination sufficiently rare to make it the more desirable.[16]

Cook could afford the largesse. The Anderson photos had become instant best-sellers, not only in New York but in Charleston. In addition to the $50 he collected from Anthony and Faris for the copy negatives and the $13.50 he charged the Sumter officers, Cook recorded a dozen separate transactions in his account book between February 11 and April 4 for photographs of Maj. Anderson. The twelve buyers bought a total of forty Anderson pictures, mostly *cartes de visite* and large format images, and paid Cook a total of $50.75.[17]

Most of the correspondence between Cook and Crawford pertained to the business of buying photographs, but there was time for personal notes, too. Cook must have sent along a copy of the February 11 article in the *Charleston Courier* with the wry headline, "Major Anderson Taken," because Crawford wrote on March 3 that Anderson "was amused at the newspaper." If friendliness and generosity were good for business, Cook also wasn't shy about asking for something in return, even if it didn't pan out. In the March 12 letter, Crawford wrote, "Major Anderson desires me to say that he is much obliged to you for your request, but that he has no photograph of any of his children that he could conveniently find." This was a curious request and must have indicated that Cook, always the opportunistic businessman, had determined that there was a market for such photos.[18]

Of equal curiosity is a particularly solicitous letter sent by Crawford to Cook on March 20 requesting images of Fort Moultrie. The old fort, which had existed in various forms since the Revolutionary War, had been where Anderson was stationed until his move to Sumter. The Confederates then quickly converted Fort Moultrie

Photographer A. J. Riddle of Macon, Georgia, who would be best remembered for his photographs of Andersonville prison, also took this *carte de visite* portrait of an unidentified Confederate captain and his slave and manservant, smartly outfitted in an eight-button Confederate shell jacket and matching trousers. This is one of less than six known wartime images showing a slave wearing a Confederate uniform. (From the collection of David Wynn Vaughan)

This unknown Georgia Rebel at left was more defiant than most of the thousands who posed for their portraits during the war. In addition to holding a Bowie knife and a pistol, he is wearing a battle shirt and an upside-down U.S. belt plate in this ambrotype. Above is a sixth-plate ambrotype of private James M. Stedham of the 25th Alabama Infantry Regiment taken in 1861 or 1862. Stedham was captured by Sherman's troops in Georgia and died of acute dysentery a month before the end of the war in an Indiana prisoner-of-war camp. (From the collection of David Wynn Vaughan)

into the primary Rebel bastion in opposition to Sumter. Crawford wrote:

> I must trouble you once more. I understand you have some good views of Fort Moultrie outside and in. They are stereoscopic views, I believe. Will you do me the favor to send me one of each? I would like to have a good view of Moultrie from the outside especially. Send these if you please at once. I hope that you received my check and that it was all right. We do not know anything of any movement yet.[19]

Crawford's final sentence indicates that Cook had asked the question of the moment in Charleston and throughout the country: Would Anderson withdraw? Rumors of the possibility were rampant. On some days, it seemed a certainty, even for the Union men. The *Courier* had reported on March 11 that Anderson indeed would evacuate Fort Sumter and go to Fort Monroe, Virginia. On March 26, Crawford addressed the subject again: "We know nothing of any order for our withdrawal and as yet are entirely ignorant as to when it will be issued."[20]

With the burning question of the day left unanswered, Cook, nonetheless, promptly complied with Crawford's request for stereoscopic views of Fort Moultrie. Crawford's final letter to Cook, dated April 1, 1861, is by far the most urgent of all his communications:

> Yours of Saturday [March 30] reached me yesterday with four stereoscopic views of Moultrie. I wish to acknowledge them and wish you to send me others at once. They are the only souvenirs I shall have and I hope you will lose no time in supplying me. Send me duplicates of every view. The ones you sent have been much admired and as there is no telling at what moment we will receive our orders. I ask you again to lose no time in sending me duplicate copies of all the views of Moultrie and its surroundings that you can obtain including two more copies each of those four views you have already sent. They will be the most acceptable product to my friends and I do not wish to leave without them. Please send them at once.

Later, Crawford implored again: "Let me know at once."[21]

There is no record of whether Cook provided these additional stereo views, and no Cook views of either Fort Sumter or Fort Moultrie from 1861 have been positively identified today. Cook's account book documents only one sale of stereo views to Dr. Crawford. An entry for February 8—the day Cook visited the fort—says, "Dr. Crawford 12 stereoscopes @ .25–3.00."

Cook may have sold Crawford stereo views during his visit, or the entry may reflect a later sale, since the $13.50 that Crawford paid in mid-March is posted under February 8. There is only one other entry for Crawford, and it comes on April 4, 1861—three days after Crawford's final letter and just eight days before the bombardment—with Cook recording a sale to "Dr. Crawford" of one dozen "*visites*" for six dollars.[22]

One can only speculate whether Crawford's request for stereo views of the Confederate fort troubled Southern leaders, assuming they ever knew. Mail service to and from the fort apparently remained inviolate until April 8, and mail in general continued to flow between the North and South until June 1. Were the Union officers simply seeking more souvenirs of their unique moment in the spotlight of history? Or were they intent on using 3-D photography of Fort Moultrie as a tool to get the best possible visual understanding of the Confederate stronghold? Was George S. Cook an unwitting partner in providing photographic intelligence to the embattled stronghold? Photo historian Harvey S. Teal believes that "since the Major and his forces had occupied Fort Moultrie and other military positions around Charleston only two months earlier, the requests for these photographs probably were motivated by a desire to send copies to loved ones and not for spying purposes."[23]

The question of espionage, however, cannot be overlooked. Doubleday, for one, wrote that Cook "proved afterward to be a lieutenant of a Charleston company" who "came as a spy, and, no doubt, thought he had done a very clever thing." Cook, indeed, was a member of a home guard unit. But as far as Doubleday was concerned, it made little difference, since other Southern visitors, including military officers, had been allowed to roam the fort at will. It should be noted as well that if the Fort Moultrie views were, indeed, significant, Crawford never mentioned it in his comprehensive 1887 study, the *History of the Fall of Fort Sumpter*, nor did he write a single word in the book about Cook's visit or their correspondence.[24]

Whether it had hidden motives or not, Cook's camera work at Fort Sumter was another milestone in the history of American photography. It is a dramatic example of the impact photography had on a national scale and a revealing glimpse into the business of photography at its most basic level: the interaction between a photographer and his customers. Whereas Anderson wanted four copies of his own *carte de visite*, Anthony was producing 1,000 a day for the rest of the nation. As the standoff at Fort Sumter dragged into April and the political fever intensified, many Northerners undoubtedly bought Anderson's *carte de visite* and secured it in their parlor photo album on the same page as their photograph of Lincoln.

On the afternoon of April 11, three Confederate officers took seats in a small boat and were rowed out to Fort Sumter to deliver to Anderson Confederate Commander P. G. T. Beauregard's final ultimatum for surrender. In his gallery on King Street, Cook was tending to the needs of six paying customers who came through his door to spend a total of $39.50. Among them were three Confederate officers—a colonel and two captains—who spent $10 each on large format images in black frames. Cook meticulously recorded these sales in a small account book that was, by and large, a dry, daily chronology of dates, names, photos, and dollar amounts, with the weather sometimes noted in the margin. It became a journal only on the most historic and notable days. April 12, 1861, was one of those days.[25]

> April 12: Shut up, war, war, war.

There is a sense of irritation in those words as Cook logs the interruption of normal business— a lost day—as the bombardment of Fort Sumter began. Cook did not write, "nothing done," as he had on so many days during the previous fall. The war had not just closed his gallery; it was "shut up." The excitement nonetheless gripped Cook, and he could not help but write a few more sparse details in his account book. In tiny handwriting in the margin, Cook squeezed in:

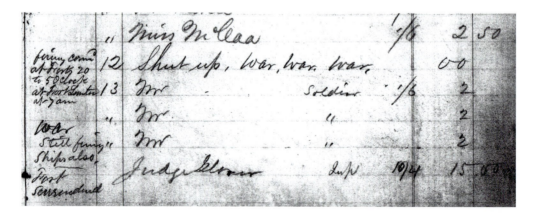

This page from George S. Cook's 1861 account book includes April 12, the day the Civil War started. As the entries show, Cook's business came to a halt, but only for a day. Although he briefly but dramatically notes the start of the hostilities in the left margin, Cook did not follow his Anderson accomplishment by photographing Fort Sumter after the surrender, leaving that to other Charleston photographers. (Courtesy of the Valentine Richmond History Center)

Firing com[menced] at Forts 20 to 5 O'clock. At
Fort Sumter at 7 a.m.

The next day, Cook was again open for business,
but he noted in the margin:

War. Still firing. Ships also.

"Fort surrendered."[26]

For thirty-three hours, Confederate guns had
pounded the fort. "Splendid Pyrotechnic Exhibition," read the headline in the next morning's
Charleston Mercury, which reported:

> At the break of day, amidst the bursting of
> bombs and the roaring of ordnance, and before
> thousands of spectators, whose homes, and lib-
> erties, and lives were at stake, was enacted this
> first great scene in the opening drama of what,
> it is presumed, will be a most momentous mili-
> tary act. It may be a drama of but a single act.[27]

It would be far more than a single act, of
course, and the irony of the *Mercury*'s declara-
tion was rivaled only by the irony that no one was
killed in this first engagement of the bloodiest of
American wars. Only a few combatants received
injuries of any serious nature. The bombardment also may have had more civilian witnesses
than any other contest of the war. The night before, thousands had gathered along the battery
and on the rooftops of Charleston's elegant
homes in eager anticipation. When nothing happened and midnight came and went, the restless
throng dissipated, only to rush back after those
booming first shots.

"Lights flash on as if by magic from the windows of every house, and in the twinkling of an
eye, as it were, an agitated mass of people are
rushing impetuously toward the waterfront of
the city," recalled a *New York Herald* correspondent years later. Once again a huge crowd
filled the battery; many remained through the
day and into the evening. "There they stood,
with palpitating hearts and pallid faces, watching the white smoke as it rose in wreathes upon
the soft twilight air and breathing out fervent
prayers for their gallant kinsfolk at the guns,"
wrote a reporter for the *Charleston Courier*.[28]

What a scene it must have been: officers bark-
ing orders, cannoneers sweating over their pieces,
politicians red-faced with bluster, ladies swoon-
ing with excitement, onlookers flushed with
whiskey, and a cause. Looking upon this scene,
as he surely must have, one can only wish that
Cook, in this instance, had been a bit more of a
photojournalist and a bit less of a businessman.
With history literally exploding in the front yard
of his soon-to-be-finished home on the Battery,
why Cook did not grab his camera and rush there
to document, if nothing else, the vast crowds
watching the bombardment is a question that can
only be answered with conjecture. Even as his
competitors rushed to get in on the action, there
is no evidence that Cook photographed any aspect of the bombardment or its aftermath.[29]

Anderson and his small band battled gamely
for a day, a night, and the better part of another
day, but the outcome was a foregone conclusion.
The fort had forty-eight guns, but only the eighty-
five officers and men, so they could only man a
few guns at a time. The Confederates had more
than 4,000 men and at least seventy guns that
ultimately fired 3,307 shots at the fort, which
was an average of two a minute. By April 13,
Fort Sumter was a battered, burning hell. Three
times or more, the three-story barracks caught
fire; each time the officers and men managed
to extinguish the blazes. Union gunners fired
almost 1,000 shells at Fort Moultrie and the
other Rebel batteries arrayed against the fort.
They scored 163 mostly inconsequential hits
against the Rebel's much-talked-about "secret
weapon," the Floating Battery, a barge-like raft
sheathed in iron that concealed four guns. Conditions in the fort became more desperate as
supplies dwindled to four kegs of usable powder
and almost no food.[30] Doubleday recalled:

> By 11 a.m. the conflagration was terrible and
> disastrous, One fifth of the fort was on fire,
> and the wind drove the smoke in dense masses
> into the angle where we had all taken refuge. It
> seemed impossible to escape suffocation. Some

lay down close to the ground, with handkerchiefs over their mouths, and others posted themselves near the embrasures, where the smoke was somewhat lessened by the draught of air. Every one suffered severely. . . . The roaring and crackling of the flames, the dense masses of whirling smoke, the bursting of the enemy's shells and our own which were exploding in the burning rooms, the crashing of the shot, and the sound of masonry falling in every direction, made the fort a pandemonium.[31]

That afternoon, Anderson accepted Beauregard's terms of surrender. The next day became known as "Evacuation Day" in the South and was filled with the formal ceremonies of surrender. Then, as if on cue, a last-act tragedy occurred. Anderson was conducting a hundred-gun salute to the Stars and Stripes within the fort when an accidental explosion of cartridges killed one Union gunner, mortally wounded another, and injured four. Anderson shortened the salute to fifty shots and around 4:00 p.m. boarded the steamer *Isabel* with his men, but by then the tide had gone out, and they were unable to leave Sumter's wharf until the next morning.[32]

As the *Isabel* finally pulled away at around 8:00 a.m. on April 15, it may have passed a small boat that arrived that morning with a young local man named Alma A. Pelot, assistant to Jesse H. Bolles, who owned the "Temple of Art," one of Charleston's leading photographic studios. Pelot brought with him at least one camera, a half-dozen or more glass plates, bottles of chemicals, and a tent-like, portable darkroom. By the end of the day, according to all available evidence, Pelot had become the first photographer of the Civil War.

As with many Civil War photographers, little is known about Pelot. He was a native of Charleston and still a young man in 1861. He was listed as a daguerreian in 1859, when he lived in Charleston at 230 King Street, the same address of J. Alma Pelot's commercial school. Bolles employed Pelot in 1860, but his job was not destined to last. In 1862, Pelot enlisted in Confederate service. After

the war, he established a gallery in Augusta, Georgia, where he took photographs for more than forty years.[33]

The story of Pelot's visit to Fort Sumter is documented in brief articles in the April 16 issues of the *Charleston Mercury* and the *Courier.* The latter newspaper reported:

> By special permission of General Beauregard, our young native artist, Mr. Alma A. Pelot, assistant to Jesse H. Bolles, has taken full and perfect representations of the internal appearance of Fort Sumter, on the morning after the surrender. These pictures for the time will afford appropriate ornaments for our Drawing Rooms, Scrap Books and Albums, and a most acceptable present to distant and anxious friends.

The *Mercury* reported that Pelot took images from "five different points of view."[34]

No sales figures have survived, but the instant success of these images is implied by the pattern of advertisements that Bolles had published in both Charleston newspapers, beginning with the issues of April 16. His first paid announcement—the same in both papers—was a moderately large display advertisement of one column by about two inches. It said the five views would be "ready for delivery to-morrow afternoon, 17th inst." Nine days later, Bolles *doubled* the size of the ads in both papers. He reported that sixteen views were now available, suggesting that he or Pelot considered the first venture profitable enough to make a second visit to the fort, or at least to print all the negatives Pelot had exposed on his first visit. The April 25 *Mercury* ad was two columns wide and two inches deep, an immense display ad by the paper's standards. "Forts Sumter, Moultrie and the Floating Battery— Sixteen Views of the Most Important and Interesting Points . . . The Pictures Are Now On Exhibition," the ad said.[35]

The Fort Sumter photographs had to compete with other bombardment souvenirs being advertised in Charleston after the surrender. On April 19, a local publisher began offering "the Full Account of the Battle of Fort Sumter in

FORTS SUMTER, MOULTRIE
AND THE
FLOATING BATTERY.

————o————

SIXTEEN VIEWS OF THE MOST IMPORTANT AND INTERESTING
POINTS OF
FORTS SUMTER, MOULTRIE AND THE FLOATING BATTERY,
Taken immediately after the surrender, previously to any repairs or changes whatever,
BY DOLLES, SOUTHERN ARTIST.

The PICTURES are now on Exhibition, and will be ready for delivery to Subscribers this day and during the
week. Terms reasonable.
JESSE H. BOLLES'
TEMPLE OF ART,

April 25 —   CORNER OF KING AND LIBERTY STREETS.

On April 25, 1861, Charleston photographer Jesse H. Bolles took out a two-column advertisement in the *Charleston Mercury* to advertise his gallery's photographs of Fort Sumter and other Charleston Harbor features after the Union surrender. The apparent success of earlier ads prompted Bolles to buy the larger, two-column notice, which is reproduced here at its actual size in the newspaper. This may be the largest advertisement for war photographs in any American newspaper during the Civil War. The photo is a reproduction from one of Bolles's original prints of the Confederate Floating Battery. (*Top*: Library of Congress; *bottom*: Hallmark Photographic Collection, Hallmark Cards, Inc., Kansas City, Missouri)

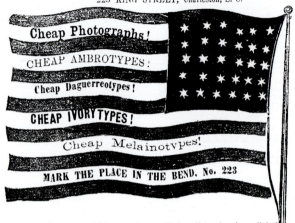

In 1858, veteran Charleston daguerreian artist James M. Osborn joined forces with F. E. Durbec and opened a multifaceted photographic establishment that offered just about any type of image available, as is made plain by their 1860 advertisement in the Charleston business directory. Although Osborn & Durbec were among the war's first photographers, it put them out of business by 1862 or 1863.

Pamphlet Form." Three days later, the *Courier* reported that merchants Spencer & Teague, located directly across King Street from Cook's gallery, "have made and supplied many tokens from the flag staff of Fort Sumter in the shape of trinkets and studds."[36]

At least ten of the sixteen images issued by Bolles can be accounted for today, including the Floating Battery image and several from Sumter that are identified as having been taken on April 15. The most famous of these April 15 photographs—an image that shows the interior of Fort

Sumter with the Confederate flag flying atop the flagstaff—has been widely credited to the photographer F. K. Houston, but it is most likely Pelot's work. Houston did not operate a gallery in Charleston until 1871.[37]

Another photographer did visit Fort Sumter after the bombardment, however, and his name was J. M. Osborn, with "Osborn & Durbec's Southern Stereoscopic and Photographic Depot" at 223 King Street at the "Sign of the Big Camera." Osborn's partner, F. E. Durbec, probably remained at their gallery to handle the daily business while Osborn embarked on his ambitious mission to document the points of interest in Charleston Harbor.

Osborn & Durbec did not run advertisements in either paper, but the *Courier* published a news item about their images, though not until April 23:

> We learn that Mr. Osborn, of the firm of Osborn & Durbec, the well known photographists, has, by special permission, been allowed to visit Fort Sumter, and has taken twenty-six different views of the fort, internal and external. Mr. Osborn has also visited Morris and Sullivan's Islands, and has taken several views of these points, all of which we may expect to see in a few days.[38]

Another *Courier* article on May 6 said, "The views of Fort Sumter comprise the whole interior, in twenty sections, for the Stereoscope, and six large Photographs for framing. Also, on hand, one hundred different Stereoscopic Views in Charleston and vicinity, Views of Plantations in the State, etc."[39]

Osborn & Durbec are known to have taken at least forty-three stereo views after the surrender, consisting of the twenty views of Fort Sumter, ten or more views from Fort Moultrie, six Morris Island scenes, four that comprised a "Coles Island" series, and at least three more from Sullivan's Island. Thirty-nine are known to exist today, most in full stereo and a few as half-stereo, two-dimensional images. Together, these views comprise the largest known group of Confeder-

This detail from an original Osborn & Durbec stereo view is one of only two known photographs of Southern photographic outfits in the field during the Civil War. The Osborn & Durbec darkroom tent, with their label on the side, sits behind the second of two mortars of the Trapier Mortar Battery, which fired on Fort Sumter from Morris Island. (From the collection of Robin Stanford)

ate images of the war, stereoscopic or otherwise, as well as one of the most complete contemporary photographic records ever made of the site of a Civil War engagement.[40]

Issued on colorful bright orange or lime green mounts, the Osborn & Durbec stereo views graphically show the damage inflicted on Forts Sumter and Moultrie by the thousands of shells fired during the bombardment. At Sumter, Osborn's twenty views show the bastion in a state of partial ruin, from the pockmarked exterior walls to the shell-damaged and fire-ravaged barracks within. In many photographs, the Rebels, who did the damage, are shown cleaning it up. Osborn ventured onto the parapet, where he photographed top-hatted South Carolina dignitaries inspecting a damaged gun. He went into one of Sumter's casemates, defying low-light conditions, to make a photograph of the big guns that Anderson's men fired. He took stereographs of the Fort Moultrie barracks that faced Sumter and bore the brunt of the Union response. He carried his stereo camera within the "Iron Clad Battery" on Morris Island to make a stereo view of the place where fiery secessionist Edmund Ruffin discharged one of the opening shots at Sumter.[41]

Osborn paid reasonably close attention to the techniques of stereoscopic photography and usually made sure the image contained an element in the foreground or mid-ground to provide good 3-D effect. He was even more attentive to making individual images work together for a wider perspective. Many of the views, particularly those of Fort Sumter's exterior and interior, can be placed side by side to create multiplate panoramas.

As a group, there are at least sixty known images taken in and around Fort Sumter after the surrender. Most, if not all, of these can be traced to either Pelot and Bolles or Osborn & Durbec. It is quite possible that other Charleston photographers also visited the fort, but documentation exists only for those two Charleston galleries.[42]

And what of George S. Cook? Perhaps Cook was still basking in the glory and financial reward of his Anderson images and decided he didn't need to revisit the fort. A number of accounts place Cook at Fort Sumter after the surrender, but no documentation or images have thus far surfaced to support such claims. In fact, the entries in Cook's account book, written in his own hand, show he was in his gallery, busy with customers, each and every day of the week, except Sunday, from April 13 through the rest of the month, and in May as well. There is no record of a visit to Fort Sumter in the account book, which *did* document the visit of February 8.[43]

The Charleston newspapers no doubt would have heralded any post-bombardment images taken by Cook, just as they had mentioned the photos taken by the others and Cook's images of Anderson. Cook had a standard, daily advertisement in the *Courier* offering "Life-Size Portraits In Oil and Pastel" that had run since February 15. After the bombardment, it remained unchanged.[44]

As the shells flew on April 13—the second day of the bombardment—Cook was not among the spectators. He was back at work tending to the needs of four customers, including three anonymous soldiers who bought sixth-plate tintypes for two dollars each. Cook had a half-dozen customers on Monday, April 15, eight the next day, ten on April 17, and on a clear and windy April 18, no fewer than sixteen paying customers.[45]

A number of these customers bought Anderson photos, which again became brisk sellers after the bombardment. On April 15, the day after the surrender, Cook sold eleven images of Anderson in three separate transactions. The next day he sold five more in two sales. By the end of the month, Anderson sales had slowed to a trickle, but in the three weeks following the bombardment, Cook's gallery sold forty images of Anderson in a dozen different transactions, taking in a total of $39 in gross sales. While this represented only a small fraction of his total gross sales of $1,166.25 for the same three weeks, Cook's photographs of Anderson appear to be the best-selling images he had ever taken as a photographer up to that time.[46]

Cook's place in the history of Civil War photography would have been assured by his Anderson images alone, but his adventures were far from over. His ultimate fate, like that of the South, was not destined to be pleasant. Yet the slave-owning, native Yankee, who parlayed his experience as a daguerreian artist to become one of the most important photographers of the Civil War, seems almost to have become a historian by accident—a man who recorded history simply by showing up. Later in the war, Cook would take the world's first combat action photographs—not because he set out to do so but because he happened to be in the right place at the right time. If Cook, like Brady, yearned to preserve the war's historic sights and scenes for posterity and history, he did not say so, at least not in any surviving documents or records. He was a businessman, and though he sold a good number of celebrity photographs, his most lucrative trade, by far, was taking photographs of individuals in his gallery. That is where he could be found during the war, even when history was unfolding on the doorstep of his soon-to-be-finished house.

The first opportunity to photograph the Civil War had happened in the South, and if Cook was missing in action after the surrender of Fort Sumter, his competitors more than ably filled the gap. In the North, the same opportunity would not come until the summer of 1861, when an overconfident and under-prepared Union Army marched out to challenge the Rebels at Bull Run.

4

BRADY AT BULL RUN

For the first six days of the war, Washington, D.C., was unprotected. The first defenders to arrive were five companies of Pennsylvania troops, who reached the capital on April 18. That night, to protect the new president from a suspected assassination plot, Kansas Senator-elect Jim Lane and several dozen of his "Frontier Guard" bivouacked in the East Room of the White House, one of the most elegant camp settings ever enjoyed by a militia unit. Thousands of militiamen and new recruits from every Northern state soon streamed into Washington. The entire country was beginning to mobilize, North and South alike. From Adrian, Michigan, to Americus, Georgia, local photographers took their cameras to the windows and roofs of their galleries, or out onto the street to photograph their local boys preparing to march off to war.[1]

An obscure New Orleans photographer named J. D. Edwards undertook one of the earliest, and one of the most historically important, wartime photographic expeditions. Unlike the vast majority of Southern photographers, Edwards saw opportunity in leaving his studio and venturing into the field, where he followed Confederate units from New Orleans to Pensacola, Florida, in April

1861 as they mobilized against the last remaining Union bastion in the South, Fort Pickens. It was widely expected to be the next major battleground after Fort Sumter, though the Confederates eventually abandoned the effort, leaving the fort in Union hands throughout the war. During the mobilization in the spring of 1861, Edwards prowled the forts, gun emplacements, and camps, which were teeming with Mississippians, Alabamians, and Louisianans. By climbing to the top of the towering, new 160-foot lighthouse just west of Fort Barrancas and shooting photos of the Confederate camps and the Gulf of Mexico, he took what are considered to be the first aerial photographs of the war. He may also have taken photographs of Union ships and coastal installations for the Confederate Secret Service.[2]

"THE WAR!" Edwards advertised in New Orleans newspapers on May 14, 1861. Without even mentioning his own name, Edwards advertised "39 different photographic views, taken by an accomplished artist on the spot. . . . They are very large and taken superbly. Price $1 per copy." Two of Edwards's images were reproduced as woodcut engravings in *Harpers Weekly* on June 15 and July 12, but he received no credit. He published his advertisement for only three days and then promptly dropped from history. The war apparently drove Edwards out of business, as it did most Confederate photographers, but before disappearing into obscurity, he created the single, most comprehensive photographic record of Confederate camps, installations, and soldiers.[3]

As militia units from New York, Pennsylvania, Massachusetts, and other states poured into Washington, camps sprang up throughout the area. The demand for photographers suddenly became enormous. For a freshly minted soldier in the field, there could exist no better souvenir of this grand adventure than a photographic portrait in uniform. Tintypes and ambrotypes were taken by the tens of thousands.

Camp Cameron, located on Meridian Hill about two miles northwest of the Capitol building, was the home of the elite 7th New York Regiment, a militia unit comprised of the city's wealthiest, most influential young men. Mere portraits would not satisfy these confident warriors. In May 1861, they arranged with Washington photographer Wm. M. Smith, a self-described "stereoscopist" with a gallery at 482 H. Street, to make custom stereo views at their camp. Smith went to the trouble of printing a custom label for the reverse side (also known as a "backmark") that included blanks where the owner could write in his tent and company numbers (but, curiously, no space was alloted for his name). The few extant original prints of these stereo views show small groups of soldiers standing or sitting in front of a tent, sometimes posed in the act of reading a newspaper or letter or cleaning a musket.[4]

M. B. Brady was responsible for some of the most distinctive portraits from this period, and his gallery also issued many images of the 7th New York. Brady was personally acquainted with many of the members of the regiment before the war, sharing a bond so close that in his last days in the 1890s, when he was penniless and bedridden, veterans of the 7th Regiment were among those who came to his aid. Brady issued portraits of the men as *cartes de visite* and mounted them on cards bearing a generic "Illustrations of Camp Life" label. Many are full-length shots, often with the soldier posed next to a tent or a tree, and they have a look unlike most other images of soldiers in the field. Whether it is the stance, the tilt of the head, the look in the eye, the background, or the arrangement of the subjects, these Brady portraits stand above the norm.[5]

In New York, the E. & H. T. Anthony & Company was expanding its catalog of stereoscopic views almost daily. On April 20, 1861, an unnamed Anthony photographer snapped four instantaneous views of the Great Union Meeting at Union Square, with Anderson as one of the featured speakers. The latest instantaneous photographs from Broadway now showed huge recruiting banners stretched across the width of the great thoroughfare. Anthony wasn't about to ignore the photographic opportunities in Washington either. At Brady's urging or perhaps on his own accord, Anthony dispatched one of the country's most experienced photographers, George N. Barnard, south to the capital and sent his stereoscopic print shop manager, Jacob F. Coonley, with him.[6]

Barnard had spent almost a decade in Oswego before moving to Syracuse in late 1853. In 1854, he became seriously ill. He also separated from his wife that year (but never divorced). These upheavals may have spurred Barnard to seek new opportunities. He eventually sold his gallery and in 1859 moved to New York. There, he went to work for Anthony at around the same time that his new employer began issuing the company's own extensive series of stereo views. Barnard may have been responsible for many of the Anthony stereo views issued in 1859 and 1860, including the instantaneous views of New York City, but he can only be positively credited for a series of 191 views of Cuba. Barnard traveled there in the spring of 1860 to take both instantaneous and regular wet plate, stereo photographs of a country that had long fascinated Americans.[7]

Barnard and Coonley arrived in Washington a

Illustrations of Camp Life.

Brady,   Washington.

Illustrations of Camp Life.

Brady,   Washington.

Whether presented as individual portraits, pairs, or group photographs, M. B. Brady's "Illustrations of Camp Life" series from 1861 had a distinctive style. The soldier above is a member of the 4th Michigan regiment. The pair above right are from an unidentified New York volunteer regiment, while the group photograph shows members of the 10th Massachusetts. (From the collection of Michael J. McAfee)

Illustrations of Camp Life.

Brady,   Washington.

few days after Lincoln's inauguration on March 4, 1861. Coonley recalled some twenty years later:

> A great many notables both military and civilian began to frequent the Capital, and we were kept very busy in making pictures of them for publication. Within a very few days [after Fort Sumter's surrender] Washington and its environs was swarming with soldiers, who reached it almost hourly. We were engaged making portraits in the Brady gallery until July, when I went into the field for the purpose of making pictures of the officers and subordinates in the army of the Potomac.[8]

Barnard also visited Camp Cameron, and with another photographer, C. O. Bostwick, made at least a half-dozen stereo photographs that the Anthony Company sold commercially as stereo views and single-image card photographs. When fourteen rambunctious members of the 7th New York made a human pyramid four levels high, Barnard and Bostwick captured the scene in a view that was marketed as "Gymnastic Field Sports of the Gallant 7th."[9]

On May 5, 1861, Union Gen. Benjamin F. Butler occupied Relay House on the Baltimore and Ohio Railroad, just south of Baltimore, and eight days later marched into Baltimore. Butler's soldiers set up camp on the hills high above the railroad junction and soon found themselves posing for an Anthony stereo photographer, probably Coonley, who captured them giving each other haircuts, writing letters, making dinner, weighing out rations, reading news from home, and generally milling about.

The Anthony Company issued thirty-eight stereo views taken in the area of Relay House and Annapolis. Though no photographer was credited, Coonley wrote that his photographic journeys in 1861 included taking views in Annapolis, making him the likely photographer of the Relay House views as well. Together with the handful of scenes that Barnard and Bostwick took at Camp Cameron, the Relay House views were part of a small Anthony series entitled "Camp Scenes." For unknown reasons, this group of eighty-three war views was never incorporated into the comprehensive "War for the Union" series issued in 1865, which became the primary compilation of Anthony war photographs. Even after the war, views from the Camp Scenes series were sold separately. While none of the negatives appear to exist, many original albumen prints have survived in wonderful condition. The men in these views were, as the labels said, "Basking in the Sunshine," or "Taking It Easy." Like the scenes from Camp Cameron, the men appear lighthearted and carefree, as if the war was a lark.[10]

But that laid-back attitude was wearing thin in the North. By the summer of 1861, as the thermometer rose in the sultry capital, so did the pressure to take action. On June 26, Horace Greeley's *New York Tribune* proclaimed: "Forward to Richmond! Forward to Richmond! The Rebel Congress Must Not Be Allowed to Meet there on the 20th of July." President Lincoln convened Congress in Special Session on July 4 to ratify war measures, and twelve days later, Union Gen. Irvin McDowell led a force of about 35,000 men out of Washington.[11]

Of the thousands of camp photographs that had been taken in the previous weeks, perhaps the final image taken before the army pulled up stakes was a group photograph of a dozen Union soldiers, primarily from the 8th New York, gathered in front of their tents. These were young Americans with last names like Briggs, Hart, Enders, and Duffy. One soldier had a musket in hand and a bedroll over his shoulder, ready to march. The image looks similar to the many other group photographs taken in the camps around Washington in the spring of 1861. What makes it unique is the handwritten inscription on the back: "Half an hour before the start at 3 o'clock to Fairfax Courthouse, Virginia," on July 16, 1861.[12]

McDowell and his army crossed the Long Bridge and camped at Fairfax Court House on July 17. They clashed with the Confederates the next day at Blackburn's Ford, losing almost eighty men. The news of the fight at Blackburn's

Ford swirled through the sweltering capital on Saturday, July 20, as did word that McDowell would attack again the next day. Just west of Centreville, beyond a creek known as Bull Run, Confederate Gen. P. G. T. Beauregard waited with his army stretched along a six-mile line.[13]

Civilians scrambled to obtain passes into Virginia. Hundreds filled picnic baskets for their expeditions to bear witness to the rout of the Rebels. A group of twenty-five to thirty newspaper correspondents had already joined McDowell's army for the march. The general de-

This Civil War–era engraving shows the New York headquarters at 501 Broadway of E. & H. T. Anthony & Company, the nation's leading supplier of photographic materials and images. The company provided photographic materials "of every description" as well as more than 4,000 different card photographs, including 110 major generals, 550 statesmen, 116 authors, and 66 prominent women.

The photographs that New Orleans photographer J. D. Edwards took at Pensacola, Florida, in the spring of 1861 include this view of Company B of the 9th Mississippi Regiment, the "Quitman Rifles," from the area of Holly Springs, Mississippi. The Confederate kneeling and frying food is said to be Kinlock Falconer, who would one day serve as a major on the staffs of Generals Joseph Johnston and Braxton Bragg. (Library of Congress)

In the spring of 1861, a new look appeared in Anthony's latest instantaneous views of Broadway in New York City. Recruiting banners for New York regiments hung the entire width of the thoroughfare. In this previously unpublished stereo view, this huge banner, seen from behind, urged "Scotchmen for the Union" to join the 79th New York Regiment, formerly a militia unit of Scottish immigrants. The Cameron Highlanders, as they were known, were mustered into service on May 29, 1861. (From the collection of Jeffrey Kraus)

Company C of the 8th New York, known as the "Washington Greys," posed for Brady's camera at Arlington Heights on July 16, 1861, thirty minutes before starting their march toward Bull Run. (From the collection of Michael J. McAfee)

cided that the best chance to keep the press out of the way was to keep the correspondents together.[14]

Anthony photographer George Barnard may have been among the group. An account published after Barnard's death in 1902 said:

> Taking his camera, which weighed something more than the modern instrument, he engaged a seat in a carryall, but he got no pictures that day. On the return he overtook a poor fellow, sorely wounded in the leg, trying to get back to Washington. He stopped and put him in his place, shouldered his heavy instrument, and after weary walking he reached Washington, footsore and tired.[15]

M. B. Brady also was part of the entourage, wearing a straw hat and a white linen duster that stood out in the heat and dust of the march. The story of Brady's Bull Run adventure remains uncertain, but brief accounts have survived in

Brady's own words thirty years after the battle, in the memoirs of a New York newspaper correspondent who covered the battle, and in reports from contemporary photographic journals.

Brady told journalist George Alfred Townsend in 1891 that he had made arrangements to follow the army into the field well in advance of McDowell's July march, but only after encountering a "good deal" of trouble. Brady recalled that before the war he had often purchased wild ducks at a steamboat crossing of the Susquehanna River and presented them as gifts to Gen. Winfield Scott and other "choice" friends in New York. Scott had been commander-in-chief of the U.S. Army since 1841 but was too old and obese by the time of the Civil War to mount a horse. Brady sought out his old friend to get permission to go into the field to photograph the war.

> He told me, to my astonishment, that he was not to remain in command. Said he to me: "Mr. Brady, no person but my aide, Schuyler Hamilton, knows what I am to say to you. Gen. McDowell will succeed me tomorrow. You will have difficulty, but he and Col. Whipple are the persons for you to see." I did have trouble, many objections were raised.[16]

It is unknown what objections Brady encountered in getting permission to go into the field with the army, but he overcame them. Given Brady's connections and his stature as a photographer, and given the fact that he was allowed to take two wagons, it is reasonable to suggest that he probably was afforded the same, if not better, access as the more than two-dozen newspaper correspondents who were granted permission to go. Brady's own description of the adventure, as told to Townsend, is frustrating in its brevity:

> I went to the first battle of Bull Run with two wagons from Washington. My personal companions were Dick McCormick, then a newspaper writer, Ned House, and Al Waud, the sketch artist. We stayed all night at Centreville; we got as far as Blackburne's Ford; we made pictures and expected to be in Richmond next day, but it was not so, and our apparatus was a good deal damaged on the way back to Washington; yet we reached the city.[17]

In the dark first hours of July 21, 1861, the Union Army marched out of Centreville toward Bull Run. McDowell sent most of the army due west on the Warrenton Turnpike toward the Stone Bridge over Bull Run but diverted 13,000 men under Gens. David Hunter and Samuel P. Heintzelman to the north and west, where they were to cross Sudley Springs Ford, turn south, and attack the Confederate left flank. Both Heintzelman and Hunter were friendly to the media, but only Brady and a few other reporters joined their flanking march. Most of the reporters remained near the Federal center and were at Stone Bridge at sunrise to watch the Union artillery open fire on the Confederates.[18]

The first published account of Brady at Bull Run appeared on August 17, 1861, when the *New York Times* reported that Brady had returned from Washington with a "magnificent series of views of scenes, groups, and incidents of the war which he has been making for the last two months." Brady had visited all the camps in the Washington area, the brief article said, and he "went upon the field of battle at Bull Run, accompanied Heintzelman's column into the action, and was caught in the whirl and panic which accompanied the retreat of our Army."[19]

The most detailed account of Brady's activities appears in the memoirs of William A. Croffut, a young correspondent who covered Bull Run for the *New York Tribune* and who also joined Heintzelman's advance. Croffut recalled the rigors that he, and by inference Brady, endured during the pre-dawn march that preceded the battle:

> In the darkness of night we woke and took a hasty cup of coffee at three o'clock, and started on the long and circuitous march for Bull Run, said to be four miles away. We marched a couple of hours in the darkness, then three or four hours more through the thickest of dust and under the hottest of summer suns. When we were pretty nearly exhausted we halted in a narrow lane.[20]

There, Croffut was relieved to find another civilian, Sen. Henry Wilson of Massachusetts, chairman of the Senate's Military Committee, who expressed his satisfaction with "the splendid array of troops." A colonel told them the men were marching to Sudley Ford to flank the Rebel Army. Croffut writes:

> Shortly another civilian came up and joined us. Like myself, he wore a long linen duster, and strapped to his shoulders was a box as large as a beehive. I asked him if he was the Commissary.
>
> "No," he laughed; "I am a photographer, and I am going to take pictures of the battle."
>
> I asked him if he could get the fellows who were fighting to stand still and look pleasant. With a very serious face he said he supposed not, but he could probably get some scenes that would be worthwhile. His name was Brady, he added, and the protuberance on his back was a camera. . . . I saw him afterwards dodging shells on the battlefield. He was in motion, but his machine did not seem effective, and when about two o'clock a runaway team of horses came dashing wildly past us, dragging a gun carriage bottom side up, I saw Brady again and shouted, "Now's your time!" But I failed to stir him. I have often wondered how many pictures he took that day and whether he got out of the battle on our side or the other. I know that he was in a good many battles after that and he sold his pictures to the government for $60,000 [actually $25,000] when Grant was President.

Portable wet plate photographic outfits did exist during the Civil War that were small enough to be carried on a man's back, and the description of Brady wearing a linen duster fits with the single photograph related to Bull Run that he is known to have produced. It is a photograph, not surprisingly, of Brady himself, standing in his studio upon his return from the battlefield, still wearing his straw hat and his soiled duster.

The Union flank attack that Brady and Croffut witnessed had forced the Confederates to retreat south to Henry House Hill, where McDowell attacked in the early afternoon. As the battle for control of the hill raged back and forth, Confederate Gen. Barnard Bee, moments before being mortally wounded, pointed toward

This image of Mathew Brady "returned from Bull Run" is one of the strongest pieces of evidence that he did go there. Brady is shown wearing his now-soiled white linen duster, and the tip of a sword scabbard sticks from below the duster. The photograph is said to have been taken the day after the battle. (Library of Congress)

the troops of fellow Gen. T. J. Jackson and said, "There is Jackson standing like a stone wall," conferring upon "Stonewall" Jackson his famous nickname. The tide changed, first with the capture of two Union batteries that precipitously advanced up the hill and, then, around 4:00 p.m., with a crushing attack by Confederate reinforcements on the Union right flank and rear. Defeated and demoralized Union troops began fleeing back toward Centreville. At Stone Bridge, the soldiers became hopelessly mired among hundreds of terrified spectators and civilians. The panic that ensued eventually spread throughout the army.

Almost a century later, a generation of Americans would read of Brady's adventures at Bull Run in the best-selling biography by Roy Meredith, *Mr. Lincoln's Camera Man, Mathew B. Brady*, which was published in 1946 by Charles Scribner's Sons. When the tide turned, Brady fell into headlong retreat with the rest of the army, Meredith wrote, and spent the night in the woods of northern Virginia, sleeping on the seat of his wagon "with a bag of oats for his pillow." A Zouave from a New York regiment wandered by, shook Brady's foot to awaken him, and warned him "that the woods were full of stragglers from both armies." He gave the photographer a broadsword for protection, after which "Brady remained alone, with the

sounds of the stricken battlefield filling the night, and with the rain beating down on the wagon top."[21]

Meredith admits in his bibliography that his narrative is largely a product of his imagination, although Brady apparently did return to Washington with a sword, since one appears in his post-battle portrait. Meredith's account of Brady's night in the woods cannot be documented, but the photographer must have endured the same terror-filled flight that many civilians experienced that day, including Croffut.

The *Tribune* correspondent spent much of the afternoon helping carry the wounded back to a makeshift hospital inside Sudley Church. "The pulpit had put on the appearance of a drug store, and the communion table had become the horrible amputation table, while the floor was covered so thickly with wounded

The assertion that Brady was seen in the field wearing a backpack camera outfit is plausible. Pictured here are two contemporary backpack outfits. The dapper photographer at left is wearing a French outfit, while the British outfit at right came complete with a chair. (*Left*: courtesy of Scully & Osterman, *right*; courtesy of Shire Publications from *Victorian Photographers at Work* by John Hannavy).

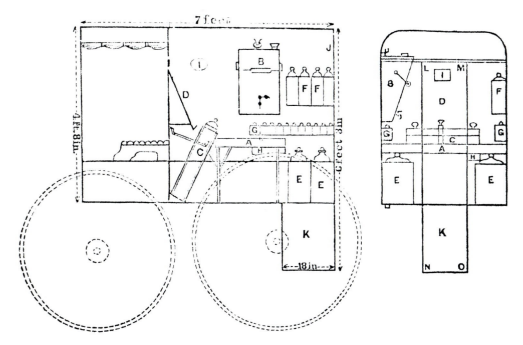

A blueprint for Civil War photographer George G. Rockwood's photographic field van was published in the *Philadelphia Photographer* in August 1865. "After three years use, I see no reason for changing it in any way, except to add little conveniences," Rockwood wrote. Among its features were (A) sink; (B) water tank; (C) hard rubber field bath; (D) shelf for plate holder; (E) chemical supply bottles; (F) and (G) large and small bottles of mixed developer, collodion, etc.; (H) tool drawer; (I) yellow "safe light" glass; (K) standing place for operator.

and dying that it was difficult to get across it by stepping carefully," he recalled.[22]

When the Union Army lost Henry House Hill, those near Sudley Church—where the morning's assault had begun—did not immediately feel the panic that followed. Croffut wrote:

Not till two hours after the battle closed were there any serious signs of disorder among the Union troops on the right. Then came all sorts of rumors about "the Black Horse Cavalry" being in close pursuit, which resulted in a hasty retreat through the darkened woods. This midnight experience seems a wild phantasmagoria as I recall it.[23]

On August 1, less than two weeks after the battle, the *American Journal of Photography* provided a largely fanciful account of the photographic adventures at Bull Run:

We have heard of two photographic parties in the rear of the Federal Army, on its advance into Virginia. One of these got so far as the smoke of Bull's Run, and was aiming the never-failing tube at friends and foes alike, when with the rest of our Grand Army they were completely routed and took to their heels, leaving their photographic accoutrements on the ground, which the rebels, no doubt, pounced upon as trophies of victory.[24]

The *Journal* added, "The other party, stopping at Fairfax, were quite successful. We have before us their fine stereo-view of the famed Fairfax Court House." No names are mentioned, but the first party's experience fits that of Brady. The "other party" is an unnamed Anthony photographer, possibly Barnard, whose view of Fairfax Court House is the only widely distributed wartime photograph that can be directly linked to the campaign. The Anthony Company's Fairfax Court House stereo view was labeled "War Views. No. 825," and the backmark reads, "Fairfax Court House and Its Surroundings. Taken just after the

Grand Army passed to fight the battle of Bull Run."[25]

Another contemporary trade periodical explicitly places Brady at Bull Run. *Humphrey's Journal*, arguably the leading American photographic periodical of the time, reported on August 15, 1861, that Brady "has been in Virginia with his camera, and many and spirited are the pictures he has taken. His are the only reliable records of the fight at Bull's Run." Humphrey launched into the fanciful suggestion that the Rebels mistook Brady's camera for a "great steam gun discharging 500 balls a minute. . . . But, joking aside, this collection is the most curious and interesting we have ever seen."[26]

Humphrey then alluded to images that show masses of troops at a distance:

The groups of entire regiments and divisions, within a space of a couple of feet square, present some of the most curious effects as yet produced in photography. Considering the circumstances under which they were taken, amidst the excitement, the rapid movements, and the smoke of the battlefield, there is nothing to compare with them in their powerful contrasts of light and shade.[27]

No photograph of this description is known to exist today.[28]

In his 1955 biography, *Mathew Brady, Historian with a Camera*, author James D. Horan described in an endnote the possible existence of another mystery image from Bull Run: "At least one historian recalled that he had once seen a Brady photograph of a frightened mob of retreated soldier and civilians at Bull Run. Efforts to locate this photograph, however, have never been successful."[29]

Brady never advertised or promoted any image like the one described by Horan's unnamed historian. A listing of "Brady's Photographic Views of the War" in the November 1862 edition of the Anthony Company's catalog of card photographs describes more than 300 war photographs, but not one is identified as having been taken during the campaign of First Bull Run in 1861. Had

Brady taken any, he would have cataloged and marketed them.[30]

So the first bloody battle was history, but there were no photographs of it, or its aftermath, despite the best intentions of Brady and others. The tragedy of that day would reverberate throughout the North and South, mostly in the harrowing tales the soldiers told in their letters home and in the long casualty lists that were published in scores of hometown newspapers. Hundreds of the men who fell would be buried in mass graves on the battlefield, but the remains of a few, including those of Gen. Barnard Bee, would be sent home. Bee died on the day after the battle—a gloomy, rainy Monday—and his body was shipped home for burial in his native Pendleton, South Carolina.

In Charleston, in the wake of Bee's death, George S. Cook suddenly began receiving requests for Bee's photograph. There is no record Bee ever sat for Cook, but Cook must have obtained a copy negative from another photographer. Beginning with the sale of a Bee photograph to a Confederate major on July 31, Cook would record seven different sales of *cartes de visite* and larger format photographs of the fallen South Carolina hero in the following six weeks, and Bee's image would replace that of Anderson as the gallery's best-seller.[31]

Business was good for Cook, although the summer brought its usual slump. During May 1861, the first full month of the war, Cook grossed $898.25; on some days he saw a dozen or more customers. Business had slowed to about $400 a month during the sweltering, low country summer days of 1861, but it was still far better than it had been in 1860; even on the slowest days, Cook usually recorded two or three sales.[32]

Cook had been in Charleston now for more than a decade. In January 1861, neither slow sales nor war stopped him from buying a lot on the Battery and starting construction on a three-and-a-half-story house that faced Fort Sumter and was flanked by some of the most

George S. Cook took the war's first photographs of prisoners on October 11, 1861, at Castle Pinckney in Charleston Harbor, and the images underscore the fact that the Union captives of First Bull Run had perhaps the best accommodations of any prisoners of the Civil War. This photograph shows prisoners of the 69th New York, an Irish regiment. One of them had formerly worked with Christy's minstrels, who played at 444 Broadway, prompting the men to designate their cell the Musical Hall. (Library of Congress)

luxurious mansions in the city. Cook may have been a native of Connecticut and a frequent visitor to the North, but his tastes and habits had become Southern. His new home featured detached servants' quarters, and 1860 tax records show that he owned one slave, for which he paid $3 in tax.[33]

Although Cook failed to photograph Fort Sumter after the surrender, he did take advantage of another war-related photographic opportunity in early October 1861. One hundred fifty-six Yankee soldiers who were captured at Bull Run had been transferred to Castle Pinckney in Charleston Harbor. Completed in 1810 and one of only three castle-type, brick forts erected in the country, Castle Pinckney was built on a shoal

off Shutes Folly Island, where Charlestonians had hanged captured pirates in the early eighteenth century. The island sits in Charleston Harbor about a mile northeast of the Battery. On the evening after Christmas 1860, in retaliation for Union Maj. Robert Anderson's occupation of Fort Sumter, the South Carolina militia had scaled Castle Pinckney's brick walls and taken possession of the fort in the first Rebel seizure of federal property. As prisoners from Bull Run were sent South, Castle Pinckney was hastily turned into a prison. Casemates were converted into cells, and the hotshot furnace was used as a bake oven.[34]

Cook carried his camera to the fort on October 11, 1861, a gorgeous, clear Friday in coastal

South Carolina. He had endured a slow week at the gallery—only one customer a day—following a rare stretch during the previous week when a "tooth fever" had kept him home in bed and forced him to close his gallery's doors for three days. Cook's account book entry for October 11 reads: "Prisoners and Zouaves at Castle Pinckney." There is no indication whether he went on his own or was requested to make the trip. Cook's expense records show that he paid a dollar to rent a "dray and boys [to go] to Castle P."[35]

Cook made at least fifteen photographs at Castle Pinckney, including five group shots of Yankee prisoners, six of their guards (the Charleston Zouave Cadets), and several showing both prisoners and guards. One of the group photographs of the prisoners shows nineteen men, most of whom were Cameron Highlanders. Some of these men, perhaps, were among those who answered the call of the massive recruiting banner that had hung over Broadway during the spring, urging "Scotchmen for the Union" to sign up with the Highlanders.

They went to Bull Run under the command of Col. James Cameron, brother of Secretary of War Simon Cameron. In the thick of the fight for Henry House Hill, the Highlanders had been raked by Confederate fire. Cameron had fallen dead on the field. The men of the 79th who were captured had been moved to Richmond and then to Charleston. Their treatment at Castle Pinckney was perhaps better than that received by any other Union prisoners during the war. The prisoners were fed the same rations as their guards. They created the Castle Pinckney Brotherhood, which established rules for living, cleanliness, and entertainment.[36]

One of the cadets, Sgt. Joseph F. Burke, recalled that he and his fellow guard indulged in good-natured banter about the war. The Yankees predicted that their army would soon come to their rescue and, in turn, taught the Confederates how to soften their hardtack to make it more edible.[37]

Unlike the photographs of Maj. Anderson, Cook apparently made little money from the images he took at Castle Pinckney. His account books show only four transactions involving the photographs, and only one cash sale. The last of the four transactions came on October 31, 1861, when a Confederate lieutenant named Walpole purchased three full plate prints for $4.50, including a framed print of the Cameron Highlanders. Perhaps because of the limited sales, Cook's Castle Pinckney photographs apparently remained all but unknown until they were first published in 1911 in the *Photographic History of the Civil War.* Fortunately, both negatives and original prints have survived. Thus, looking back through the lens of history, we must give credit to Cook, not Brady, as the first photographer to establish a visual legacy related to the battle of First Bull Run and, in doing so, becoming the first photographer to make images of prisoners of the war.[38]

Northern photographers would have to wait eight months, through the winter and into the spring of 1862, before they could photograph the Bull Run battlefield. That opportunity finally came in early March when the Confederates withdrew from Centreville and Manassas in the face of another big Union push, leaving the battlefield in Federal hands. Almost immediately, Brady sent photographers George Barnard and James Gibson back to the scene of the conflict.

Liberally exposing at least twenty seven-by-nine-inch plates and more than forty four-by-ten-inch stereo plates, Barnard and Gibson photographed the Confederate fortifications at Centreville, paying particular attention to the large logs (known as "Quaker guns") that the Rebels placed in the embrasures to simulate cannons. They took a number of views of the dozens of wooden shacks the Rebels had built for their winter quarters. They photographed the ruins of Stone Bridge, which the Confederates had destroyed after the battle. They also made glass plate negatives of many prominent battlefield positions, including Sudley Springs Ford, the Matthews House, the rolling hills of the battlefield, the ruins of the Henry House, the

Robinson House, the crude wooden markers on the mud bog graves of at least a half-dozen Union soldiers, and the mass grave of more than one hundred Union dead in the woods below Sudley Church. Then it was on to Manassas Junction itself, where Barnard and Gibson made their most dramatic photographs. The entire railroad junction had been burned to the ground except for a few rail cars, which Barnard photographed amidst the still-smoking ruins.[39]

The Civil War's first battlefield was finally well documented by the camera, and the images soon appeared for sale in Brady's galleries as stereo views, two different sizes of card photographs, and large format, ready-for-framing folio prints with an "Incidents of the War" imprint. They also appeared for sale in the E. & H. T. Anthony catalog of card photographs for November 1862.

The spring of 1862 brought a new campaign, as well as new opportunities to cover the war from behind the camera. As Gen. George Mc-Clellan took the Army of the Potomac into Virginia on the Peninsular Campaign, photographer James F. Gibson followed. Gibson would record that long, futile slog through the lowland forests and swamps toward Richmond. The public, however, would have to wait until the autumn to view the true horror of war, when the photographs of Alexander Gardner would escort them across the threshold and introduce them to the bloody harvest strewn across the fields bordering Antietam Creek.

5

GARDNER AT ANTIETAM

Of the tens of thousands of wire messages transmitted as U.S. military telegraphs during the Civil War, only a handful pertain to photography. One of them, sent by Alexander Gardner to employee David Knox at Brady's gallery in Washington, was received at the War Department at 10:00 a.m. on September 21, 1862, four days after the battle of Antietam:

Send four by ten glass . . . got forty five negatives of Battle. Alex Gardner. Tell Jim. Please deliver as soon as possible.[1]

Gardner urgently needed four-by-ten-inch glass plates to make additional stereoscopic views, and he didn't hesitate to use his influence to gain access to the military wires. His crisp message gave the first hint of what soon was to be recognized as an epochal moment in the history of war photography. Most of the forty-five negatives of battle were stereoscopic images that showed, for the first time, dead American soldiers on the battlefield. By mid-October, they would be on display in Brady's gallery on Broadway, under a small placard: "The Dead of Antietam." Crowds of visitors, including an unnamed *New York Times* reporter, trooped up the stairs to the second-floor reception room to stare in "terrible fascination" at these "weird copies of carnage."

"These pictures have a terrible distinctness," the *Times* reported on October 20. "By the aid of a magnifying glass, the very features of the slain may be distinguished."[2]

The photographs were the stunning payoff of a determined, systematic effort by Brady, Gardner, and their staff of photographers to capture the reality of war using the lens of a camera. With their aggressive coverage of the conflict in 1862, Brady's photographers had edged ever closer to this photographic achievement.

As the year began, Brady dispatched his young new talent, Timothy O'Sullivan, to South Carolina and Georgia to photograph Union-held areas along the coast with a stereoscopic camera. O'Sullivan returned with about fifty negatives of Forts Pulaski, Beauregard, and Walker, scenes in Beaufort, South Carolina, and several plantation views. Meanwhile, Brady photographer James F. Gibson joined Union Gen. George S. McClellan's Peninsular Campaign in Virginia in early April 1862, carrying stereo and large format cameras. By April 5, the 150,000 men of McClellan's Army of the Potomac were facing

Post-mortem photographs were popular in the nineteenth century, though few examples exist of fallen Civil War soldiers. In Virginia, however, a photographer took an image of Turner Ashby after he was killed in Harrisonburg, Virginia, on January 6, 1862. "After the fight was over we had his picture taken as he lay there— beautiful as if carved in marble, only there was a dark spot above the heart," a female witness wrote years later in *Confederate Veteran*. (Courtesy of the Fred Barr Collection, Stewart Bell Jr. Archives Room, Handley Regional Library, Winchester, Virginia)

the Confederates at Yorktown. In the vast Union encampment known as Camp Winfield Scott, Gibson occupied his own white, photographic tent, possibly with an assistant or two.[3]

Gibson is perhaps the least recognized of the war's most significant photographers. He was with Alexander Gardner at both Antietam and Gettysburg and is credited with photographs from both battlefields, but his own greatest legacy was the wide array of photographs he took while on the Virginia peninsula. The Peninsular Campaign was one of the most extensively photographed campaigns of the Army of the Poto-

mac; the camera captured military operations on land, water, and in the air.

Biographical information on most Civil War photographers is scarce, and Gibson is no exception. He was born in Scotland in 1828 or 1829. In 1860, his name appeared with that of his wife Elizabeth in the Washington, D.C., census, and the city directory showed that Brady employed him. Since Gardner was also from Scotland, he may have brought Gibson over. Gibson may not have been the easiest person to get along with, as he became embroiled in lawsuits with both Brady and Gardner during or after the war.[4]

Gibson's first documented trip into the field was when he accompanied Barnard to photograph the Bull Run battlefield in March 1862. He is jointly credited with Barnard for nineteen "folio-size," seven-by-nine-inch negatives at Centreville, Bull Run, and Manassas. Barnard, however, is credited individually for all of the stereo negatives of those same scenes. This would suggest that Barnard was Brady's lead man on the return trip to Bull Run, and that Gibson was his assistant. By the same measure, it appears Gibson was Brady's lead photographer during the Peninsular Campaign. He is credited alone for most of the stereo output, and he shares credit for eight large-plate photographs with John Wood, who appears to have been his assistant. From May through July, ranging back and forth across the peninsula from Yorktown to Fair Oaks and back to Hampton Roads, Gibson took at least 120 stereo negatives and co-produced at least fifteen large-plate negatives. In addition to these mass market images, Gibson may have spent some of his time taking individual portraits of officers and soldiers.[5]

His first dated photographs, taken on May 1, 1862, show European military officers and dignitaries visiting at Camp Winfield Scott. During the first half of May, Gibson extensively documented the area around Yorktown, including the massive siege guns that would never be used. After McClellan's vast army moved to Cumberland Landing on the Pamunkey River, Gibson made at least fifteen stereo photographs of the new camp. He photographed the sprawling encampment from an adjacent hilltop and carried his camera high into a tree, probably onto a signal platform, for some striking stereoscopic images, using a tree branch in the foreground to provide a vivid 3-D effect. Gibson's attention to panoramas is reflected by the fact that four different multi-image landscape views can be created from his fifteen Cumberland Landing encampment photographs and stereographs.[6]

Gibson also went on board the USS *Monitor* at Hampton Roads and photographed the dents in its stovepipe-shaped turret, souvenirs from its battle with the CSS *Virginia*. He probably was also responsible for a group of at least five photographs and stereographs of Professor Thaddeus S. C. Lowe, the Union Army's self-described "Aeronaut," and his observation balloon, the *Intrepid*. Time and again during the campaign, the balloon carried Lowe and one of several Union commanders to an elevation of 1,000 feet, sometimes under fire, where they made precise and detailed observations of enemy operations and modified their maps or created new ones.[7]

And, yet, no aerial photographs apparently were ever taken from Lowe's balloon. Gibson, after photographing the balloon from the ground, surely must have thought of taking his camera aloft. He had climbed a tree to take photographs at Pamunkey Landing, and no doubt he would have gladly joined Lowe in the *Intrepid*'s gondola.

The inflating of the observation balloon *Intrepid* near Gaines Mill, Virginia, by Professor Thaddeus Lowe, the army's primary "aeronaut," drew more than a few spectators to the far hillside. Lowe and various Union officers made many flights during the Peninsular Campaign, sometimes under a harassing Rebel fire. (Library of Congress)

Aerial photographs from balloons had been made before, first in Paris in 1855, then in 1860 in Providence, Rhode Island, and Boston. *Humphrey's Journal* reported both 1860 accomplishments, and Gibson was probably aware of them and equally aware that it might not be an easy task. In the sky above Boston, the gondola was so unsteady that only one of photographer James Wallace Black's eight negatives turned out. Still, in 1861 and again in 1862, the New York Photographical Society encouraged Professor Lowe to consider aerial photography and publicly offered the help of its members in making that happen.[8]

Lowe apparently had no interest. Although photographers were not specifically banned from making ascensions, newspaper correspondents were. Perhaps Lowe considered photographs unessential. The aeronaut revealed a glimpse of his feelings at the end of a December 15, 1861, report of his observations from Edwards Ferry, Maryland, into Virginia. Lowe acknowledged receiving a communication from one W. G. Fullerton about photographs being taken from a balloon, but countered, "I would say the author advances no new ideas. As soon as other matters connected with the balloons are accomplished, I shall give the photographic matter a thorough and practical test." Lowe's many reports in the *Official Records of the Union and Confederate Armies* contain no further mention of balloon photography.[9]

In late June 1862, George Barnard arrived on the peninsula and took more than two-dozen images around Yorktown and Hampton, mostly in 3-D. Soon enough, Barnard would establish his own distinctive photographic legacy with Gen. William Tecumseh Sherman in the Western theater, but it was Gibson's work that stood out in the spring of 1862. It gained almost immediate attention, prompting articles in the *New York Times*, the *New York World*, and *Harper's New Monthly Magazine*, which proclaimed, "Brady's album photographs of the war, and its persons and places, are the portraits of a living time." In

London, the *Times* published a 2,200-word review of the war photographs and portraits issued by Brady's gallery. More than half the British essay was devoted to Gibson's work, but only Brady was mentioned. The image of the shell-damaged deck of the captured Confederate gunboat, *Teaser*, was "striking," the *Times* said, and showed the boat with "deck stove in, iron stanchions gone, a great cratur [*sic*] in the hold, machinery torn into ribands [*sic*]." The reviewer also described Gibson's memorable image of Capt. George Armstrong Custer (misnaming him "Captain Custis") with his captured West Point classmate, Confederate Lt. J. B. Washington, and observed that it was Custer who looked "much more like a prisoner."[10]

The *Times* took note of what is arguably the most important image from the Peninsular Campaign, a stereo photograph taken on June 27, 1862, that shows "groups of wounded, out in the open sun, at Savage's Station." Osborn & Durbec had managed to photograph war damage at Fort Sumter, but Gibson's image at Savage Station raised the standard. For the first time in American photographic history, the camera captured a glimpse of the human toll. The Savage Station view, taken in stereo, was a candid image of tremendous immediacy, showing a makeshift field hospital with badly wounded soldiers sitting and lying in such a haphazard fashion that it illuminated the chaos of the moment, especially through a 3-D viewer. The wounded lay so thick and close, the ground looked "like a dull, heavy sea of which bodies [were] the waves," reported *Harper's New Monthly Magazine*. "This scene brings the war to those who have not been to it. How patiently and still they lie; these brave men who bleed and are maimed for us! It is a picture which is more eloquent than the sternest speech."[11]

Forced to maneuver with the rest of the army, Gibson was unable to document what was already being frightfully described in newspaper stories—the sights of a freshly bloodied battlefield strewn with bodies ripped by shot and shell.

A farmyard at Savage Station, Virginia, served as a temporary respite for wounded men of the straw-hatted 69th New York Regiment after the battle of Gaines Mill. It also gave photographer James Gibson an unprecedented opportunity. Many of these men were captured in a Confederate counterattack two days after the stereoscopic negative of this image was made. (Library of Congress)

Gibson's Savage Station field hospital photograph came close, however, even though he received scant credit for it.

Another more obscure photographer, G. H. Houghton of Brattleboro, Vermont, also carried his camera close to the action during the Peninsular Campaign. Houghton focused mostly on the Vermont troops of the Army of the Potomac, but he also captured memorable images of Gen. Winfield Scott Hancock in the field, as well as a slave family. When Vermont troops assaulted an entrenched line of Confederates on April 16, 1862, Houghton was close by. One of his images shows a battery on the move, another reveals the Rebel works; Houghton claimed the enemy still occupied them at the time. He also took several images of the fresh graves of the Vermont soldiers who perished in the bloody charge.[12]

A few months later, after the battle of Cedar Mountain in Virginia in August, Brady photographer Timothy O'Sullivan raised the standard yet again with a small series of stereo views. These shots showed a battery in movement on the day of battle, as well as dead horses on the field and the fresh graves of Union soldiers.[13]

Brady's gallery in Washington, headed by Gardner and staffed by experienced and talented photographers, had made great strides in war photography in the first eight months of 1862, but they could not know what breakthroughs

Photographers edged ever closer to the carnage of war during 1862. After the battle of Cedar Mountain in August, photographer Timothy O'Sullivan photographed fresh Union graves as well as this detail from a stereoscopic negative showing dead horses on the battlefield. (Library of Congress)

lay just ahead. What they did know was that wherever the Army of the Potomac went, they would follow with their cameras and eagerly add new images to a growing catalog of photographs that, by the late summer of 1862, included more than 260 different stereographs and several dozen large-plate photographs.[14]

On September 4, 1862, advance units of Robert E. Lee's Army of Northern Virginia began the first Confederate invasion of the North, crossing the Potomac River at fords near Leesburg, Virginia, and sending waves of shock and fear through the North. By September 6, Stonewall Jackson's men were in Frederick, Maryland, and the Confederate army occupied the town for almost a week. At some point during that time (or possibly when the Confederates occupied Frederick in 1864), an unknown photographer set up his camera in a second-story window above Rosenstock's Dry Goods and Clothing store and aimed the lens at a long line of the invading Rebels standing in column, pausing from the march. This candid image shows about eighty soldiers, most of whom have their muskets on their shoulders, some having turned to peer up at the camera. As significant as this image is to the photographic history of the Civil War, it was almost unknown in its own time. It apparently was never marketed and may have been an amateur's effort, probably by a member of the Rosenstock family of Frederick, who owns a copy of an orig-

inal print that is now lost. The existence of the photograph was not common knowledge until it was reproduced in a *Civil War Times Illustrated* article in 1965.[15]

In Washington, meanwhile, Gen. George B. McClellan had done a skillful job of reorganizing and reenergizing the Army of the Potomac following its defeat under Gen. John Pope at Second Bull Run. McClellan marched out of Washington on September 7 and set after Lee. Joining McClellan was Alexander Gardner, who was making his first trip into the field with the army. Sometime during the winter of 1861–1862, Gardner had become affiliated with the fledgling U.S. Secret Service created by friend and fellow Scot Allan Pinkerton, McClellan's mistake-prone chief intelligence officer. Known informally as "Captain Gardner," the burly Scotsman had spent much of his time in 1862 copying maps and documents and taking photographs for the U.S. Topographical Engineers.[16]

There is no evidence that Gardner took any photographs until after the battle of Antietam, but his presence in the field with McClellan from the start of the army's march is documented by the first of three military telegrams sent by Gardner to Brady's Washington gallery during the campaign. At 11:00 a.m. on September 9, Gardner sent a telegram from Rockville, Maryland, to Timothy O'Sullivan at Brady's gallery, imploring him to "come right away to Rockville,

This is the telegram, published for the first time, that photographer Alexander Gardner sent from the Antietam battlefield to David Knox at Brady's Gallery in Washington. The wire arrived at the War Department at 10:00 a.m. on September 21, 1862, with Gardner reporting that he had forty-five "negatives of battle" and needed more stereoscopic-size glass plates. (National Archives and Records Administration)

there make for Headquarters. Bring commander of telegraphic corps one horse. Alex Gardner." This is the only concrete information about Gardner's activities until he began exposing glass plates of the wreckage-strewn deathscape at the Antietam battlefield on September 19, 1862, two days after the battle.[17]

The first serious fighting of the campaign had come on Sunday, September 14, when McClellan defeated a portion of Lee's army during the battle of South Mountain. The retreating Confederates streamed off the mountain and gathered at Sharpsburg, where the entire army would soon reassemble. Lee had sent Stonewall Jackson to capture nearby Harper's Ferry, and Jack-

son accomplished that task on September 15. Twelve thousand Union soldiers surrendered at Harper's Ferry without putting up much of a fight, and their commander, Col. Dixon S. Miles, was mortally wounded. Had Miles survived, he probably would have been court-martialed for his role in the debacle. The first Northern newspaper reports, however, were glowing. The *New York Times* headline proclaimed: "Gallant Defense by the Forces Under Col. Miles."[18]

The news from Harper's Ferry struck a chord at Brady's gallery in New York. Brady and his men had spent a good bit of time at Harper's Ferry in 1861 and in the summer of 1862, taking pictures of various units and sights and, according to one private, charging "infernally high" prices for copies. Brady also had photographed Col. Miles outside his headquarters. When word arrived of Miles's demise, Brady's gallery reacted by immediately sending prints of the Harper's Ferry photographs to the major New York newspapers.[19]

"We have received some very finely executed photographs of Harper's Ferry and vicinity, by Brady, forming part of a complete series of 'Views of the War,'" reported the *World* on September 18 with the headline: "War Scenes Photographed." On the same day, the *Herald* reported, "The gallant defense of Harper's Ferry by the late lamented Colonel Dixon S. Miles invests with a vivid interest the photographs recently taken there by Mr. Brady, and now being published among his 'Incidents of the War.'" The *Herald* noted that the photographs "possess a value that the country will know how to appreciate." But events were moving far too fast for an already dated portrait of a losing commander to hold much interest. The battle of Antietam had already been fought by September 18, and the first reports from the field were beginning to appear in the papers that very day.[20]

After the battle at South Mountain, Lee regrouped outside Sharpsburg, Maryland, determined to make a stand. McClellan massed his forces on the east bank of Antietam Creek and methodically plotted strategy for an attack on September 17. The ever-cautious Union general worked from a field headquarters set up at the home of Philip Pry, whose farmhouse sat atop a hill just east of the creek, about a mile and a half from Confederate lines. Here, Gardner took one of his first Antietam images, if not the first. His original caption, which read, "View of battlefield of Antietam on day of battle, 17th September, 1862," led many books and authorities, including the *Photographic History of the Civil War*, to misidentify the smoke-shrouded clusters of soldiers in the distant right of the view as actually being engaged in combat. In 1963, however, *Civil War Times Illustrated* reported that the photograph had been taken on a prominence

next to McClellan's headquarters at the Pry House, more than a mile from the battlefield. The location was identified by lining up hills and other geographical features in the image.[21]

Gardner probably was with other members of the press most of the day of the battle, including sketch artist Edwin Forbes of *Frank Leslie's Illustrated Newspaper*, who watched the fight from a hill near the Pry House. Wrote Forbes:

The battle of Antietam was probably the most picturesque battle of the war, as it took place

Wearing his laboratory coat, with fingernails black from photographic chemicals, Scotsman Alexander Gardner poses for his own camera sitting in the "Congressional Chair," the same elegant studio chair used by President Lincoln and thousands of other portrait sitters. This is Gardner around 1863, in his prime as a photographer and operating his own Washington gallery. (From the collection of Larry J. West)

on open ground and could be fully viewed from any point north of Antietam Creek, where our reserve batteries were posted. The engagement was a spectacle which was not surpassed during the whole war. Thousands of people took advantage of the occasion, as the hills were black with spectators. Soldiers of the reserve, officers and men of the commissary and quartermasters' department, camp-followers, and hundreds of farmers and their families, watched the desperate struggle. No battle of the war, I think, was witnessed by so many people.[22]

The day after the battle, both armies remained in position, battered but resolute. Most of the ground they had fought over was a no-man's land until truces were declared to allow both sides to gather their wounded and begin burying their dead. That night, Lee decided to withdraw back to Virginia. Thousands of Rebel troops made their way from Sharpsburg to the Potomac River, where they waded across the ford at Shepherdstown under the flickering light of torches held by cavalrymen posted at intervals in the river.[23]

On September 19, probably in the morning, Alexander Gardner began taking photographs on the Antietam battlefield. Various histories mistakenly place M. B. Brady there with him. One book has Brady and Gardner together, literally "advancing with Hooker's forces." Another has Brady with his head under the focusing cloth as a shell explodes nearby. There is no credible evidence that Brady was at Antietam at all. Gardner's partner and assistant at Antietam was James Gibson, whose presence there is documented by the fact that he is individually credited with taking seven images on September 21 and 22.[24]

We have no information about where Gardner and Gibson spent the night of September 18, or how far they had to travel with their wagons to reach the battlefield on September 19. If they stayed near McClellan's headquarters at the Pry House, it was at least three miles to the Dunker Church, no matter which route they took. The photographers surely would have been told of the ghastly scenes that lay ahead of them, spurring them to move with all due haste.

Although it had no steeple and looked more like a schoolhouse than a place of worship, the whitewashed Dunker Church was the most distinctive feature in the heart of the battlefield. The Dunkers, a sect of pacifists who refused to bear arms for either side, had worshiped there on the previous Sunday, with the distant sound of artillery from the battles on South Mountain providing its own accompaniment to the prayers, hymns, and sermons of the three-hour service. Now the church's dark roof and brick walls were peppered with shell holes,[25] and its wooden floor was covered with wounded from both sides.

Bathed in the direct morning light, with the dark woods behind as a backdrop, the war-scarred Dunker Church gleamed in the sun as Gardner arrived at the scene. In an open field only a few hundred feet east of the church, a cluster of dead Rebels lay near the remains of their artillery limber. Here Gardner and Gibson went to work.

We can only theorize about which pictures they took first and what route they chose in touring the field. Their presence on the battlefield on September 19 is documented by the original captions on three separate Antietam photographs (including one of the scenes taken near the Dunker Church), which identify them as having been taken that day. Gardner and Gibson may have continued taking photographs on September 20, though none are explicitly identified as having been taken then. In any event, their initial work bears the evidence of expediency and haste. They exposed and developed as many as twenty-five stereoscopic plates on September 19. Except for the classic scene of dead Rebels with the Dunker Church in the background, which Gardner shot twice, he did not take the time to shoot more than one image from the same camera angle. In the following days, Gardner often made time to shoot a duplicate plate, sometimes as many as five plates, of the same scene, and he used both stereo and large-plate cameras. On September 19, however, Gardner limited his output, and he used only his stereo camera.

A positive reproduction of the original four-by-ten-inch glass plate negative of one of the most famous photographs of the Civil War shows the wear and tear of more than a century of use. The plate is badly cracked and the emulsion significantly eroded, but the image retains its impact. Below, the original label pasted onto the back of the stereo-view sold by Brady's gallery in 1862 was one of the most dramatic of the war. (Library of Congress)

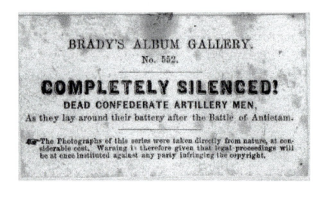

Gardner knew the stereoscopic camera would give Brady's gallery the most options for marketing the images. Each four-by-ten-inch stereo negative produced two four-by-five-inch images, which were cut down to three-by-three-inch squares for stereo views. Using the stereo negative, they could, of course, create stereo views, but they also could make *cartes de visite* and oversized album cards of about twice that size, known as "Imperial Cartes." Stereo views cost 50 cents each, album cards and *cartes de visite* were 25 cents each. Gardner's large-plate camera was particularly useful in producing group photographs; the gallery charged $1.50 for large-plate "folio" prints.[26]

Gardner also demonstrated an economy of motion while operating on the battlefield. He parked his darkroom wagon at locations where he could make many images from different angles without having to move his camera more than a few yards in any direction. This was revealed by photohistorian William A. Frassanito, who tracked down the original camera locations of most of the Antietam images, in his definitive 1978 study, *Antietam: The Photographic Legacy of America's Bloodiest Day.*[27]

Facing west toward the damaged Dunker Church, Gardner made three westerly exposures showing the church. At the same general location, he also made one southwestern view showing dead horses, and two shots that looked north, including one that showed Capt. Joseph Knap's independent battery of Pennsylvania Light Artillery just before it left the field for Harper's Ferry.[28]

Sometime during the early part of his visit to the battlefield, Gardner heard about a large group of dead Confederate soldiers lying as they fell along the fence lining Hagerstown Pike, the main road north out of Sharpsburg. He spent at least an hour there, exposing six stereo plates before possibly moving over to the East Woods, where he took two more plates. Finally, he left the northern part of the battlefield and traveled more than a mile south to reach the Sunken Road, where he exposed his final three plates on September 19 as the late afternoon sun cast long shadows over the bodies and debris of battle. Gardner had a closeup look at the horror in the Sunken Road, but he did not bestow its famous name, "Bloody Lane." Gardner's rather prosaic title was "Ditch on the Right Wing," because at the time he thought the location to be on the right wing of the Confederate line. (It is more toward the Confederate center.)

Gardner accomplished a great deal during his initial tour of the battlefield. Each four-by-ten-inch stereo negative had to be made from scratch and developed on the spot, a process that took seven to ten minutes. Gardner manned the camera, and Gibson or another assistant prepared the plates. Each plate was wiped free of dust before being coated with collodion, which was probably mixed back in Washington. "Collodion is made by the solution of guncotton in about equal parts of sulphuric ether and 95 proof alcohol," recalled war photographer George G. Rockwood. "The coating of plates was a delicate operation even in the ordinary well-organized studio." A puddle of collodion about three inches in diameter was poured from a bottle onto the center of the plate and then flowed over the entire surface with a single tilt to each corner, lest the fast-drying liquid double over on itself and ripple the coat. With the last tilt, all excess collodion was poured back into the bottle.[29]

The assistant sensitized the plate in a bath of silver nitrate for three to five minutes, working in the back of the photographic wagon. The wagon was usually a converted delivery wagon that looked unusual enough in the field for soldiers to ask, "What is it?" Eventually, it came to be known as a "what-is-it" wagon. Once the plate was sensitized, the darkroom operator bellied up to the back of the van, pulled the large tarp that was attached to the top rear of the wagon around himself, and sealed out the daylight by pulling or tying the bottom of the tarp around his ankles. Working in the dim orange or red glow that filtered through the small, oval, safe-light windows, the assistant removed the sensitized plate from the silver bath, blotted off the excess silver, secured the plate in a wooden plate holder, and closed the hinged door. Then he rushed the plate to the camera, knowing that every wasted moment threatened the possibility of a dry plate, and no picture.[30]

By this time, Gardner had already aimed the camera, now on its tripod, and stepped under the camera cloth to focus the lens. He could see the scene he was about to photograph—upside down, but in color. With the focus set, he moved the focusing frame out of the way and replaced it with the plate holder, which he attached to the camera. Then he slid the front panel out of the plate holder, or dark slide, to expose the plate to the interior of the camera. Finally, he removed both lens caps, and the light of the sun poured through the lenses to expose the plate. (Each exposure that day was probably ten or fifteen seconds.) Gardner probably counted the seconds of each exposure as he made the plate, then replaced the lens caps, replaced the plate holder's front cover, removed the plate holder, and quickly walked or ran back to the assistant at the wagon. In safelight once again, the assistant removed the plate from the holder. Holding the plate in his hand, he poured the developer over it quickly and evenly, swished the liquid over the plate for about two minutes, and then poured water over the plate to stop the action of the developer. He then gave the plate a thorough rinsing.[31]

The collodion on each plate had to be dried to a permanent hardness by exposing it to a moderate source of heat, such as a candle, and Gardner may not have had the time to do it in the field. He may have temporarily stored the plates in a mixture of dilute glycerine until that evening, when he would have rinsed, fixed, washed, and dried them before adding a protective coating of varnish. Prints would not be made in the field. They would be printed in the sunlight on the

The Stone Bridge.

SCENES ON THE BATTLE-FIELD OF ANTIETAM.—From Photographs by Mr. M. B. Brady.—[See Page 663.]

This striking image of Burnside Bridge on a sunny September morning a few days after the battle of Antietam was reproduced, with some license taken, as a woodcut engraving in a two-page spread of Antietam images in *Harper's Weekly* on October 18, 1862. The engraving was well known, but the actual photograph did not resurface until 1993.

gallery roof and fixed and toned in the dark-room. Although enlargers did exist then, the prints were most often direct contact prints created by placing the glass plate directly onto the albumen paper.[32]

Gardner and Gibson left no written account of what it was like to photograph the dead of Antietam, but it must have been challenging and exhausting. In the heat of the Crimea seven years earlier, Fenton had to battle with a "plague of flies" for possession of his darkroom, which became its own form of a torture chamber. "As soon as the door was closed to commence the preparation of a plate, perspiration started from every pore; and the sense of relief was great when it was possible to open the door and breathe even the hot air outside," Fenton recalled.[33]

The closest we can come to understanding what it was like for Gardner and Gibson to operate on the Antietam battlefield is to listen to the experiences of a modern wet-plate artist such as Civil War photography reenactor Rob Gibson, who has prepared, exposed, and developed wet plates on the Antietam battlefield during the month of September on three separate occasions:

> Their biggest enemy was time. These burial crews are trying to get these corpses buried as quickly as possible, digging shallow, mass graves, and Gardner and Gibson are racing around trying to get as much as they can in as many places as they can. They're scrambling all day long. And there may have been a third guy with them, a teamster to tend to the horses and get them water. Each time they moved, they would have to secure all the bottles, chemicals and plates. Each time they stopped, the wagon would have to be level, so the bathes weren't tipped.

James Gibson's hands would have been black with silver nitrate. He no doubt perspired excessively under the tarp while taking care not to lean his head over the plate, lest drops of sweat fall on the glass. Like Fenton, Gibson probably had to battle flies as well, which are attracted to the smell of collodion.[34]

The wagon reeked of ether, which is used in the collodion, and excessive breathing of the fumes might make one woozy. Surely, however, the smell of ether was far preferable than the overwhelming stench of death that permeated the area for days afterward. That odor was so sickening, local resident Alexander Root recalled that he couldn't eat a good meal. "The first thing in the morning when I rolled out of bed, I'd have to take a drink of whiskey. If I didn't, I'd throw up before I got my clothes all on."[35]

The photographers endured any and all hardships and kept working. Rob Gibson reflects:

> I think the biggest thing for them was knowing what they had. Considering the journey they made, and the conditions they worked under, and then driving all the way back to Washington with all those exposed plates, and arriving at the Brady Gallery on Pennsylvania Avenue, and carrying those plate boxes up the back staircase, knowing they had the photographic scoop of the century—that had to be the most thrilling feeling for those guys, and it probably outweighed everything else.[36]

In early October, when President Lincoln visited the battlefield, Gardner would return to Antietam to take more images, including two stereo plates and four large-format plates of the president. On October 4, as Lincoln concluded his three-day visit, Gardner sent a final telegram back to the gallery in Washington: "Got groups of president, Generals McClellan, Porter, Morrell, Marcy & Humphrey. Will find negatives tomorrow. Alex Gardner."[37]

Brady would come to the area, too, but not until McClellan finally advanced into Virginia in late October. Brady appears with a group of a half-dozen photographers, assistants, and servants—including David B. Woodbury—in an image taken near the Potomac River at Berlin, Maryland (about six miles downstream from Harper's Ferry), on October 28. Brady's presence is further documented in a handwritten caption on the back of a stereo view from Woodbury's personal collection that shows the pontoon bridge at Berlin. "Brady and [assistant E. T.] Whitney crossed this pontoon

No evidence exists that M. B. Brady visited the Antietam battlefield, but this photograph places him at Berlin (now Brunswick), Maryland, on the Potomac River on October 28, 1862. Brady stands second from right, next to one of his principal operators, the kneeling David B. Woodbury, who was the original owner of this unmounted albumen print. Others in the image, from left, are assistant Silas Holmes, an African American cook named Stephen, assistant E. T. Whitney, H. Hodges, and a teamster named Jim. (From the collection of Larry J. West)

Facing page: A remarkable, previously unknown, private Gardner photograph from Antietam (*bottom*) shows McClellan's staff drinking at Antietam at the time of President Lincoln's visit in early October 1862. In the top photograph, an image that was offered for public sale in Gardner's catalog, we see the staff with Gen. John Gibbon (*right*) and Gen. John Buford (*third from left*). In the private image, taken at the same spot, the generals no longer appear. From left, Maj. Henry Francis Clarke, the chief commissary of subsistence, holds a cup; the servant is standing with a pitcher; seated foreground is Capt. James Chatham Duane, chief engineer of the Army of the Potomac, while seated against the tree, smoking a pipe, is glassy-eyed surgeon George Suckley. The army's chief signal officer, Maj. Albert James Myer, pours himself a drink, while the blurred visage of Inspector General Delos Bennet Sacket lifts a cup toward his lips. Just behind Sacket is a sober-appearing Dr. Jonathan Letterman, the army's medical director; next to him, with a shot glass in front of his hands, is Lt. Col. Albert V. Colburn, assistant adjutant-general. The others are unidentified.

GARDNER, Photographer.   M. B. BRADY, Publisher.

GARDNER, Photographer.   M. B. BRADY, Publisher.

bridge with Genls McClellan and Burnside on our way to Warrenton," Woodbury wrote.[38]

As the Maryland campaign came to an end, Gardner and Gibson had more than a hundred new photographs to add to Brady's growing catalog. Today, we can document 118 images from the Maryland campaign, including 105 at Antietam and thirteen at Berlin or Burkittsville, Maryland. Of the 105 known Antietam images, seventy-eight were taken in 3-D, including all twenty images that show dead soldiers.[39]

But at least one of those images never made it into the public catalog of images for sale. It apparently was an off-the-record exposure—a private image done strictly for the personal enjoyment of the staff officers of Gen. George McClellan. The public image—the one offered for sale in the catalog—showed McClellan's staff officers sitting with Gens. John Buford and John Gibbon. After the generals departed, the staff officers broke out drinks, including a bottle and a shot glass. Gardner was good friends with these men and didn't hesitate to expose another plate—confidentially. The photograph of McClellan's staff drinking on the very day Lincoln was at Antietam trying to prod the general into action was never offered to the public. The only known print was among fourteen Antietam large-plate folio images contained in a custom-made portfolio (probably owned by one of the officers) with a gold-lettered cover, "Incidents of the War."[40]

Gardner and Gibson had used cameras to record history at Antietam in the most dramatic fashion yet, and now it was time to finish the job and make all that hard fieldwork pay off. Prints had to be made in the sunlight on the gallery roof. Captions had to be written, and labels printed. Several of Gardner's titles for the images of the dead of Antietam are uniquely descriptive and reveal his own awareness of just how unusual and graphic these images were. The original Brady backmark on the stereograph of the dead Confederates and the Dunker Church proclaims: "COMPLETELY SILENCED!" The caption for the image of a young dead Confederate reads, "He Sleeps his Last Sleep. A Confederate Soldier, who, after being wounded, had evidently dragged himself to a little ravine on the hill-side, where he died."[41]

The photographs of the dead of Antietam were the first American images of the carnage of war, but not the first in history. At least one stereo image was taken of the dead, heaped for burial, after the battle of Melegnano, Italy, during the Franco-Austrian War of 1859. A year later, naturalized Englishman Felice Beato, already a photographic veteran of the Sepoy Mutiny in India in 1857 to 1859, took several images of Chinese dead scattered around North Taku Fort during the Second Opium War in China in 1860.[42]

Gardner's photos, however, were the first to receive extensive public exposure. The *New York Times* correspondent who wrote the October 18 article thought the pictures of the dead would have repulsed him, "but on the contrary, there is a terrible fascination about it that draws one near these pictures, and makes him loath to leave."[43]

Some of the first prints of the dead were sent to *Harper's Weekly* in New York, where they were converted into woodcut engravings for publication. Brady already was a regular contributor to the nation's leading, weekly, illustrated newspaper—the *Time* magazine of its day. Engravings based on Brady photographs had appeared in twenty-five different issues in 1861, sometimes on the cover, and in eleven additional issues by mid-October 1862, but nearly all were portraits. The October 18 *Harper's Weekly* featured something different. The illustrated center spread, which featured eight pictures, was, for the first time, derived entirely from photographs. All were from Antietam, and seven of the eight converted photographs showed scenes of carnage. *Harper's Weekly* observed:

> Minute as are the features of the dead, and unrecognizable by the naked eye, you can, by bringing a magnifying glass to bear on them, identify not merely their general outline, but actual expression. This, in many instances, is perfectly horrible, and shows through what

tortures the poor victims must have passed before they were relieved from their sufferings.[44]

For Oliver Wendell Holmes, inventor of the hand-held stereoscopic viewer and eloquent essayist on the wonders of the stereo view, the Antietam images were all the more real because they were all too personal. His son, Capt. Oliver Wendell Holmes Jr., was wounded in the battle, and the elder Holmes had rushed to Sharpsburg to search for him. Father did not locate son until days later in Hagerstown, where he turned up on a northbound train car, waiting for its departure. The elder Holmes had taken the time to visit the battlefield during his search, and it looked to him "like the table of some hideous orgy left uncleared."

Let him who wishes to know what war is look at this series of illustrations. It was so nearly like visiting the battlefield to look over these views, that all the emotions excited by the actual sight of the stained and sordid scene, strewed with rags and wrecks, came back to us, and we buried them in the recesses of our cabinet as we would have buried the mutilated remains of the dead they too vividly represented.[45]

The variety and scope of Civil War photography in the coverage of just a single event, the battle of Antietam, is reflected in this display of original Antietam photographs by Alexander Gardner. Shown are vintage stereo views, album gallery cards, a *carte de visite,* and mounted and unmounted large-plate "folio" prints. The sixty-three images here represent slightly more than half of Gardner's total output during the Maryland campaign. (Photograph by Fuchs & Kasperek)

6

EMBEDDED WITH THE TROOPS

The war surged on, leaving behind a landscape of death and misery. Nearly all the dead of Antietam were buried in shallow battlefield graves within a few days, but thousands of wounded remained in makeshift hospitals that transformed nearly every farm in the area into a cradle of suffering. "Day before yesterday, I dressed the wounds of 64 different men—some having two or three each," Dr. William Child, assistant surgeon of the 5th New Hampshire Volunteers, wrote to his wife on September 22. His letter continued:

> Yesterday I was at work from daylight till dark—today I am completely exhausted—but shall soon be able to go at it again. The days after the battle are a thousand times worse than the day of battle—and the physical pain is not the greatest pain suffered. How awful it is—you have nor can have until you see it any idea of affairs after a battle.[1]

Antietam was Child's first battle. He was twenty-eight, a Dartmouth graduate, and a farmer's son from Bath, a tiny New Hampshire town in the White Mountains. Child would endure many battles in the next three and a half years. He would saw off many more limbs, dress countless wounds, and write vivid letters of his experiences to his wife Carrie. As a 5th New Hampshire surgeon, Child experienced more of the brutality of war than most non-combatants. The 5th New Hampshire lost more officers and men killed or fatally wounded in battle—295—than any other regiment in the Union Army. Child ultimately wrote its regimental history, but nothing he wrote during or after the war surpassed the eloquence of his letters from Antietam.[2] "No one can begin to estimate the amount of agony after a great battle," Child wrote on October 7.

> We win a great victory. It goes through the country. The masses rejoice, but if all could see the thousands of poor, suffering dieing [sic] men, their rejoicing would turn to weeping. When I think of the battle of Antietam it seems so strange. Who permits it? To see or feel that a power is in existence that can and will hurl masses of men against each other in deadly conflict—slaying each other by the thousands—mangling and deforming their fellow men—is almost impossible. But it is so—and why we can not know.[3]

On October 4, Child was transferred from his small field hospital at Fountain Bridge Farm, where he had set up operations after the battle, to Smoketown Hospital, located at the northern terminus of Smoketown Road about a mile and

It is 6:00 a.m. on a breezy fall morning at Smoketown Hospital near the Antietam battlefield. Dr. William Child, assistant surgeon of the 5th New Hampshire, stands at left in front of the surgeons' quarters, facing another day of caring for shattered bones and dressing oozing wounds. "Doctors Barber and Ely are still asleep," reads a notation on the reverse of this original print. The tents of Wards A and B are in the distance.

a half north-northeast of the battlefield. Smoketown Hospital was one of two large, consolidated tent hospitals established at Antietam by the army's medical director, Dr. Jonathan Letterman, who that very day was serious, and apparently sober, in the midst of his fellow imbibing staff officers as they sat for a private group portrait by Alexander Gardner.[4]

Letterman's handling of the evacuation and treatment of the wounded at Antietam was a tremendous improvement over the horrid conditions that had existed after previous battles, particularly Bull Run and Fair Oaks. After Antietam, seventy-one field hospitals were set up at farms and homes on and near the battlefield. By early October, Letterman had closed most of these and sent many hundreds of wounded, by wagon and train, to hospitals in nearby Frederick, as well as Baltimore, Washington, and other cities. Only the most seriously wounded—seven

out of ten being amputees—were kept at Antietam. They were moved to either Smoketown Hospital in the northern area of the field or Locust Spring Hospital in the southern area.[5]

Smoketown Hospital, also known as Antietam Hospital, became Child's home for two months. His daily routine involved dressing bullet wounds and stumps. "The worst part is the bad smell," he wrote. He shared a roomy tent with two or three fellow doctors and wrote his letters on the surface of a wooden box as he sat on his bed—a stretcher covered with straw and layered with five blankets.[6]

Sometime in November, or possibly late October, an unknown photographer arrived with a large plate camera and took a few photographs at Smoketown Hospital. Six images are known today, but more may well exist. Four of the pictures show the hospital wards, and one is a group photograph of the hospital's surgeons, including

The surgeons of Smoketown Hospital gather in front of the headquarters tent of hospital director Dr. Bernard Vanderkieft for a group photograph. At right is Dr. Child. Dr. Vanderkeift is fourth from left, directly in front of the tarp pole. Third from left is Dr. William Smith Ely, an assistant surgeon with the 108th New York, in whose personal collection was preserved the six known photographs of Smoketown Hospital.

Child. Another shows the doctors' quarters, with Child standing outside the tent where he composed his letters about the aftermath of Antietam, such as on October 22, when he noted: "After a great battle the whole army is like a great monster, panting for breath."[7]

The Smoketown photos establish that Gardner and Gibson were not the only photographers to visit Antietam in the wake of the battle. Unlike Gardner's photos, which created a sensation in New York and were widely sold, the Smoketown Hospital images were apparently unknown to anyone except those who appeared in them. They were apparently never advertised, and their existence would remain hidden to the greater community of Civil War scholars and enthusiasts until the 1990s.[8]

Many of the doctors and nurses at Smoketown Hospital, including director Dr. Bernard A. Vanderkieft, were ordered to Antietam from their base at U.S. General Hospital No. 1, which had been installed at the Naval Academy in Annapolis after the academy was evacuated in 1861. The Annapolis hospital's resident photographer is the most plausible producer of the Smoketown photographs. A. H. Messinger, who is known to have operated the photograph gallery at the hospital in 1864 and 1865, may have been the Smoketown photographer as well. (There is no photographer's imprint on any of the extant Smoketown Hospital prints.)[9]

Dr. Child's third child, a son, was born while he was stationed at Smoketown Hospital. Child so admired Vanderkieft, he insisted the baby be

On the evening of October 4, 1862, as President Lincoln returned to Washington after his visit to the Antietam battlefield, photographer Nicholas Brown ventured onto the fresh battlefield at Corinth, Mississippi. Pictured is one of his two known images of the Confederate dead, with Col. William P. Rogers of the 2nd Texas at left and the body of Col. W. H. Moore, a brigade commander, leaning on Rogers's shoulder. (Library of Congress)

named Bernard Vanderkieft Child. On November 28, 1862, the very day his wife was giving birth at their home in Bath, Child sent a letter that included prints of two Smoketown Hospital photographs:

> I shall today send those pictures. No. 1 is a group of the surgeons of Smoketown Hospital. . . . The one to the extreme right is Dr. Child. Picture No. 2 is the Surgeon's tents. The first tent is ours. Please take good care of the pictures— sometime I hope to be able to frame them.

Child never did frame the images but kept them well preserved among his personal possessions. He passed them on to his children before his death in 1918.[10]

As Child continued his daily rounds in the placid browning of a western Maryland autumn, steeled to the disagreeable task of changing the dressings of wounded men, several of whom died each day, the war raged on elsewhere. In late September, Confederate Maj. Gen. Earl Van Dorn launched a campaign to drive the Yankees from Mississippi and West Tennessee. That effort ended in the battle of Corinth on October 3 and 4, and a Rebel repulse. Somehow, a St. Louis–based photographer named Nicholas Brown managed to gain access to the battlefield on the evening of the 4th, when he took the only known photographs of dead on the field of battle in the Western theater. More notably, these images are the only known photographs of dead Civil War soldiers in which bodies were positively identified at the time they were photographed.

Photographers recorded images of unburied, dead soldiers in the field seven times during the war (Antietam, Corinth, 2nd Fredericksburg, Gettysburg, Spotsylvania, 1864 burials in Fredericksburg, and Petersburg), but only in the Mississippi images were any names put to any of the lifeless forms. Two Corinth images are known today, one showing Rebels, including Col. William P. Rogers of the 2nd Texas, as they fell during an assault on Federal Battery Robinette. In the other, the bodies of more than a dozen dead Confederates have been gathered together for burial, including those of Rogers and Col. W. H. Moore, whose bloodied faces are clearly visible.

Brown's images were offered for public sale, but unlike Gardner's Antietam photographs, failed to attract much attention. The images did not fall into obscurity, however, and were assimilated into the earliest photographic and visual histories of the Civil War. The image of Rogers as he fell was one of more than 200 Civil War photos faithfully drawn in pen by artist Walton Taber and published as an engraving around 1885 in the four-volume *Battles and Leaders of the Civil War.* Both of Brown's actual images were first published in the first photoengraved photographic history of the war, the *Memorial War Book*, in 1894.[11]

On November 7, 1862, President Lincoln ran out of patience with Gen. George McClellan and relieved him of his command of the Army of the Potomac, replacing him with Gen. Ambrose Burnside. Days later, just before Burnside marched toward Fredericksburg, Gardner was with the army at Warrenton, Virginia, to make a number of images in camp, including large-plate and stereoscopic photographs of Burnside and his staff. Gardner also photographed McClellan and his staff at Warrenton.[12]

Lincoln wanted action, and Burnside gave the president a disaster at Fredericksburg on December 13. Child, who was released from duty at Smoketown Hospital on December 10 to rejoin the 5th New Hampshire, reached Fredericksburg on the December 13th, "just before dark—[when] the battle was raging furiously." Child began assisting with the wounded at the first hospital he came to, then found his regiment the next day. The 5th New Hampshire and other Union regiments had been decimated in the charge against the Rebels on Marye's Heights, many of whom were well protected behind the infamous Stone Wall. Fifty-seven of some 250 in the regiment had been killed or mortally wounded, more than 115 were wounded, and only about seventy-five had returned unscathed.[13] No photographs have surfaced from the Fredericksburg debacle.

After the defeat, the Army of the Potomac moved back across the Rappahannock River to Falmouth and occupied the area for much of the next five months. In January, Burnside launched his ill-fated, rain-soaked advance that became known as the "Mud March." It ended in failure after four days and ended his command. Lincoln replaced Burnside with Gen. Joseph Hooker, who kept the army in place around Falmouth until late April.

During those early months of 1863, photographers took advantage of this inactivity. They exposed numerous large-plate and stereoscopic negatives in and around the Falmouth camps and set up their tripods on Stafford Heights to capture images of Rebel-held Fredericksburg, directly across the Rappahannock River. Alexander Gardner was there on February 14, 1863, to photograph the smoking ruins of the Phillips House—Burnside's headquarters in December—after an accidental fire gutted the mansion. James Gibson is credited with several images, including a view of the army's balloon camp and another of Fredericksburg from a Union battery on Stafford Heights. Timothy O'Sullivan also made negatives, both large-plate and stereo, from Stafford Heights, and photographed Hooker and his staff, an ambulance train, and a number of groups of officers, including one showing George A. Custer, who apparently never met a camera he didn't want to pose for.[14]

At age twenty-three, O'Sullivan was the youngest of the leading photographers of the Civil War. As it progressed, he would play an ever-greater role in its photographic documentation. Alas, as with Gibson and so many others, little biographical information exists about O'Sullivan. Even images are hard to come by of some of the photographers. *Carte de visite* portraits of O'Sullivan did not surface until the late 1970s, and identifiable images of Gibson have yet to surface. Though both men made their living at photography, self-portraits have proved to be almost as elusive as hard information.

O'Sullivan was born around 1840, possibly in

Ireland or perhaps on Staten Island, where he died an untimely death from tuberculosis in 1882. In an application to become a photographer for the U.S. Treasury Department in 1880, O'Sullivan wrote that he was born in the city of New York. His death certificate, however, said he was born in Ireland and was forty-two years old when he died on January 14, 1882. Brady provides a shred of information about O'Sullivan's early years in an 1880 letter that recommended O'Sullivan for the Treasury position: "I have known Mr. Sullivan [*sic*] since boyhood and know that he is a thorough expert at his business and a very reliable man." Brady's niece, Alice Handy Cox, told author James D. Horan in 1954 that, according to the family's oral history, O'Sullivan went to work for Brady "when he was a boy . . . and Mr. Brady taught him how to be a photographer." As with all Civil War photographers, the best available chronicle of O'Sullivan's life, by far, is the vast portfolio of photographic images he left behind.[15]

When Brady opened the Washington gallery in 1858, O'Sullivan went to work for him there under Gardner's tutelage. O'Sullivan's career in the field apparently began with the photographs he took in coastal South Carolina and Georgia in early 1862, then picked up noticeably in Virginia in 1863. Gardner's semi-official position in the army obligated him to photographically reproduce maps for distribution to the top commanders, and in an 1880 letter applying for the Treasury job, O'Sullivan wrote that he was in charge "of all the map work done for the army during the war." Although O'Sullivan's statement is almost surely an exaggeration, map copying may have occupied much of his time in 1862, before he returned to the field in early 1863.[16]

During the extended stay at Falmouth in 1863, the Army of the Potomac became more organized in the way it kept track of photographers approved to do business with the forces. Army clerks started a register and began documenting, division by division, not only all of the "photographists" but the newsboys, purveyors and caterers, mail carriers, sutlers, booksellers, and stationary salesmen. Each division had its own approved photographist, who usually had one or more assistants. Most of these photographers were solely devoted to taking soldier portraits and took few, if any, stereo views or scenes in the field. Not all of the cameramen met with official approval. For example, the name "Photographist John H. Thomas," who was with Gen. David B. Birney's 1st division, 3rd Army Corps, was lined through, with the handwritten notation "revoked." The reason for his termination was not recorded.[17]

The Army of the Potomac's 1863 register (one exists for 1865 as well) lists thirty-two photographers and thirty-eight assistants (including six photographers and ten assistants whose names are lined through). The register even includes a page for Hooker's general headquarters, and as one might expect for a command headquarters, the officially approved photographers were the leaders in their craft. Hooker's photographers were "A. Gardner" and "T. H. O'Sullivan," with a note by O'Sullivan's name elaborating that he would be "taking views on the march."[18]

No similar register for any other Federal Army exists today, though from 1863 to 1865, the Department of Virginia and North Carolina logged a "list of permits . . . as granted by Maj. Gen. Benj. Butler" that includes the names of more than a dozen photographers, the dates they received permits for bringing in photographic materials, and, in one instance, the payment of a $6 permit fee. Civilian photographers provided most of the photographic needs of the army, from the reproduction of maps to the creation of a sixth-plate tintype for the lowliest private. The most significant exception was Capt. Andrew J. Russell, who became the official photographer of the U.S. Military Railroads on March 1, 1863.[19]

From February 1863 through the end of the war, Russell produced hundreds of images and stereo views on several different sizes of glass negatives, including huge fourteen-by-seventeen-inch plates. Most of the images depicted the

In this little-known camp group photograph, Capt. A. J. Russell, official photographer of the U.S. Military Railroads, stands second from right, just inside his tent, with his hand across his camera. (From the collection of Larry J. West)

railroads of northern Virginia and the army's relentless determination to keep them open. During the war, elaborate, custom-made sets of Russell's photographs, often with eighty-two images each, were widely distributed to the Union's top leaders, including President Lincoln, Vice President Hannibal Hamlin, Secretary of War Edwin M. Stanton, three other cabinet members, twenty-three Union major generals, fifteen brigadier generals, ten civilians, and even the admiral and captain of the Russian fleet.[20]

Russell was almost thirty-four-years old when he took the assignment, apparently without having any previous photographic experience. Born on March 20, 1829, he grew up in Nunda, New York, and trained to be an artist. His paintings included landscapes, portraits of local leaders, and, at the beginning of the war, a traveling war diorama used to encourage army enlistment. He

recruited a company of soldiers and was enrolled as captain of Company F, 141st New York Volunteers on August 19, 1862. Russell was with his regiment until some time in February 1863, when he was detached from the unit and sent to Alexandria, Virginia, to take pictures for Brig. Gen. Herman Haupt, the chief of the United States Military Railroads (USMRR). Russell learned the wet plate process from Egbert Guy Fowx, an independent civilian photographer who maintained a brisk portrait business with one or more army units while also freelancing. Fowx took large views and stereo views for the army, and for Brady and/or Anthony as well.[21]

Haupt, who created Russell's position, was a brilliant civil engineer whose single-minded pursuit of his own initiatives led to frequent disputes with his commanders, but also an array of innovations. From devising the spectacular "beanpole" bridges that appeared from a distance to be built of matchsticks to inventing the one-man pontoon boat for inspecting bridge foundations, Haupt excelled in finding efficient, simple solutions for fixing the war-battered railroads in Virginia and for keeping them open for the army.[22]

To spread his innovations to other Union armies and theaters of the war, Haupt distributed written reports to other commanders. He decided that he must also include photographs to illustrate his writings. "And, with the view to make use of a photographic instrument found in the storehouse of the Orange Line [in Alexandria, Virginia], Capt. A. J. Russell of the 141 N.Y. Vols was detailed to the Military Railroads as the operator or artist," said an official report on Russell's activities.[23]

This nine-page report was written on February 24, 1864, by J. H. Devereux, superintendent of the military railroads, to justify not only allowing Russell to continue with his photographic work but to greatly expand the distribution of his photographs to military officers and government leaders. In making his arguments, Devereux provided a revealing glimpse of Russell's one-man photographic department: "The Photograph Department begins and ends with him. No salaried assistant has ever been employed, and the work is done by the Captain, the Captain's servant, and a laborer." Russell's work was a huge bargain for the government, Devereux argued. Expenses for one year, including the cost of a new camera, had been $1,878.72. "This has produced (by Capt. Russell's estimate at ordinary trade prices) $7,000.00 worth of pictures."[24]

The dissemination of Russell's photographs had begun on March 5, 1863, only five days after Russell's appointment, when former Assistant Quartermaster C. B. Ferguson received three large individual pictures of the Potomac River. More images were distributed in April, including the first sets of photos. Then, on May 18, 1863, two weeks and a day after the second battle of Fredericksburg, Haupt authorized the extensive distribution of Russell's work. Sets of thirty-

three large photographs, likely including images of Fredericksburg, were delivered to Lincoln, Stanton, Secretary of State William H. Seward, Treasury Secretary Samuel P. Chase, and several others.[25]

In the weeks and months to come, more and more photographs would be distributed to more and more people, both inside and outside the army. By mid-February 1864, more than 6,500 large photographs and 368 small photographs had been distributed to President Lincoln and sixty-seven others in the administration or the military. Lincoln received 151 large photographs and eighty-eight small images (no doubt including some stereo views) on four dates: May 18, July 23 and 24, 1863, and February 1, 1864.[26]

Brig. Gen. Montgomery C. Meigs, who had overall command of the military railroads as quartermaster general, received more than 150 Russell images during the war. In Meigs, Russell could have had no stronger supporter. Meigs was an artist and an experienced amateur photographer whose own greatest contribution to the photographic history of the United States is a group of at least five images—some in stereo—of Lincoln's first inauguration, showing the gathering throngs and the ceremony itself.

Meigs, however, had to pull back on the reins after reading Devereux's February 1864 report, which concluded with a grandiose plan for the widest distribution of Russell's photographs yet. Designated recipients now included dozens of Union major generals and brigadier generals, two colleges, all cabinet secretaries and heads of executive departments, and "one set to all Foreign Ministers." Meigs crossed off the foreign ministers, the cabinet secretaries, the department heads, and all the brigadier generals. "The distribution of these photographs has been too large," he wrote. Hereafter, photographs would be distributed only to those who could use them directly for the benefit of the military railroads.[27]

Most of the hundreds of photographs that Russell produced for the department are prosaic images taken to illustrate the many facets of military rail transport, including bridges, support facilities, railroad destruction, and repair. The warfare around Russell, however, was inescapable. His work sometimes took him close to the front lines, and his status as a military officer gave him unparalleled access. When Russell came upon his first opportunity to photograph the conflict itself—and to capture actual scenes of battle—he took full advantage, acutely aware of his role in preserving history. Russell could not ignore the obvious lure of battlefield photography, as Devereux clearly understood.

Simultaneous with Russell's railroad photography, "gradually a new series of photographs was forming. . . . [Some] plates [were] being taken of war scenes, preserving for the Government, almost without cost, delineations of its struggle," wrote Devereux. Russell's photographs would be "invaluable as time [progressed], carrying mementos of strength and pride to the present generation, and sublime in their lessons and worth to those who [were] to come after." Devereux also noted Russell's unique access: "Frequently these pictures were secured when no other person and no other circumstance would have ever immortalized them in truthful representation," he wrote. In modern parlance, Russell was embedded with the troops.[28]

On one occasion, Russell was so close to enemy soldiers he could see—and photograph—their faces. On April 8, 1863, Russell or an assistant took his camera up to Stafford Heights across from Fredericksburg and warily approached the east end of the destroyed railroad bridge across the Rappahannock River. He was to take photographs of the bridge so that, should Hooker capture Fredericksburg and push the Confederates south, engineers could see what they needed to do to rebuild it. In a series of five photographs and using some form of a telephoto lens, Russell photographed not only the bridge but also a group of Confederates who came out to pose for him once they were certain he was not a threat. In any war, photographs of an active enemy are remarkable; Russell's are probably the first in history.[29]

Some of Russell's best-known and most dramatic images were taken with a massive fourteen-by-seventeen-inch "Camera Box and Holder" that he received in late March from Holmes, Booth & Haydens, a New York supplier. Russell had a wide-angle Harrison Globe Sine twelve-inch focal lens to use with it and a camera he found in the Orange Line storehouse, which apparently was used for stereoscopic photography.[30]

Russell placed the order for the huge camera with the New York supplier soon after he was appointed to his position on March 1, because by March 21, he was known to have impatiently demanded its whereabouts. "Hurry up the express folks," he wired to Holmes, Booth and Haydens. "I am confused and delayed on account of its non-arrival." Twice he wired the delivery company, Adams Express, finally exclaiming on March 26, "Forward it at once. Very important." The next day, it finally arrived.[31]

Less than six weeks later, on May 3, 1863, Russell had the opportunity to carry this massive camera to the threshold of battle and onto a Civil War battlefield soon after the fighting, just as Gardner had done at Antietam. Unlike Gardner, however, Russell took photographs of the actual battle being fought in the distance, and he may have possibly made his appearance on the field as soon as twenty minutes after the fighting, when the bodies were literally still warm. That day, in the aftermath of the second battle of Fredericksburg, which was part of the overall battle of Chancellorsville, Russell took his turn raising the bar of Civil War photographic achievement. More than any other photographer had to that point, Russell was able to follow an army in action.

It is quite possible, even probable, that among the first to see Russell's historic images was President Lincoln. If so, their impact may have been tempered by their association to Chancellorsville, which was yet another devastating defeat for the Army of the Potomac. On April 27, after more than three months at Falmouth, the army had gone on the offensive again, crossing

Previously unpublished as a group, these three images (*facing page and above, left*), by A. J. Russell or an assistant, tell the story behind the famous photographs of Rebel officers and soldiers posing for Union cameras across the Rappahannock River in Fredericksburg. The first two images are from the personal collection of Joel Clough, a railroad engineer who on April 7, 1863, ordered the inspection of the destroyed bridge for possible later repair. The photographs were made around noon on April 8. In the first image, Russell is southeast of the bridge and Marye's Mill, and only a single person sits on or near the bridge. Russell's telephoto lens captures a clear view of the stately pillars of the Marye House, in the background directly above the mill. As Russell moves to a position just northeast of the mill for his second shot, his presence has attracted wary attention. More than a dozen Confederates are eyeing the cameramen, but most keep their distance and remain close to the shelter of the mill. The Confederates finally have become comfortable in the presence of Russell's camera in the third image and other variants. Russell has moved onto his end of the bridge, and the Rebels pose on their end. It was not the first time the bridge had been used in that manner (*above, right*). In an Alfred R. Waud sketch published in *Harper's Weekly* four months earlier, on December 13, 1862, Union and Confederate soldiers exchange salutations. (*Facing page*: From the Joel B. Clough Collection, items reproduced by permission of The Huntington Library, San Marino, California; *above, left*: the Western Reserve Historical Society; *above, right*: Library of Congress)

Long thought to show Union troops at the siege of Petersburg, the images on these two pages actually show Brooks's Division of the Sixth Corps gathered in abandoned Confederate works on the west bank of the Rappahannock River, *Time-Life* researchers the late Brian C. Pohanka, Harris J. Andrews, and Larry Strayer determined in 1983. These A. J. Russell images, including the classic above, were probably taken on April 29 or 30, 1863, and show an army ready to move at a moment's notice. Confederate pickets were only about 400 yards distant. (Courtesy of the Western Reserve Historical Society)

the Rappahannock upstream from Fredericksburg. Russell remained with a large force that stayed behind to confront the Confederates in the city. By April 30, Hooker was at Chancellorsville Court House, and Russell was with the 6th Corps troops of Brig. Gen. William Brooks, who had crossed the Rappahannock about a mile below Fredericksburg in pontoon boats and occupied abandoned Rebel rifle pits on the west bank of the river. These troops were on the front line at Fredericksburg, and Russell took several images of the Union soldiers packed into the trenches

of a bivouac, huddled together in a compact line. The most famous of the images shows a cluster of Union soldiers in the foreground, some wearing forage caps and overcoats against chilly, wet weather, and nearly all of them bearing looks of grim determination.[32]

These men would see battle on May 3, and Russell would, too. Shortly after sunrise on that clear, warm morning, Russell extended the legs of his tripod and set up his huge, new camera on Stafford Heights. From this bluff, he had a panoramic view of Fredericksburg and Marye's

Heights beyond, with the stately pillars of the Marye House shining white in the morning sunlight.

At Chancellorsville, Stonewall Jackson had already flanked Hooker, and the battle raged into its third day. As Lee pressed Hooker's battered army into an ever-tightening semi-circle of defense, Gen. John Sedgwick received urgent orders to drive the Rebels out of Fredericksburg and hit Lee's rear. That meant another assault on the dreaded Stone Wall at Marye's Heights.

The crucial infantry attack began around 10:30 a.m. One of the five views Russell took from Stafford Heights that morning shows what may be the opening Union artillery volley shortly after dawn. The landscape beyond the city is perfectly clear, and Russell's massive camera captures the vista in minute detail, including a light-colored, rounded anomaly that could be the smoke of Union batteries at the western edge of the city.[33]

Another Russell photograph of the same scene appears to be quite different. The panoramic, ten-by-thirteen-inch albumen print preserved at the Western Reserve Historical Society is labeled in pencil as "Fredericksburg, Day of Battle, May 3/ 63." In this view, the white haze of smoke is visible in several areas between the city and the heights. Smoke pours off the heights beyond the city, where several Confederate brigades are in line.[34]

Making another photograph, Russell turned his camera a bit more northwest and exposed a plate of a scene that included the entire destroyed railroad bridge, as well as a tree with two soldiers sitting in its upper branches, their attention riveted toward the city and the hills

This magnificent plate shows two soldiers in a lone tree on Stafford Heights "watching the fight" as the battle of second Fredericksburg grinds on in the distance on May 3, 1863. The image also gives a clear view of both sides of the destroyed railroad bridge, where Russell photographed the Rebels on April 8. (Courtesy of the Western Reserve Historical Society)

Facing page: Published together for the first time, these three A. J. Russell prints, made from fourteen-by-seventeen-inch negatives, show the progression of the second battle of Fredericksburg on May 3, 1863. In the first image, taken from Stafford Heights with the rising sun illuminating Fredericksburg on a clear morning, all is quiet, save for a possible puff of smoke just beyond the city at left center, possibly the start of artillery fire. The second image, looking slightly more south, shows battle smoke spread across the battlefield. On the left, smoke seems to be pouring from heavily defended Lee Hill. On the right side, smoke has enshrouded Marye's Heights. Finally, in the third image, Russell has moved upstream toward the pontoon bridge, preparing to cross into the city. He stops, however, to make one more image, which shows that the smoke of battle has obliterated the distant scene and is creeping into the city itself. (Courtesy of the Western Reserve Historical Society)

This A. J. Russell classic of the Stone Wall at Marye's Heights after the second battle of Fredericksburg may not have been taken as soon as twenty minutes after the fight, as some original labels claim, but it was no more than a couple of hours. Russell's battle panoramas and his photographs of the aftermath underscore how close he was to the action on May 3, 1863. (Courtesy of the Western Reserve Historical Society)

This reproduction of parts of the first and fourth pages of the six-page distribution list of A. J. Russell photographs by the U.S. Military Railroads shows President Lincoln receiving photographs on May 18 and July 23, 1863, and February 1, 1864. It also documents the release on June 23, 1863, of a single photograph to the sergeant of the 6th Maine who stormed the Stone Wall, undoubtedly a print of Russell's classic. (From the National Archives and Records Administration)

beyond. The original penciled caption on this twelve-by-fifteen-inch view is "Fredericksburg—Battle Progressing—May 3/63—Soldiers Watching Fight."[35]

When the Union infantry assault began in earnest, it took the Yankees only about thirty minutes to sweep the outnumbered Confederates from the heights. As this was happening, Russell was moving north along the riverbank toward the pontoon bridges that crossed the Rappahannock, obviously intent on crossing the river and moving toward the Marye's Heights battlefield the moment the fighting was finished. For his next shot, Russell mounted his camera on a much lower area of the heights, which was closer to the river and nearer the pontoon bridge he would need to cross to reach the battlefield. In this thirteen-by-sixteen-inch image, also dated May 3 and labeled "Battle Progressing," smoke, having almost entirely obscured the horizon, can be seen drifting into the city and literally wrapping around St. George's Episcopal Church.[36]

Almost immediately after taking this image, Russell crossed the river on the pontoon bridge with Haupt. Making their way through the city, they found no signs of life at the Stone Wall, only the litter and death of battle. Here, Russell took perhaps his most famous war photograph. It shows several dead Rebels behind the Stone Wall. He then took the short walk to the back side of Marye's Heights, where he photographed Haupt viewing the shattered remains of an artillery battery.

Russell's photograph at the Stone Wall gained instant recognition among his peers. It was the only image that Devereux specifically mentioned in his 1864 report, noting that the "Stone Wall is a characteristic picture" that exemplified Russell's unrivaled access to the scenes of conflict. Only a few officers below the rank of general were ever given copies of Russell's photographs, and one of those happened to be a lowly sergeant from Maine who had fought in the May 3 battle and had apparently come to the railroad department in Alexandria to inquire about the availability of a certain photograph he'd heard about, or perhaps even seen. An entry on the USMRR distribution list of photographs for June 23, 1863, reads: "Sarg't 6th Maine, who stormed Stone Wall—1 Picture."

While Devereux was correct in saying that the military railroad photograph department began and ended with Russell, other civilian contract photographers were, in fact, taking images for the army in 1863 and 1864. These included Fowx and Washington photographer R. W. Addis, who took a series of at least twenty-five images of the 50th New York Engineers at work in the field, including one picture that places him, on May 3, 1863, as close to the second battle of Fredericksburg as Russell. This Addis image, measuring five-by-seven inches, shows the same pontoon bridge that Russell crossed before he photographed the Stone Wall.[37]

Sedgwick's victory at the Stone Wall did not prevent the army's overall defeat at Chancellorsville. On May 5, Hooker's beaten army started retreating back across the Rappahannock. Lee soon began to plan a second invasion of the North, and A. J. Russell headed back to Alexandria to print hundreds of copies of his photographs for exclusive distribution to the highest levels of civilian and military leadership in the United States.

As the war tramped into the summer of 1863, bodies and photographs alike continued to accumulate. The wholesale slaughter was terrible to contemplate, and a shaken, divided nation asked itself how much more could be endured. In the first week of July, after the smoke of battle had cleared, the answer was revealed in a series of stark images taken among the fields and boulders near the Pennsylvania crossroads town of Gettysburg.

7

GETTYSBURG

By the end of May 1863, Robert E. Lee was set to invade the North once more, Union Gen. Ulysses S. Grant had laid siege to Vicksburg, Mississippi, and, in Washington, photographer Alexander Gardner had left the employ of M. B. Brady and struck out on his own. Gardner's new photographic gallery on the northwest corner of 7th and D Streets in Washington, D.C., boasted the latest equipment, ideal lighting, and a chemical department of "such perfection that the sitting for a Carte de Visite rarely exceed[ed] five seconds! Oftener not more than one or two!" The first notice of Gardner's Gallery was in the May 26 edition of the Washington *Daily National Intelligencer*, where an advertisement boasted that "excellent" photographs had been taken as late as 6:20 in the evening. It was impossible for anyone within eyesight of the gallery to miss it because seven huge signs festooned the upper walls of the front and east side of the four-story commercial building. The sign on the front facade, "VIEWS OF THE WAR," was almost twice the height of the studio's third-floor windows. Another sign, "GARDNER'S GALLERY," stretched the length of the building at its roofline, with letters two-feet tall.[1]

After five years as manager of Brady's Washington gallery, Gardner would now be competing against him. Much has been written about the split, but almost all of it is based on speculation and circumstantial evidence. No one is even sure when the parting happened, except that it was sometime after November 1862 and before the debut of Gardner's new gallery in May 1863.[2]

The split is usually depicted as acrimonious, but most writers overlook the possibility that Gardner may have left Brady simply because he wanted to go on his own. If a problem spurred the breakup, it was most likely about money. Brady was plagued by financial trouble throughout his career. Another possible indicator of financial problems is the fact that Gardner took with him more than 400 stereoscopic and large-plate negatives of war scenes, including all of the Antietam photographs, all of O'Sullivan's work in South Carolina and Georgia, and most of the photographs from Cedar Mountain, northern Virginia, Bull Run, Manassas, and the Peninsular Campaign. Brady retained as many as ninety-five stereoscopic negatives and an unknown number of large plates, including all of his 1861 images from the Washington camps, images from Harper's

Unlike M. B. Brady, Alexander Gardner did not put himself in his Civil War photographs. He was not publicity shy, however, when it came to promoting his gallery at 7th and D streets in Washington, D.C., which was covered with signs. The gallery was above Shephard & Riley's Bookstore and first advertised for business in the *Washington Intelligencer* of May 26, 1863. (Library of Congress)

Ferry in the fall of 1862, two Bull Run battlefield stereo views from March 1862, one Cedar Mountain stereo view, and forty stereo views from Yorktown, Virginia, and the Peninsular Campaign. Some of Brady's other photographers also left with Gardner, including James Gibson and Timothy O'Sullivan.[3]

One theory about the breakup has been repeated so often that it is widely accepted as fact: Gardner left because Brady failed to credit the individual photographs to the photographers who took them. The evidence on this point is mixed and, once again, circumstantial. It is true that Gardner, once on his own, routinely gave credit to the photographer of each image, both on original prints and in his sales catalog, but it was an unusual practice. Anthony did not give credit, nor, among others, did D. Appleton, a large New York stereo view marketer, or the London Stereoscopic Company. Aside from Gardner's men, the only photographers who received credit were

those who marketed their own work, such as the Langenheim brothers or Osborn & Durbec in Charleston.

Brady, however, did not prevent Gardner and his other war photographers from taking credit for their images while under his employ. Original large-plate albumen prints from the Antietam battlefield and Warrenton, Virginia, in the fall of 1862—some of the final images Gardner produced while with Brady—clearly carry equal billing for both men and specify their respective roles in the production of the images. Imprinted on each mount at lower right, just below the albumen print, is "M. B. Brady, Publisher." At lower left appears: "Gardner, Photographer." A standard feature of many Civil War prints was a copyright line, and on most of the Antietam prints, this line, too, carried Gardner's name.

In the clerk's office of the U.S. District Court of the District of Columbia, the year 1862 was marked by a sudden frenzy of photographic copyrighting by Brady and some of his operators. It is a curious phenomenon that merits further study. When Brady copyrighted his first photograph in Washington in 1859—an image of the Buchanan administration—it was only the fifteenth photograph that had ever been registered at that office. Only a few dozen copyrights of any kind were filed annually, mostly for books, music, poems, plays, and the occasional beverage title or medicinal preparation. During the war's first year, however, Brady copyrighted a dozen separate war images. In 1862, his gallery seemingly overwhelmed the office, copyrighting 174 images, each of which had to be meticulously recorded by hand in the clerk's copyright book. During all of 1862, the clerk's office registered only thirty-four other copyrights.[4]

Brady was more concerned about piracy than most photographers. The "Brady's Album Gallery" labels on the backs of original stereo views and album cards issued in 1862 carried this admonition: "The photographs of this series were taken directly from nature, at considerable cost. Warning is therefore given that legal proceedings will be at once instituted against any party infringing the copyright." Brady's gallery failed to come even close to formally copyrighting everything it produced. The 174 copyrights that flooded the clerk's office in 1862, nearly all for stereoscopic photographs, represented less than half of the gallery's output of more than 400 images that year. Each Brady-mounted print nevertheless carried a copyright line.

Until May 5, 1862, every Brady's gallery photograph that was copyrighted was done so in Brady's name. On that day, Brady secured in his own name copyrights for four northern Virginia stereoscopic images: Taylor's Tavern, Falls Church, Bailey's Crossroads, and Centreville. Then, mysteriously, Brady's photographers began copyrighting their images in their own names, and Brady's name disappeared from the District of Columbia copyright books altogether until 1865. On May 5 and two other dates in May, George Barnard and James Gibson secured a joint copyright for a total of sixty-six stereo views produced at Manassas, Bull Run, and Yorktown. Gardner and Gibson jointly copyrighted forty-eight Peninsular Campaign stereo views on July 21. Gardner returned alone on October 7, 1862, to copyright sixteen Antietam stereographs (once again, a fraction of his output and including no large-plate images).[5]

It is not known why Brady ceased copyrighting his gallery's images in his own name in mid-1862. Perhaps it was a result of pressure from Gardner and the other photographers; perhaps Brady willingly changed his gallery's copyright procedure. All that may ever be known for certain is that at least six months before Gardner and Brady split, Brady's photographers were taking credit for their own work. Copyright credit, however, did not translate to public credit. In 1861 and 1862, the media always described all images from Brady's gallery as "Brady" photographs. This was particularly true with the Antietam photographs, regardless of how meticulous Gardner was in putting his name on every mounted print.

"These terrible mementos of one of the most sanguinary conflicts of the war we owe to the enterprise of Mr. Brady of New York," wrote Oliver Wendell Holmes. The *Harper's Weekly* credit line for its Antietam woodcuts said: "Photographs by Brady." The *New York Times* headlined its article: "Brady Photographs." Was this Brady's doing? Or did Holmes and the newspapers' headline writers simply take it by custom that any photograph from Brady's gallery, no matter whose name was on the copyright line, was a "Brady photograph?" In 1862, a photograph from Brady's gallery may have been thought of in the same manner that people today consider a movie directed by Steven Spielberg to be a "Spielberg movie," with no regard for the collaborating cinematographers, except in the credits.[6]

Given Gardner's philosophy about proper credit, it is reasonable to suggest that he was irritated, or even furious, about the lack of public recognition for his Antietam work. But it is only speculation. Gardner may well have been resigned to the custom of the time and decided without rancor that when he opened his own gallery, he would do it his way and give credit. Perhaps the parting was amicable and businesslike, and Gardner kept the majority of the 1861–1862 battlefield negatives as fair settlement for what Brady owed him. We simply do not know.

After Lee's second invasion of the North ended with the battle of Gettysburg, on July 1, 2, and 3, 1863, Gardner and Brady both traveled to Pennsylvania to photograph the battlefield. They traveled in separate photo wagons, arriving at different times, and surely their mutual intent was to produce better photographs, or in today's photojournalistic parlance, to "outshoot" one another.

Gardner, accompanied by James Gibson and Timothy O'Sullivan, beat Brady to the battlefield. Gardner and his crew apparently arrived on the evening of July 5, two days after Pickett's thousands had hurled themselves in bloody futility against a solid Union line on Cemetery Ridge. Gardner and his associates arrived in time to capture, once again, images of the dead on the battlefield—both Yankees and Rebels—before they were covered by dark Pennsylvania soil. Brady and his operators, David Woodbury and Anthony Berger, did not begin taking photographs until around July 15, well after the bodies were buried. But Brady's photographs exude their own style—not gritty and graphic, but expansive and contemplative. Many were sizeable landscapes or panoramas with a strategically placed observer or two, sometimes Brady himself, to encourage the viewer of the photograph to form a personal vision of what the battle must have been like.[7]

At Gettysburg, Gardner and Brady, each with his own eye and unique photographic perspective, produced classic images destined to become ranked among the war's most famous. Gardner and his men, the quintessential news photographers, produced "Harvest of Death" and "Home of a Rebel Sharpshooter." Brady, the portrait and landscape artist, produced, with his assistants, "Three Rebel Prisoners." Although photographers frequently traveled together during the war and photographed the same subjects, Gardner and Brady were not together at Gettysburg, and, excepting the distinctive Evergreen Cemetery gatehouse and Little Round Top, they photographed different subjects and different areas of the battlefield. Even at Little Round Top, where they both took stereoscopic photographs, Gardner and his men concentrated on the trenches; Brady captured the broad vistas. Due to timing, atmospheric conditions, and creative instincts, and owing nothing to intention, the end result was that they complemented one another's work. Brady's wide-screen vision was one perspective; Gardner's hard-news photojournalism was quite another. For history's sake, the breakup was all for the best.[8]

It must be stressed that for more than a hundred years after the Civil War, no distinction was made between the Gettysburg photographs of Gardner and those of Brady. Usually, Brady received the credit for all of the battlefield images. William A. Frassanito, who is perhaps better known for his detective work in discovering the original locations of scores of Gettysburg images, first separated the photographs of Gardner and his men from Brady's images in his unique 1975 study, *Gettysburg: A Journey in Time.* Today it is routine to distinguish between the work of Gardner, Brady, and other Civil War photographers, but when Frassanito first began studying Civil War photographs in the 1950s as a youngster, no such distinctions were made.

The ascension of Gardner to his rightful stature in the history of Civil War photography has come at considerable expense to Brady's reputation. Past generations had come to associate Brady's name with any Civil War photograph, as if he were responsible for every one. As Gardner began to receive his due, writers also began to assert that Brady probably personally took no photographs at all during the war. In the ebb and flow of historical revision, Brady holds the singular

The difference between Alexander Gardner's Gettysburg photographs and those of M. B. Brady is the difference between live bodies and dead ones. The enterprising Gardner was first on the battlefield, and he focused on the still-unburied dead. Brady arrived too late to photograph bodies, but not too late to imbue his inimitable style on the images. (*Top*: Library of Congress; *right*: from the collection of John J. Richter)

distinction of being credited for taking every Civil War photograph, and also discredited for not taking a single one. Frassanito recognized the proper balance. Gardner's contribution had been overlooked, and often ignored. Even after Gardner is given his due, however, "we are left with a deep sense of appreciation for [Brady's] efforts and accomplishments on the battlefield," Frassanito writes. "His irreplaceable series of photographic documents will forever play an integral role in the interpretation of our nation's tragic experience at Gettysburg."[9]

Only shreds of written information exist to illuminate the story behind the trips Gardner and Brady made to the Gettysburg battlefield. On the morning of July 5, Gardner was at the Farmer's Inn in Emmitsburg, Maryland, just nine miles south of the battlefield, when Jeb Stuart's Rebel cavalry swept through around dawn and briefly detained Gardner (and possibly O'Sullivan or Gibson). Gardner's fifteen-year-old son Lawrence was attending Mount St. Mary's College, and the photographer had likely stopped in Emmitsburg to check on the lad's well-being.[10]

Later that afternoon, in the company of Charles H. Keener, a U.S. Christian Commission volunteer from Baltimore, Gardner and his crew made their way to the battlefield. It is a shame that Gardner did not record his first impressions of what he saw on that July 5. He undoubtedly knew he was approaching a great battlefield; he would have already heard stories of the fight while he was in Emmitsburg, and those he met on the road as he traveled north more than likely would have embellished these tales. The stench of death hung heavy in the dank, summer air and probably alerted his senses long before the battlefield was in view. The blazing midsummer sun, leavened by the occasional downpour, cooked the pot of offal, releasing an ever-thickening malodorous miasma of rot and putrefaction.

Keener and his companions reached Gettysburg at 6:00 p.m., before the shadows began to lengthen in the fragile light. Keener recounts his experiences in a letter:

> We passed over the battlefield for more than 3 miles, where we had a fresh view of things as they looked two days after the battle. First we saw the smoking ruins of a house and barn; fences were all leveled; breastworks were thrown up on all sides; the road barricaded; dead horses laid about by dozens, and filled the road with a horrible stench.[11]

Gardner was no stranger to the horrors of a battlefield, but even he must have been awestruck by the vast panorama of destruction that spread out before him as his wagon crested the small rise on Emmitsburg Road at Sherfy's Peach Orchard. Here, the road crossed what is now Wheatfield Road and turned slightly to the east, revealing the vast plain of combat between Seminary Ridge and Cemetery Ridge. It is a breathtaking panorama seen by every traveler entering from that route, but whereas memorials dominate today's vista, the scene on the morning of the second day of battle was far more unsettled.

Arriving at around 9:00 a.m. on July 2 from Emmitsburg, Capt. James Edward Smith of the 4th New York Independent Battery recalled:

> As we approached the ground between the two armies in the vicinity of the "Peach Orchard," I noticed that the fences had been cleared away, and all preparations made that usually precede a battle; even then the pickets and skirmishers were uneasy and kept up a desultory fire, little puffs of thin blue smoke dotting the plain before us, indicating quite distinctly the respective lines of the two greatest armies on earth, at this hour.[12]

Gardner saw the same landscape after it was decorated by the detritus of two long days of fighting. Immediately to his right, the peach trees of Sherfy's Peach Orchard were broken and torn in their precise rows after desperate infantrymen pruned one another's ranks in repeated attacks and counterattacks, often in close-quarters fighting. Spreading out before him for two miles to the north, like a vast arena, the shallow, mile-wide swale between Seminary Ridge and Cemetery Hill would have been littered with debris and populated by small groups of men holding picks and shovels, with handkerchiefs probably covering their mouths and noses. Sitting on their wagon, or standing beside it, Gardner and his companions may have spoken with some of the soldiers exhausted by the disagreeable business of grave digging. These men, roiled by combat, fear, and too much death, may not have been overly communicative, but they could have given Gardner a few clues as to the true scope of the tragedy. At this moment, his journalistic soul must have been charged with the thought of his work ahead, but his human soul must have recoiled at what lay about him. Perhaps these inherent qualities directed him toward the spots where the dead still lay unburied.

Gardner, O'Sullivan, and Gibson may have started taking photographs that evening, but more likely it was not until the morning of July 6. Unlike Antietam, where Gardner used only his stereoscopic camera during his initial work, the three of them used the stereo camera and large-plate camera simultaneously from the start.[13]

Gardner seemed to be unsure exactly how to assign credit for the more than fifty stereoscopic negatives he and his crew took at Gettysburg, because it appears that he arbitrarily devised a system designed to give equal credit to all three photographers. Gardner's stereo negative numbers for the Gettysburg series run from 226 to 274. Gardner lists himself as the photographer of No. 226, O'Sullivan of No. 227, and Gibson of No. 228. He systematically repeats this rotation—Gardner, O'Sullivan, Gibson—through the rest of the series. O'Sullivan was listed as the photographer of every large-plate Gettysburg image.[14]

Gardner and his team most likely began their work with the group of unburied Federal soldiers seen in the "Harvest of Death" images, because the Union dead would have been buried first. These images were taken on a relatively level section of the battlefield, probably in the center or southern area, and not far off Emmitsburg Road, which was Gardner's route into the

battlefield. Their precise locations have yet to be determined.[15]

On July 6, Gardner and his men most likely took their cameras to the Rose Farm, where they photographed groups of dead Rebels, a badly mutilated corpse, and the half-buried remains of South Carolina soldiers. Frassanito's discovery of the Rose Farm as the location of these images, and the resulting discoveries of the significance of the fighting there on the second day's battle, are hallmarks of his Gettysburg studies.[16]

Gardner, O'Sullivan, and Gibson appear to have moved from the Rose Farm to Devil's Den and Little Round Top, where they apparently concentrated their efforts on July 7. The crew's photographs at or near Devil's Den included the famous "sharpshooter" images. Just west of the Den, Gardner and his team made three stereo negatives and a large plate of a dead Confederate infantryman (the plate is titled "A Sharpshooter's Last Sleep"), then moved the body seventy-two yards to the east to the nook they called "Home of a Rebel Sharpshooter." This more dramatic location in Devil's Den itself was a sharpshooter's nest formed by two convergent boulders and a hastily constructed barrier of smaller stones. Here, the team took one stereo negative and one large plate. Historian Frederic Ray's revelation in 1961 that the same body was photographed in another position before being moved to the sharpshooter's nest was brought to full fruition by Frassanito's discovery in 1967 of the original camera locations. These findings, however, inadvertently led to a common misconception that Civil War photographers frequently moved bodies to achieve better photographs. In fact, this is the only known instance. Gardner and other photographers sometimes added props, such as muskets, canteens, shells, and such, but with the exception of this corpse, they left the bodies alone.[17]

In the vicinity of Devil's Den, the team also photographed dead Confederates on the east side of Plum Run in an area they called the "Slaughter Pen." The discovery of this location as the

This Gardner's Gallery image of the Fahnestock brothers' store in Gettysburg, which housed the office of the U.S. Sanitary Commission, is the most recent major Gettysburg photographic discovery. The stereo view of this scene had been known, but this large-plate version by photographer Timothy O'Sullivan did not surface until 1997 and is published in a book for the first time. (Courtesy of the New York Public Library)

site of several key images of the dead of Gettysburg was Frassanito's first major find in his research into Gettysburg battlefield photographs. From the Slaughter Pen, Gardner, O'Sullivan, and Gibson apparently moved onto Little Round Top to photograph Union breastworks and positions. They had to stop working from time to time during the four or five days they spent on the battlefield to wait out passing showers and storms. On the morning of July 8, the heavy downpour that soaked Gettysburg for about eight hours finally gave way to clear skies around 11:30 a.m. Whether Gardner and his men took images that afternoon is uncertain, but they were back at work the next morning, as evidenced by the morning shadows and water puddles in their images of the Evergreen Cemetery gatehouse on July 9, their final day on the battlefield. That

afternoon, the team apparently wrapped up their work by taking their only photographs in Gettysburg proper: a stereo negative, credited to Gardner, of the headquarters of the Sanitary Commission on Baltimore Street and a large plate of the same scene, credited to O'Sullivan, that has only recently resurfaced.[18]

O'Sullivan and Gibson then split from Gardner and trailed after the Army of the Potomac, whose headquarters moved out of Gettysburg on July 7. Gardner may have stayed behind, perhaps to pick up his son Lawrence at Mount St. Mary's, before returning to Washington with the battlefield negatives. As he had after Antietam, Gardner used the military telegraph to transmit a message to O'Sullivan. The short message, though undated, gives us an illuminating glimpse into the work of the war photographers.[19]

T. H. O'SULLIVAN
HEADQUARTERS ARMY POTOMAC

I have just got back from Gettysburg. Woodbury and Berger were there. If they come your length I hope you will give them every attention. Tell Jim that McGraw is dead. I will write. Alex. Gardner.[20]

As Frassanito has noted, the thirty-four words in Gardner's telegram contain a surprising wealth of information. Not only does it establish that Gardner parted company with O'Sullivan and Gibson, who went with the army, it reveals that Gardner encountered Brady's photographers, David Woodbury and Anthony Berger, who also planned to follow after the army. Gardner's hospitable request to "give them every attention"

does not sound like a man harboring hard feelings toward his former employer, particularly since nearly half of the valuable and limited space in his wire is devoted to that subject. The telegram also reveals that, as the photographers took one gruesome picture after another, the fate of a wounded friend preyed on their minds. The identity of "McGraw" is most likely Lt. Hugh McGraw of the 140th New York, who was wounded in his right leg at Little Round Top and had it amputated at a field hospital, but died on July 8. Gardner obviously learned of McGraw's death after he parted company with Gibson and O'Sullivan, and the need to pass along the sad news was another reason for the wire message.[21]

While exploring the background of M. B. Brady's stereoscopic negative of the John Burns house at Gettysburg from a high-resolution Library of Congress download, researcher and collector John J. Richter discovered the previously overlooked presence not only of Brady but of his portable developing tent on a tripod, which is set up behind the well house. A contemporary engraving of a dark tent on a tripod shows how the operator works within the tent while shutting out the sunlight. (Library of Congress; detail by John J. Richter; engraving courtesy of Scully & Osterman)

Brady arrived on the battlefield around July 15. He may have been delayed by travel restrictions and post-battle chaos in south-central Pennsylvania. Woodbury and Berger probably arrived from Washington with the photo wagon a few days earlier and were awaiting Brady's arrival from New York when they ran into Gardner.[22]

One can imagine Gardner telling Woodbury and Berger that, yes, he had made photographs of the dead, but that all of the bodies had now been buried. With no human carnage to record, the alternative was battle damage. Brady and his men roamed the area taking pictures for several days, perhaps as long as a week. Before Brady arrived, Woodbury and Berger had plenty of time to scout the many different areas where fighting occurred at Gettysburg, and they were probably the ones who located and identified the area of fighting on the first day of the battle. They also found Culp's Hill, a prime location for photography. Gardner had missed both areas.

Brady and his men took four stereoscopic photographs on Culp's Hill, each providing a dramatic 3-D view of scarred and damaged trees. These images graphically show why Culp's Hill was by far the most popular and most visited area of the Gettysburg battlefield for some twenty years after the fight—until new growth finally concealed the scars of war. In one Brady image, an assistant lies on his back in a grove of scarred trees, both knees pulled up. Was Brady's man trying to simulate the rigor-mortis stiffened bodies so familiar from Gardner's Antietam negatives? Was he trying to fake a Gardner photo? If not, Edward Anthony was, because the original caption on this stereo view (issued exclusively by the Anthony Company beginning in 1865) includes "in the middle ground a dead soldier." Later versions omitted the lame attempt to hype a Brady photograph with Gardner-style content.

Brady was fond of putting himself in photographs; he appears in at least six of his images at Gettysburg. Twice as often, though, he used assistants or others. His primary motivation seemed to be the desire to add a human element—either himself or someone else—into the landscape. Brady, however, is usually a subtle presence in his photographs rather than a commanding feature. He appeared alone in only one Gettysburg photo and refrained from stepping into the spotlight at moments ripe for self-promotion, such as with citizen hero John Burns or with the three Rebel prisoners. Brady did appear in one image with Burns, but his presence is so subtle that he remained undetected until 2004.

Brady's poor eyesight is usually offered by revisionists as the reason he personally took no photographs during the Civil War. This story surfaced a decade before the Civil War, during the daguerreian era, when the *Photographic Art-Journal* reported in March 1851, "Brady is not an operator himself, a failing eyesight precluding the possibility of his using the camera with any certainty, but he is an excellent artist." Throughout his life, Brady corrected his bad eyesight with glasses and, as countless bespectacled photographers can attest, would have had no trouble operating a camera.[23]

If in many cases Brady was not the actual photographer, it was because he did not see it as his job. It is likely that he saw his role not as a camera operator but as the gallery owner—the leader. His operators may have prepared and exposed the wet plates while he mingled with his guests, but Brady was, nonetheless, the man with the vision. Whether it was selecting the scene, dictating a camera angle, adjusting a politician's clothing, or placing himself or assistants in a scene, Brady played a creative role in many "Brady" photographs. His artistry is present in many of his Civil War images, and the unique Brady eye that created his distinctive, 1861 camp images returns in his Gettysburg series. With an abundant variety of landscapes present in the geologically rich environs of Gettysburg, Brady created at least three, two-plate panoramas with his large-plate camera and captured other sweeping vistas and scenes with single plates, both stereoscopic and large-format. His feel for celebrity is seen in his images of Burns, the local

Gardner's photographs of the dead at Gettysburg were not reproduced in *Harper's Weekly* until July 22, 1865, months after the war was over. This full-page woodcut engraving combines elements of five different Gardner photographs into a single scene. (Library of Congress)

resident who took up his flintlock musket and fought with the Union soldiers during the first day's battle. Brady's sense of artistic composure reveals itself most prominently in the exquisite placement of the three Rebel prisoners. Brady may not have actually worked the camera, but the scenes were his creation.

The known output by Brady and his crew at Gettysburg is rather small—sixteen large-plate photographs and twenty stereoscopic photographs. He missed some obvious opportunities, most notably Devil's Den. Neither Brady nor Gardner photographed the area of Pickett's Charge, probably because it had no truly distinctive landmarks—the scrubby "Copse of Trees" hardly qualified then—and its significance may have remained unknown to them since their visit came so soon after the battle. Gardner, O'Sullivan, and Gibson produced at least eighty-seven images (thirty-five large plates and fifty-two stereo negatives) at Gettysburg, or about the same number of total images as Gardner and Gibson had produced during their first Antietam visit (about eighteen large plates and seventy stereos).[24]

The bodies at Gettysburg were just as grotesque as those at Antietam; some scenes, such as the eviscerated corpse at the Rose Farm, were worse yet. The impact of these photographs, however, was not the same. This time, with the war well into its third year, there would be no articles and no spreads in the illustrated news weeklies to acclaim Gardner's first great photographic accomplishment since striking out on his own. What little publicity did result would go to Brady, yet again. Eleven of Brady's images were reproduced as woodcut engravings in the August 22, 1863, edition of *Harper's Weekly*, even though the *Harper's* sketch artist, Alfred Waud, was with Gardner and his men at Gettysburg and posed for their stereo camera in Devil's Den. Gardner, working apart from Brady, had beaten his old boss to the battlefield and captured the only photographs of the dead at Gettysburg. He had scooped Brady in the field, but Brady, the master of promotion, had scooped Gardner in the press. When the thousands of readers opened their *Harper's Weekly* to see the graphic coverage of Gettysburg, from photographs converted into woodcut engravings, once again the credit line they saw was "Photographs by Brady."[25]

By 1863, photo piracy of Civil War images apparently was no longer seen as the threat it appeared to be in 1862, at least as far as securing copyrights. Gardner was not particularly concerned about ensuring formal copyrights for his Gettysburg images, even though each print always carried a copyright line. Not until December 31, 1863, did Gardner appear at the court clerk's office in Washington to file copyrights— in his name—on twenty-one Gettysburg stereo views: ten that were his, seven of O'Sullivan's, and four that were Gibson views. Those were the last photographs he formally copyrighted in that office during the Civil War.[26]

It is important to note that Brady and Gardner were not the only photographers at Gettysburg in 1863. In fact, Brady arrived not only after Gardner's team but after Philadelphia photographer Frederick Gutekunst took seven plates around July 9 to 12, 1863, including the first image of Burns. Local Gettysburg photographers Isaac and Charles Tyson took a series of plates in August, while several photographers, apparently including Gardner, took images of the November 19 dedication of the Soldier's National Cemetery, where Lincoln delivered his Gettysburg address. In the following years and decades, Gettysburg would become the most photographed of all American battlefields.[27]

Most of the soldiers who fought at Gettysburg probably never had the opportunity to see any of the photographs by Gardner, Brady, or the other photographers until long after the battle, or long after the war, if ever. This did not lessen the significance of photography in the life of the everyday soldier. Many of the soldiers who marched to Gettysburg carried with them a pho-

This sixth-plate ambrotype, taken by an unknown photographer, is the only known image of Amos Humiston, who died at Gettysburg during the first day of the battle. His body was found within the town of Gettysburg with one hand clutching an ambrotype image of his three children. (Courtesy of David Humiston Kelley)

tograph or two, maybe even three. A soldier would discard many items, perhaps even letters, before a campaign, but not his images. "He tucks his little collection of photographs, which perhaps he has encased in rubber or leather, into an inside pocket, and disposes other small keepsakes about his person," wrote John D. Billings in *Hardtack and Coffee*. The countless family likenesses and personal portraits that were mere commerce for photographers meant far more to those whose loved ones were pictured.[28]

As with any other product, the customers were apt to complain, most often about high prices and poor quality. The task of sitting for a photograph was itself nerve-racking. The *American Journal of Photography* observed in 1863:

This *carte de visite* of "The Children of the Battlefield" by Philadelphia photographers Wenderoth, Taylor & Brown was one of fourteen known card versions of the original ambrotype of the Humiston children. (From the collection of Mark H. Dunkelman)

You have a vague expression that to look smiling is ridiculous, and to look solemn is still more so. . . . You desire to look intelligent, but you are hampered by a fear of looking sly. You wish to look as if you were not sitting for your picture; but the effort to do so fills your mind more completely with the melancholy consciousness that you are. [The iron head brace] gives you exactly the appearance as if somebody was holding onto your hair behind.[29]

Self-conscious or not, everyone got through it, leaving the soldiers to worry about their pictures making it home safely, and those at home to worry about whether their likenesses reached their men in the field. "Not infrequently a number of bags go out from the Washington office entirely filled with sun pictures, enclosed in light but bulky cases. Most of these pictures are taken on the Melainotype [tintype] Plate for

the reason that it is light, durable and easily sent in a letter."[30]

Sgt. Amos Humiston of the 154th New York Regiment felt no differently than any other soldier when a small package arrived from home with an ambrotype portrait of his three children. Eight-year-old Frank was sitting on the left, while Alice, six, was on the right. Four-year-old Fred was sitting between them in a high chair. Writing home on May 9, 1863 (in fractured English, corrected here), Humiston exclaimed:

I got the likeness of the children and it pleased me more than anything that you could have sent me. How I want to see them and their mother is more than I can tell. I hope that we may all live to see each other again, if this war does not last too long.[31]

Born to an upstate New York farmer in 1830, Humiston abandoned a career as a harness maker at age twenty, after a five-year apprenticeship, to cast his fate to the seas. He sailed the Pacific on a whaling ship for three voyages, ultimately returning to his native Owego more than three years later to resume harness making. By 1861, Humiston was a thirty-one-year-old father of three and the proprietor of a harness shop in Portville, New York. He had married his wife, Philinda, on the Fourth of July in 1854.[32]

When the war came, Humiston held off from enlisting until July 26, 1862. In November, now in the field, he fell ill for several weeks. In December, once again in good health, he wrote to Philinda: "I can tell you how I would like to be with you Christmas and New Years and enjoy one of your dinners again and have the babies on my knee to hear them prattle as they used to." In January 1863, he was promoted to sergeant; by late February he was sick again, suffering from chronic diarrhea for several weeks. In May, the 154th was mauled at Chancellorsville. Humiston was struck by a spent ball and momentarily stunned, but reported, "I am in the land of the living after the battle." In nearly every letter home, Humiston expressed his longing for his family. In March, he even composed a poem to Philinda.

> You have put the little ones to bed, dear wife
> And covered them o're with care
> My Frankey, Alley and Fred
> And they have said their evening prayer.
>
> Perhaps they breathed the name of one
> Who is far in southern land
> And wished he, too, were there
> To join their little band
>
> I am very sad tonight, dear wife
> My thoughts are dwelling on home and thee
> As I keep the lone night watch
> Beneath the holly tree.
>
> O when will this rebellion cease,
> This cursed war be o'er.
> And we our dear ones meet
> To part from them no more?

On May 24, he expressed concern that "the little ones will forget that they have got a pa." He told his wife, "Be a good girl and keep your courage up." It was the last letter Philinda Humiston ever received from her husband.[33]

Previously unpublished in a book, this 1867 stereo view by Gettysburg photographer Charles J. Tyson provides photographic documentation of the area on Stratton Street where Humiston's body was found. The original caption reads: "The Rail fence marks the spot where Serg't. Hummiston [sic] fell." (From the collection of John J. Richter)

Although Humiston is shown lying in a field rather than in town, his tragedy was depicted in "An Incident of Gettysburg—The Last Thought of a Dying Father," a woodcut engraving published in *Frank Leslie's Illustrated Newspaper* on January 2, 1864. The limber and dead horses in the background are vaguely reminiscent of a Gardner stereo view. (From the collection of Mark H. Dunkelman)

The 154th went into battle on the first day at Gettysburg. They fought within the town itself, on the northeastern outskirts in front of a brick-making plant. They deployed in a line, with the 27th Pennsylvania on their left and the 134th New York on the right. Almost immediately, eight Confederate regiments attacked. Outnumbered by more than three to one, the Union defenders on either side of the 154th melted away.[34]

"Boys, let's stay right here!" shouted Lt. Jack Mitchell of the 154th. A round or two later, even Mitchell knew it was hopeless. "Boys, we must get out of here!" he shouted, and the company fled back toward the city, every man for himself. The fighting deteriorated into isolated hand-to-

hand contests. Many in the regiment surrendered on Stratton Street, next to the brickyard. The fastest runners in the regiment escaped. Whether he fought or he ran, Humiston didn't make it. A bullet? A bayonet thrust? We do not know—only that he was mortally wounded and came to his final resting place along a rail fence on Stratton Street. When he died, he was clutching in his hand the ambrotype of Frankey, Alley, and Fred.[35]

And that is how his corpse was found. He had no equipment, no corps badge, no sergeant's chevrons, and no identification—nothing except the ambrotype of the three children. The body apparently was found by the daughter or son-

EMANCIPATED SLAVES.

Brought from Louisiana by Col. Geo. H. Hanks. The Children are from the Schools established by order of Maj. Gen. Banks.

| WILSON CHINN. | | MARY JOHNSON. | | ROBERT WHITEHEAD. | |
| CHAS. TAYLOR. | AUGUSTA BROUJEY. | | ISAAC WHITE. | REBECCA HUGER. | ROSINA DOWNS. |

Entered according to Act of Congress, in the year 1863, by PHILIP BACON, in the Clerk's Office of the United States for the Southern District of New York.

Photographed by **M. H. Kimball, 477 Broadway, N.Y.**

"OH! HOW I LOVE THE OLD FLAG."

REBECCA,

A Slave Girl from New Orleans.

A popular fund-raising initiative during the Civil War featured the sale of large photographs and *cartes de visite* of emancipated slaves, particularly children, from New Orleans. To make a point, many of the mulatto children depicted in the images are extremely light-skinned. On the reverse of the "Rebecca" *carte*, which was photographed by Charles Paxson of New York, an imprint says: "The net proceeds from the sale of these Photographs will be devoted to the education of colored people in the department of the Gulf, now under the command of Maj. Gen. Banks." (*Top*: Courtesy of the Western Reserve Historical Society; *left*: from the collection of Michael J. McAfee)

in-law of a former borough tavern keeper, Benjamin Schriver, who had moved to Graeffenburg thirteen miles west of Gettysburg. Sometime in July 1863, the ambrotype of the anonymous children came into Schriver's hands, and he showed it to four men who stopped in his Graeffenburg tavern after their carriage broke down. They were headed to Gettysburg as volunteers to help the wounded. One of the men, forty-nine-year-old Dr. John Francis Bourns, a Philadelphia physician, convinced Shriver to give him the ambrotype so he could try to find out who the children were. Bourns told Schriver that after his work was finished in Gettysburg, he would return to Philadelphia, copy the image, and use the media to spread the story.[36]

Bourns had *carte de visite* copies made from the ambrotype, and he took the story to the Philadelphia newspapers. It broke on October 19, 1863. "Whose Father Was He?" headlined the *Philadelphia Inquirer.* In the following weeks, the story was reprinted in other papers, and around the second week of November, Philinda Humiston saw it. Through intermediaries, she sent a query to Bourns, who rushed her a copy of the *carte de visite* with the picture she already knew so well. The poignant episode was widely covered both before and after the children and their father were identified. *Frank Leslie's Illustrated Newspaper* ran an article and woodcut engraving on January 2, 1864. The *carte de visite* of the Humiston children sold well, with the proceeds going to the fatherless family. Poems and sheet music further popularized the incident.[37]

The story might have slowly faded from public consciousness, but Bourns had other ideas. An ambitious, complex man, Bourns was not without pretense. He had added the "o" to his actual surname, which was Burns. The Humiston saga soon evolved into a quest by Sunday Schools across the North to establish a home in Gettysburg for orphans of fallen soldiers. With Bourns organizing and leading the effort, it was funded in no small measure by the continued sale of the "Children of the Battlefield" *cartes de visite.*[38]

On November 20, 1866, the Homestead orphanage was formally inaugurated in a two-story brick house along Baltimore Pike on the northern slope of Cemetery Hill. Twenty-eight soldiers' orphans came to live there, along with Philinda Humiston and her three children. Gen. U. S. Grant was among the many dignitaries who visited. In time, however, the day-to-day life at the Homestead left much to be desired. In October 1869, Philinda Humiston married Asa Barnes, almost a stranger to her, and moved out of the orphanage. According to Humiston family lore, she was so dissatisfied with life at the Homestead that she married Barnes just for the sake of leaving. He was twenty-four years older than Philinda and had sent a letter proposing marriage after visiting the orphanage and meeting her once. There is little doubt that all four Humistons were glad to leave. Afterward, conditions at the Homestead only became worse.[39]

Around 1871, a new administrator, Rosa J. Carmichael, arrived highly recommended by Dr. Bourns. The first years under Carmichael were quiet, but rumors of mistreatment began to spread. The Gettysburg chapter of the Grand Army of the Republic (GAR), the Union veterans organization, undertook an investigation on June 11, 1876, twelve days after Carmichael refused to allow the orphans to participate in the annual Memorial Day procession. She was arrested on the charge of cruelty to an orphan. That fall, she was convicted of aggravated assault, fined $20 plus court costs, and released. She returned to the orphanage, but conditions continued to deteriorate until June 1877, when a GAR leader blew the lid off the scandal in an exposé published in a Philadelphia newspaper, reprinted a week later in a Gettysburg paper.[40]

The thirty orphans had not been schooled in two years because Carmichael had driven away the last teacher. She had a nineteen-year-old male "taskmaster," who beat the younger children. Girls had been seen on the Homestead grounds wearing boys clothing. On a bitterly cold Christmas Eve in 1876, she had penned a four- or five-year-old boy in the outhouse, where he remained until midnight when his screams finally led neighbors to intercede.[41]

The stories told over the back fences and in the barrooms of Gettysburg were even more hair-raising. Carmichael was said to have suspended children by their arms in barrels and hidden bruised victims from visitors. "Most scandalous of all were tales of a dungeon in the Homestead cellar, a black hole eight feet long, five feet deep and only four feet high, unlit and unventilated, where she shackled children to the wall," historian Mark Dunkelman writes. By the end of 1877, the Homestead was closed, and its remaining residents were moved to other homes. Carmichael disappeared from public view. The household goods were sold at a public auction, and the local GAR post bought a pair of iron shackles said to have been used by the cruel administrator. A photographer made an image of the shackles, providing a photographic coda to a story that started because of another photograph.[42]

8

THE DAWN OF COMBAT PHOTOGRAPHY

When George S. Cook crept onto the parapet of Fort Sumter on September 8, 1863, and aimed his camera at Union ironclads, their guns blazing less than 1,000 yards away, he was achieving a milestone that his fellow photographers, North and South, could keenly appreciate. Cook was the first photographer to capture a verifiable image of battle while under fire himself. Russell, and perhaps Fenton before him, had managed to take a photograph of distant battle smoke, but neither was in the midst of the conflict while taking pictures.

Cook himself apparently never advertised or made much of his accomplishment, though it was one of the best-covered photographic achievements of the war, with newspapers in the North and South publishing articles about it. But fantasy became mixed with reality as the story evolved over time. There can be no doubt that he took two photographs of the gunboats of the Union fleet in action again Fort Moultrie, with cannon smoke spewing from the USS *New Ironsides.* New evidence has surfaced, however, proving that Cook's so-called "exploding shell" photograph, supposedly taken the same day, is a painting. Replacing it as a matter of interest, a new scene of battle has surfaced that may be the most spectacular Civil War battle photograph of all. Former daguerreian artist Philip Haas and his partner, Washington Peale, took the photograph on the beach at Morris Island in the summer of 1863. Labeled "Unidentified camp scene," the photograph was finally recognized in the year 2000 for what it was—a panorama of the battle in Charleston Harbor, with a towering plume of gunsmoke coming off the *New Ironsides.*

Haas had lied about his age so he could go to war. He was fifty-three, with his business in apparent decline, when he enlisted with the 1st New York Engineers in September 1861, claiming he was only forty-three. Perhaps the recruiter had accepted him with a wink, for Haas had been around so long he had daguerreotyped John Quincy Adams.

By the spring of 1862, the 1st New York Engineers were in South Carolina, and Haas was detailed to shoot photographs. Peale, the son of Philadelphia artist James Peale Jr., then came on as a partner. During the thunderous summer of 1863, Haas and Peale roamed Morris Island with their camera, visiting camps and forward batteries as the battle raged for control of Charleston Harbor.[1]

This detail from half of a stereoscopic negative shows Sam Cooley, his assistants, and his equipment somewhere in the field, probably in South Carolina. Cooley, who stands at right, called himself a "U.S. Photographer," but he worked for the government only by contract. (Library of Congress)

The sea islands and coastal areas of South Carolina that Union forces controlled during the war made up less than 5 percent of the geographic area of the state, yet this small area was teeming with photographers. In addition to Haas and Peale, photohistorian Harvey S. Teal has documented the names of seventeen other Union photographers who worked in this confined area during the war. Hundreds of their images have survived, either as negatives or prints or both. In addition to scenes in the field, the photographers took countless thousands of photographs of soldiers and sailors. Teal writes: "It is very doubtful that any other area of the South or, for that matter, the North received similar photographic documentation."[2]

Attached to the 10th Army Corps was photographer Samuel A. Cooley, who also promoted himself as the official photographer of the army's Department of the South. By the end of the war, Cooley had galleries in Beaufort, Folly Island, and Hilton Head, South Carolina, and in Jacksonville, Florida. He was also a semi-official military photographer for Quartermaster General Montgomery C. Meigs. Cooley's stereo output included at least 135 views of scenes in those places, as well as Morris Island, Port Royal Island, Savannah, Georgia, and Fort McAllister.

Although his primary purpose was to take a photograph of Company G, 48th New York, inside Fort Pulaski, Georgia, in 1862 or 1863, New Hampshire photographer Henry P. Moore also captured one of the first pictures of a baseball game in action in the background. The batter is at far left, with his right knee bent in as if ready to take a pitch. (Courtesy of the Western Reserve Historical Society)

Another Yankee photographer in South Carolina was Henry P. Moore of Concord, New Hampshire. Moore made trips to South Carolina in 1862 and 1863, taking dozens of camp and plantation images, as well as one of the first photographs of a baseball game.[3]

Boosted by the tremendous demand for images by soldiers, the Northern photography business was booming in 1863. "The profession was never before so prosperous as it has been during the past year," the *American Journal of Photography* reported on January 1, 1863. The periodical painted a bleaker picture in the South:

There has been little photography in Jeffdom for the past two years. It is only in Charleston and perhaps Richmond that any photographs at all are made. By favor of our British cousins who run the blockade with powder and guns, our friend Cook of Charleston still has a precarious stock of photographic materials and still makes a business in the shadows of the people.[4]

Cook, in fact, had an enviable wartime business that defied the Federal blockade of Southern ports and kept getting better as the conflict continued. For the twelve months of 1863, the war's middle year, Cook's gallery had 4,042 customers, an increase of almost 58 percent over the 2,559 customers of 1862, which was a whopping 96 percent increase compared to the 1,307 customers of 1861. The increases in Cook's business, which continued even as Union shells began to fall on Charleston, can probably be attributed to the steady decline, as the war continued, in the number of other photographers in the city. By 1863, Cook may have been the only Charleston photographer still open for business.[5]

Cook was a major supplier of photographic goods to other Southern photographers, and his account books reveal that he continued this business throughout 1863, though at a greatly reduced pace from 1861. His records nonetheless painted a brighter picture of photography in the South than the *American Journal of Photography* reported. Cook sold $4,180.50 of stock supplies to eight other Southern photographers in 1863, including operators in Jacksonville, Florida, Charlotte and Wilmington, North Carolina, and Columbia and Spartanburg, South Carolina. Photography in the Confederacy may have been considerably diminished in 1863, but it was by no means dead.[6]

Cook was forty-four years old in the summer of 1863 and was a shrewd operator in all manner of ways. He may have avoided military service using the popular Civil War method of paying someone else to do it. On February 25, 1862, Cook recorded in his expense records the payment of $25 to "Thos. Hagen, Substitute for the war." As if to cement the deal, Cook's next expense, dated March 1, was a $200 "donation to the Confederacy."

A month later, Cook began pouring his burgeoning wartime profits into a new venture: blockade runners. His 1862 account books list eleven transactions, either purchases or dividends, in connection with the stock of Charleston shippers and traders who were smuggling goods in and out of the city past the blockading Union Navy. Most of his early investments were with shipping agent J. A. Enslow and his "Enslow's Schooners," including several stock purchases or dividends ranging from $500 to $1,650

Alfred Moore Rhett is pictured in this wartime *carte de visite* by George S. Cook. Rhett was commander of Fort Sumter from April to September 1863 but is better known for slaying Col. W. Ransom Calhoun, a nephew of John C. Calhoun, on September 15, 1862, in the most infamous duel in Charleston during the Civil War. Calhoun had demanded the duel after being publicly ridiculed by Rhett. (Courtesy of South Caroliniana Library, University of South Carolina, Columbia)

that were specifically linked to a vessel named "Catawba, alias Nelly." Cook probably also relied on blockade runners to bring in chemicals and other photographic supplies from Europe, but his wartime account books do not prove this. The books document many purchases of bulk chemicals and supplies during the war but give no indication where they come from.

By the summer of 1863, Cook had been a photographer for some twenty years. He had operated a gallery in Charleston since 1849. As another hot Charleston July stretched into August,

BURSTING OF A SHELL IN THE STREETS OF CHARLESTON, SOUTH CAROLINA.

British author and illustrator Frank Vizetelly was reading about the battle of Waterloo in his Charleston Hotel room when the first shell of the Union bombardment of Charleston fell into the city about 1:30 a.m. on August 22, 1863. This is Vizetelly's dramatically enhanced illustration of the explosion of the first shell as it appeared in *Harper's Weekly* on January 9, 1864. "My first feeling was that of utter astonishment; but a crash, succeeded by a deafening explosion in the very street on which my apartment was situate, brought me with a bound into the centre of the room," he wrote.

Cook was averaging about ten customers a day. They would troop up the stairs at 235 King Street to be received on the second floor. Having dispensed with cordialities and business matters, Cook or an assistant would escort patrons up to the studio on the third floor. Its massive, west-facing skylight illuminated the subject with sunlight as he or she stood next to a softly painted backdrop featuring a pot of flowers. In his account book, Cook would document each transaction, usually identifying the patron by name. Sometimes he would jot down a mailing address and shipping instructions.

Every third or fourth customer was a military officer. Two-thirds of Cook's clients were men. The typical customer bought three to six *cartes de visite*. A half-dozen would generally cost $10 (or more if hand-tinted). Every so often, Cook would be asked to leave the studio and carry his camera to someone's home or a funeral parlor to photograph the body of a deceased loved one. The practice, unheard of today, was common in the nineteenth century. On August 17, 1863, for example, Cook's gallery charged $50—Cook's flat fee for a postmortem photograph—for the image of Mr. P. O. Connor's deceased child.[7]

That same day, Union batteries on Morris Island and navy ships began hammering Fort Sumter with shellfire. Rear Admiral John A. Dahlgren, commander of the Union Navy's South Atlantic Blockading Squadron, was bound and determined to win back Fort Sumter—where the Confederates had started it all. During the next seventeen days, Federal forces fired 6,878 shots into Fort Sumter, killing two men, wounding fifty, battering its masonry walls, silencing its few

Most of the photographers of Charleston, South Carolina, were clustered here along King Street, which was well within the range of Union guns during the bombardment of Charleston. This print from a stereo view shows King Street in 1865 or 1866. George S. Cook's studio is on the second and third floors of the fourth building on the left. Just before Cook's building, as the detail shows, was the photo gallery of Charles J. Quinby, who hung his "Quinby & Co. Artists" sign out over the walk. (From the collection of Jack Thomson)

remaining guns, and reducing it to rubble, shell by shell.[8]

After the Rebels declined an invitation to surrender on August 21, a 16,500-pound Parrott gun, known as the Swamp Angel, began hurling 200-pound, incendiary shells into Charleston from its swamp-bound perch on Morris Island, a record-setting distance of some five miles. The bombardment of the city radically changed the contest, sending waves of fear through the city's residents and rendering mere spectators into unwitting participants. It was one thing for the civilian population to watch a battle in the harbor, but quite another to come within the ring of fire. For the first time since the beginning of the war, George S. Cook took note of an event in the margin of his otherwise business-only account book, next to the date of August 22:

Shelled the city from 2 to 4 a.m. 14 shells.[9]

The first shell shrieked into the city and exploded in the street near the Charleston Hotel, where British illustrator and journalist Frank Vizetelly, unable to sleep in his hotel room, was reading an account of the battle of Waterloo in *Les Miserables*. Pandemonium reigned in the hotel hallway.

> At first I thought a meteor had fallen; but another awful rush and whirr right over the hotel, and another explosion beyond, settled any doubts I might have had: the city was being shelled. Whirr! Came another shell over the roof, and down on their faces went every man of them into tobacco-juice and cigar ends and clattering among the spittoons.

The following night, the Swamp Angel hurled another thirty-five shells into Charleston, then exploded while firing the thirty-sixth shot and pitched itself up onto the sandbagged parapet of its own emplacement. For the time being, the shelling of Charleston stopped.[10]

On September 6, the Confederates abandoned the strategically important Battery Wagner on Morris Island. It had withstood repeated attacks by land and sea, including the July 18 assault of the 54th Massachusetts Colored Infantry, which was made famous by the 1989 movie *Glory*. With Morris Island and Battery Wagner conquered, Union forces redoubled their efforts to take Fort Sumter.

"I sent a flag demanding surrender of Sumter. Answer: 'Come and take it,'" Dahlgren wrote in his diary on September 7. As a preliminary action, Dahlgren directed the monitor USS *Weehawken* to cut off communications between Sumter and points south. As the *Weehawken* tried to negotiate the narrow channel between Fort Sumter and Cumming's Point immediately to the south, it ran aground in eleven feet of water.[11]

The monitor remained stuck through the afternoon and night, though the Confederates failed to notice until the next morning. Cook was rowed across to Fort Sumter under the cover of night on September 7. The sight that greeted Cook in the daylight of September 8 must have stayed with him for the rest of his life. The massive, red brick fort that he saw during his 1861 visit, its three levels graced with dozens of beautifully arched casemates, was a wreck. The third floor of the barracks was missing entirely, and the parade ground was a sea of debris. The interior of the north face had borne the brunt of the artillery fire from Morris Island. The upper wall was somehow still intact, but the shells had opened an ever-widening hole.[12]

The amount of destruction had prompted Cook's return in the first place, after he received a request from Confederate general headquarters. Could he photograph the damage in Fort Sumter wrought by more than 6,000 shells? In the words of the *Charleston Daily Courier*, "Gen [Thomas] Jordan sought to obtain the services of a photographic artist . . . to preserve a faithful delineation of the ruins of Fort Sumter, and to show to future generations what Southern troops can endure in battle." J. M. Osborn, whose own gallery, Osborn & Durbec, had long since gone out of business, was Cook's assistant on the trip.[13]

A high-resolution, digital scan of the original twin negatives of George S. Cook's historic first combat-action photographs taken from the bomb-damaged parapet of Fort Sumter provides the clearest view of the scene ever published. These scenes of the Union ironclads in action in Charleston Harbor were taken on September 8, 1863. The white masking applied to the top of both negatives does not affect the view of the ships, and it is plainly obvious in both images, which were taken moments apart, that the lead gunboat, the USS *New Ironsides*, is firing at Fort Moultrie. The detail, taken from the right negative, reveals what appears to be a flag hanging from a pole on the trailing monitor-class gunboat, as well as groups of harbor obstructions between the ships and Fort Sumter. (Courtesy of the Valentine Richmond History Center)

At 7:00 a.m. on September 8, the day of Cook's visit, the commander of Fort Sumter, Major Stephen Elliott Jr., belatedly realized that the *Weehawken* was stuck. "The monitor near Cumming's Point is evidently aground. Fire should be opened on her, as the thin part of her hull is probably exposed," Elliott telegraphed Fort Moultrie. As soon as Fort Moultrie began firing, Dahlgren sent in the entire fleet to defend the stranded gunboat. "The diversion made by the rear admiral to cover his endangered monitor . . . led to what was probably the severest naval engagement in American history up to that time," wrote John Johnson in the *Defense of Charleston Harbor*. The massive, ugly USS *New Ironsides* was joined by the monitors *Patapsco*, *Lehigh*, *Nahant*, *Montauk*, and *Passaic*, "and for nearly three hours [they] delivered by far the heaviest cannonade heard from the naval force off Charleston Harbor."[14]

The *Weehawken*, though aground, was hardly defenseless. At 9:07 a.m., the second shot from the *Weehawken's* fifteen-inch gun glanced off the muzzle of an eight-inch Columbiad in Fort Moultrie and ricocheted into some shell boxes. They blew up in quick succession, and a hail of shrapnel tore through the men of Company E, 1st South Carolina Infantry. When the explosions stopped, sixteen Confederates were dead, twelve more were wounded, and Union sailors were cheering from their vessels. Company commander Capt. R. Press Smith escaped harm by diving into a ditch. The fort's guns fell silent for a time as Moultrie's commander, Col. William Butler, scrambled to replace the shattered company with another company, whose members had to sprint over from nearby Battery Beauregard while under fire. For the Confederate defenders of Charleston Harbor, it was one of the most tragic moments of the entire war.[15]

The engagement continued for more than four hours. The grounded *Weehawken*, after scoring its devastating hit on Fort Moultrie, turned its gun on Sumter and fired forty-six shells into the island fort. From the parapet, avoiding incoming shells from the *Weehawken* that were "knocking about some bricks and dust," Elliott watched a noisy spectacle unfold before his eyes as if in slow motion. "The engagement this morning was one of the most beautiful sites [*sic*] you can imagine," he wrote that day in a letter to a friend. "All the ironclads were within a mile of us and not firing on us at the time, which improved the view considerably." Elliott's dramatic telegrams to Fort Moultrie provided a blow-by-blow account.

9:45 a.m. The monitor [*Weehawken*] has been hit three times on water line.

10:35 a.m. The monitors have been hit repeatedly. Those next Moultrie have drawn her fire from the one aground, which is to be regretted. The Ironsides is 1,460 yards from this fort.

11:15 a.m. Ironsides was heavily hit just now, throwing great deal sand off her deck. Enemy very busy at their old works on Morris Island. One Parrott gun from there opened on fort just now.

Noon. Fragments of Ironsides torn away by shot from Sullivan's Island just now.[16]

During the battle, Cook made his way up to the northeast corner of the parapet, where he perched a camera on a piece of broken gun carriage and aimed it toward three enemy gunboats in line, perhaps a thousand yards away and making a slow pass by Fort Moultrie. The *New Ironsides* was in the lead, her guns blazing. Two monitors followed, one after another and low in the water, the guns of their cylindrical turrets locked on the enemy fort. Cook exposed one plate, handed it to Osborn for developing, took a fresh plate from him, and secured it on the back of his camera. Before he exposed the second plate, Cook moved the camera to his right about one inch. This gave him the necessary separation for a stereoscopic view. When Cook exposed the second plate, the gunboats were slightly farther east in the harbor. Other than that, the second image looked identical to the first. While Fort Sumter was under fire that day, Cook managed to take the first two photographs in recorded history that clearly show the enemy in battle, thus becoming history's first combat photographer.

A Charleston correspondent of the *Mobile Daily Advertiser* wrote on September 11:

Shot and shell were flying in profusion, but, nevertheless, arranging their chemicals in one of the dark crevices of the fort, and making use of a broken gun carriage in place of the customary tripod, the work was begun. Subsequently, an admirable battle scene was taken, representing the Ironsides and two monitors, wreathed in their own smoke, while delivering their fire on Fort Moultrie. I learn that it intended, after a time, to make these pictures public, and to reduce them to stereoscopic dimensions.[17]

The *Charleston Daily Courier* ran its own article about the photos on September 12, under the headline "The Ironsides and two Monitors Taken—A Bold Feat," calling it "one of the most remarkable acts . . . ever recorded in the history of war." The *Courier*'s article also explicitly mentioned the combat action photographs: "The artists turned their attention to the fleet, and had the good fortune to secure, amid the smoke of battle in which they were wreathed, a faithful likeness of the Ironsides and two Monitors." While Cook made pictures, Union ships were "throwing their eleven- and fifteen-inch shells against and into Sumter, rendering personal exposure hazardous in the extreme. The feat itself is unparalleled, as far as we know, and no little praise is due to the gentlemen who had the hardihood to risk their lives for the purpose of securing an heirloom so precious." The *Courier* reported that Cook wanted even more. "Mr. Cook requested permission to go outside of the Fort and take a picture of the exterior from the water, but it was thought that this would draw additional fire from the fleet and the project was abandoned."[18]

The only hint that Cook's activities on the parapet might have been noticed by the Union fleet came in this cryptic entry from Dahlgren's own report of the engagement of September 8: "Some movement in Sumter seemed to draw attention from the *Weehawken*, which, with a few well-directed shells, settled that business." The Union fleet suffered no serious damage during the battle, but it was bruised and battered. The *New Ironsides*, while firing 483 shots, was hit at least seventy times. "Seventy hits can be counted, but the woodwork on the spar deck is so much cut up that we were probably struck near a hundred times," reported the ship's carpenter. "The spar deck represents a complete mass of ruin." All of the monitors took hits and had some damage; most also had a wounded sailor or two. The *Patapsco* shot a hole through its own smokestack, choked its engines, and had to be towed off. The *Weehawken*, though still under fire, managed to free itself and steamed off to safety that evening with an exultant crew. The *Weehawken* had fired eighty-two shells, including the devastating second shot into Fort Moultrie,

and had been hit twenty-four times, suffering no serious damage. One sailor had suffered a broken leg and two others were slightly wounded. (Three months later, the *Weehawken* foundered and sunk at anchorage in Charleston Harbor, taking a third of its men with it.)[19]

The naval battle of September 8 has been overshadowed in history by what came next. At 1:00 a.m. on September 9, several hundred Union Marines, in two columns of small boats, made for Fort Sumter in a nighttime assault. Elliott was well prepared to greet them. The defenders raked the attacking force with musketry. Rebel batteries bombarded them with shot and shell. The fighting was over in twenty minutes. The Union loss was six killed, nineteen wounded, twenty-five missing, and 102 captured. In Sumter, not a defender was hurt.[20]

Cook did not mention his Fort Sumter visit in his account book, but the five entries for September 8 document that he was not working in the gallery that day, because all were written in an assistant's hand. Cook was back in his studio on the ninth, which was fortunate. It was one of the busiest days of the month, with eighteen customers, and it was made even more hectic by the necessity of making prints from the negatives of Fort Sumter. Cook took three large-plate views within the fort, at least seven stereo views, and the two images of the ironclads in action. By September 12, he had prepared thirty-six copies of the larger views and seventy-two stereoscopic views for the Confederate general headquarters. During the next five months, he would distribute or sell at least forty-five sets of views in more than twenty separate transactions.[21]

A dozen negatives from Cook's September 8 visit to Fort Sumter survive today in the Cook Collection at the Valentine Richmond History Center in Richmond, Virginia, including eight stereoscopic negatives and both images of the ironclads in action. The two battle negatives were, indeed, reduced to stereoscopic dimensions. The two separate plates were, and still are, secured

The mystery of the so-called "exploding shell photograph" began and ended on a parlor table in Charleston, South Carolina. Published here for the first time is the full frame of the negative that was used to produce the various extant prints of the "exploding shell" image, revealing that the "photograph" supposedly taken by George S. Cook actually was a painting by Lt. John R. Key. The original negative was masked to obliterate everything in the image except the painting. It had been thought that Key based his painting on a Cook photograph of an exploding shell. Key, in fact, probably based his painting on three half-stereo prints by Cook that together (*below*) form the same panorama that Key painted. (Courtesy of the Valentine Richmond History Center)

side by side on a separate plate of glass for printing stereoscopic views. The other Sumter images are interior views of the damage. Most combine with two or three other images to form wide-angle panoramas.[22]

Not long after the engagement of September 8, Lt. John R. Key, a young Confederate officer and artist, apparently used a three-image, Cook photographic panorama of the interior of Fort Sumter to paint a scene of the battle, complete with a shell exploding in the parade ground. In time, this painting came to be known as a photograph and is presented as such in a number of works, including both major compilations of war photographs, the *Photographic History of the Civil War* and the *Image of War*, as well as in my own previous work, *The Civil War in Depth*. I had always assumed the photograph was heavily retouched and that the Key painting was drawn from the photograph, not vice versa. I never thought to ask how Cook's camera managed to capture the impossibly wide swath of the fort depicted in the so-called "exploding shell" photograph.

In the full plate of this Haas and Peale battle action masterpiece from 1863 (*facing page, lower left*), a plume of cannon smoke floats away from the USS *New Ironsides* and spreads over Charleston Harbor. The greatest dramatic impact, however, is contained in the panorama taken from the center of the image. In the detail, dozens of soldiers are riveted by the battle. The panorama also reveals the presence of five Monitor-class ironclads in action—the *Passaic*, *Montauk*, *Nahant*, *Patapsco*, and *Lehigh*. The discovery of this picture within a picture was made by Charleston historian Jack Thomson. (Library of Congress; detail by John J. Richter)

The issue was resolved beyond doubt when I inspected the original negative in the Cook Collection at the Valentine. This negative is the source for all known "exploding shell" prints. The negative has been carefully masked to show only Key's painting and not the parlor table it is sitting on, nor the three chairs behind it. The painting was placed on the parlor table so Cook could make the copy negative. The so-called exploding shell photograph is, and always has been, the Key painting. There is no record, however, of Cook ever passing off this image as a photograph, nor is there any evidence that Cook advertised any of his Fort Sumter images.

The irony of the exploding shell painting is that, while it was being passed off to generations of Americans as a true battle action photograph, another battle action photograph from Charleston Harbor—this one unmistakably real—was waiting to be rediscovered. This Haas and Peale photograph of the *New Ironsides* in action may stand as their single greatest photographic contribution to the visual history of the war. Somehow, it was not recognized for what it was for more than 140 years. It was not published in a book until 2000, even though it has been readily accessible at the Library of Congress since 1966. It was one of twenty-five original, four-by-

This Haas and Peale scene from Morris Island is known as "unidentified camp," as is the scene of the *New Ironsides* in action. The photograph is thought to show the photographers themselves, Washington Peale and Philip Haas, standing near the spot where they took their battle photograph. (Library of Congress)

seven-inch, Haas and Peale glass plate negatives acquired by the library—all showing scenes on Morris or Folly Island in the summer of 1863.[23]

Eight of the twenty-five negatives, including the battle photo, are labeled "Unidentified camp" scenes. This nondescript title may have helped obscure the true subject of the battle photograph. More than fifty people are visible standing on the beach, but not one is facing the camera. All peer up the beach toward Charleston Harbor, riveted by the spectacle before them. Smoke erupts from the port side of the *New Ironsides*, hugs the surface of the water, and then arcs hundreds of feet into the sky.[24]

When Charleston historian Jack Thomson first saw this image some years ago, he immediately noticed the smoke and was drawn deeper into the scene. What were those strange structures on the water line that looked like distant buildings? When Thomson had the image en-

larged, he found the five monitors, their smokestacks and distinctive cylindrical turrets clearly outlined at water level. The image is undated, but after studying tides and shadows, Thomson came to believe it was taken at maximum low tide, at about 10:00 a.m. on September 8, 1863. The date cannot be proven conclusively, but it is possible, even likely, that the fight over the stranded *Weehawken* not only yielded Cook's combat action photographs but became the first battle in history to be captured by two cameras in two different places, representing both sides of the conflict.[25]

The Haas and Peale image slipped into obscurity and was soon forgotten, though perhaps not by the photographers themselves. Another Haas and Peale negative in the Library of Congress was exposed at the same vantage point as the action photo. The background is quiet in this view, but in the foreground are two men who

On Morris Island, the old Confederate battery Gregg was renamed Fort Putnam when occupied by Union forces, and a Parrott gun was aimed high to allow the shells to make the five-mile trip into the city of Charleston. The bombardment devastated the city but did not level it. The brick building (*right*) at the corner of East Bay and Elliott streets was shot through by shells but still standing at the end of the war, as this reproduction of half of a stereo view by photographer William E. James shows. (*Left*: Library of Congress; *right*: from the collection of Jack Thomson)

are probably Haas and Peale themselves. Perhaps they well knew the historic value of the action photograph they had made and posed at the site as a way to commemorate the feat.[26]

Years later, wartime photographer Timothy O'Sullivan, who took so many unforgettable images of his own, recalled the photographic work in Charleston Harbor. O'Sullivan seemed to morph both the Cook and Haas and Peale photographic achievements into a single, muddled legend:

> In 1863, while photographing Fort Sumter and the Confederate batteries in the vicinity of Charleston, a courageous operator saw his camera twice knocked over by fragments of shell, his camera-cloth torn and the loose, white sand of Morris Island scattered over plates and chemicals. The veteran artillerists who manned the battery from which the views were made wisely sought refuge in the bomb-proofs to secure themselves from the heavy shell fire which was opened upon their fortification; but the photographer stuck to his work, and the pictures made on that memorable occasion are among the most interesting of the war.[27]

After the failed assault of September 9, Union guns fell silent for a time, and Charleston settled back into its wartime routine. Customers continued to stream into his gallery, but time was running out on George S. Cook, just as surely as it was running out on the Confederacy. September gave way to a busy October for Cook, but on October 26, the Union guns aimed at Fort Sumter began to roar once more. A total of 18,677 shells rained down on Fort Sumter, day and night, for the next forty-one days. About halfway through this "Second Great Bombardment" of the fort, some of the Union Parrott guns on Morris Island were turned west and elevated to a high angle. On the night of November 16–17, they began firing on Charleston again. Fifteen shells cut through the night sky toward the cradle of the Confederacy. From that night on, the city was under nearly daily bombardment until its evacuation in February 1865.[28]

W. Chris Phelps writes in *The Bombardment of Charleston 1863–1865*:

As Union shells fell daily on the city of Charleston in late 1863 and early 1864, photographer George S. Cook sometimes noted the hostile fire in the margins of pages in his account books. On December 31, 1863, he noted artillery strikes at nearby buildings or businesses. (Library of Congress)

Never before had artillery pieces thrown their projectiles such great distances, nearly five miles, and for such an extended period of time, 545 days. . . . Not until the German bombardment of Leningrad in World War II, which lasted more than 800 days . . . would the Union bombardment of Charleston be surpassed.

Yet, for at least eight months of it, and probably longer, George S. Cook continued to operate a gallery in Charleston, serving a steady flow of patrons who continued to come through his door.[29]

No American city is quite so charming as Charleston, nor quite so prone to trouble—both natural and man-made. Since its founding in 1670, Charleston has been hit by two earthquakes, four fires, and at least six hurricanes. Long before its troubles during the Civil War, Charleston endured a forty-day siege and two years of British occupation during the American Revolution. When the bombardment of the city began in earnest in November 1863, a large swath of Charleston was already in ruins. A wind-whipped fire on December 11, 1861, cut a path one- to three-blocks deep through the heart of the city, stretching its entire width.[30]

At first, the shells struck in lower Charleston, closer to the point of the peninsula that it sits on. Many residents had already left the city after the shelling in August. More left that November, but a greater number simply moved out of the lower part of the city. Some Yankee shells were loaded with "Greek Fire," an experimental incendiary mixture, and though none harmed the city as badly as the fire of 1861, they were a constant threat. Charleston firemen extinguished ninety-eight fires during the bombardment, usually under heavy fire since the Union gunners made a habit of targeting fires for more intense barrages. The effective range of the Union guns was 8,140 yards, which covered about a third of the city, but shells could reach all but the most northwestern section. Cook's studio was at the edge of the effective range, but still well within the line of fire.[31]

"Shelling," wrote Cook in the margin of his account book for November 20, 1863. He had nine sales that day.

"Shelling—one in Beaufain," Cook wrote on Saturday, November 21. The gallery was even busier that day—fourteen sales and $140 in gross receipts—but the shells were falling closer. Beaufain Street meets King Street a half block south of Cook's studio.

The following Monday, Cook wrote an unusual entry in his account book: "Nothing done. Wilson deserted his duty." Perhaps his assistant, Wilson, was somehow affected by the bombardment, but regardless, Wilson was back at work the next day, and Cook did not dock his pay. With each new day of the bombardment, however, conducting business in Charleston became more difficult.[32]

On November 23, the *Courier* suspended publication for a week while it moved out of range. By November 30, the Mills House was closed, and the Charleston Hotel had given notice of closing. "There are very few travelers and visitors except on official demand," the paper reported. Rooms that had cost $2.50 a night were now $10. The citizens, however, became used to the shells, a few of which came screaming in,

George S. Cook's Losing Battle against Confederate Inflation

The chart presented here, compiled from 9,522 individual entries in the five daily account registers of George S. Cook from 1860 to 1865, reveals dramatic statistical evidence of how the Charleston photographer fought an aggressive but ultimately hopeless battle against inflation due to the ever-shrinking value of Confederate money.

From April 13, 1861, the day after the start of the bombardment of Fort Sumter, until March 8, 1864, when Cook's final existing wartime register reached its final page, Cook recorded 8,210 entries, almost half of those (4,042) in 1863 alone. The Confederacy might have been slowly strangling from the Federal blockade of Southern ports, but Cook's investments in blockade runners (also noted in his account books) provided him with a source of photographic supplies at least into 1864.

By late 1863, as the city began to come under daily Federal bombardment, Cook may have been the only photographer in Charleston whose gallery remained open. This fact is reflected in the dramatic upsurge in Cook's business from a moribund 1860 through a robust early 1864. Before the war started, Cook was barely surviving, and his daily entries for dozens of days in the fall of 1860 read "nothing done." With war came a level of business unlike Cook had ever seen. The number of customers at Cook's gallery at 235 King Street almost doubled from 1861 to 1862, and rose again in 1863 by almost 58 percent. Invariably, April and May were his busiest months, and Cook logged in his register a one-month record of 549 customers in May 1863, or an average of twenty-one customers each day he worked that month. (His single-day record during the war was forty-two customers on April 17, 1863.)

The patrons came in ever-increasing numbers despite the spiraling prices Cook charged for his work. At the beginning of the war, Cook typically charged $2.50 for a sixth-plate image. By July 1862, the price had jumped to $4, and in May 1863, it was $6. Just five months later, in October, Cook now demanded $10 in Confederate paper money for a sixth-plate view. In February 1864, the price was $15, and in the first week of March 1864, the final full week in Cook's wartime registers, he had raised it to $20—ten times the cost of the same image three years earlier.

These price hikes are reflected in the huge increases in Cook's gross receipts during the war. For instance, from 1862 to 1863, whereas the number of customers jumped by 56 percent, Cook's gross receipts more than *tripled*, from $12,732 to $39,653.50. In raw gross receipts, Cook's biggest month of the war was February 1864, the final full month documented by his daily account books, when he took in $5,162 from 350 customers. When adjusted for inflation, however, that figure plummets to $245.76. The inflation figures, which represent a roughly month-by-month assessment of the purchasing power in gold of Confederate Treasury notes, were compiled and published in Official Publication #13 of the Richmond Civil War Centennial Committee and were available online in 2005 at two websites.

The chart's final two columns, which show the average amount of money Cook took in from each customer and the same average adjusted for Confederate inflation, are the most graphic in showing Cook's losing battle against inflation. The average is remarkably consistent in late 1860, 1861, and even through 1862 as it hovers just under $5.00 per customer. But as Cook increases his prices, the average jumps to almost $10 a customer in 1863 and $15 by 1864. Meanwhile, inflation has almost no effect in 1861, but by the end of 1862, Cook's $4.97 average per customer is actually worth only $2.48. And by 1864, the average of $14.98 is eviscerated to a mere 68 cents. After the war, when Cook resumes business in the second half of 1865, the average returns to just under prewar levels at $4.44 per customer.

Date	Inflation Rate $1 Gold =	Customers	Gross Receipts	Inflation Adjusted Gross	Average per Customer	Inflation Adjusted Average
1860						
Aug.*	—	25	74.50	—	2.98	—
Sept.	—	20	156.50	—	7.82	—
Oct.	—	51	346.50	—	6.79	—
Nov.	—	78	346.75	—	4.44	—
Dec.	—	102	416.75	—	4.08	—
1861						
Jan.	—	88	530.00	—	6.02	—
Feb.	—	148	907.75	—	6.13	—
Mar.	—	151	788.25	—	5.22	—
Apr.	1.00	199	1,160.75	1,160.75	5.83	5.83
May	1.05	208	898.25	855.47	4.31	4.11
June	1.05	120	472.50	449.99	3.93	3.75
July	1.05	91	380.25	361.14	4.17	3.98
Aug.	1.05	67	443.85	422.71	6.62	6.30
Sept.	1.05	47	199.50	190.00	4.24	4.04
Oct.	1.10/1.12	56	163.75	147.53	2.92	2.63
Nov.*	1.15	36	195.24	169.77	5.42	4.71
Dec.*	1.20	96	339.25	282.70	3.53	2.94
1862						
Jan.	1.20	138	530.50	442.08	3.84	3.20
Feb.	1.25/1.40	161	555.20	420.36	3.44	2.61
Mar.	1.50/1.65	245	970.50	617.58	3.96	2.52
Apr.	1.75/1.80	331	1,362.00	767.45	4.11	2.31
May	1.90/1.95	398	1,734.50	901.18	4.35	2.26
June	2.00	118	562.50	281.25	4.76	2.38
July	2.00	236	1,022.50	511.25	4.33	2.16
Aug.	2.20	106	574.45	261.11	5.41	2.46
Sept.	2.50	159	954.50	381.80	6.00	2.40
Oct.	2.50	173	1,108.75	443.50	6.40	2.56
Nov.	2.50	228	1,534.75	613.90	6.73	2.69
Dec.	2.50	266	1,822.50	729.00	6.85	2.74
1863						
Jan.	2.50	271	1,670.50	668.20	6.16	2.46
Feb.	3.00/3.10	315	2,193.50	719.36	6.96	2.28
Mar.	3.25/5.00	324	2,427.50	605.47	7.49	1.86
Apr.	5.00	454	3,298.00	659.60	7.26	1.45
May	5.00/6.00	549	4,749.50	870.72	8.65	1.58
June	6.50/7.50	443	4,738.00	680.29	10.69	1.53
July*	8.00/10.00	259	1,980.50	222.80	7.64	.86
Aug.	10.00/15.00	256	2,257.50	263.35	8.81	1.02
Sept.	15.00	271	2,981.00	198.71	11.00	.73
Oct.	15.00	333	4,449.00	296.30	13.36	.88
Nov.	15.00/15.50	253	3,993.00	261.75	15.78	1.03
Dec.	15.50/21.00	314	4,915.50	275.55	15.65	.87
1864						
Jan.	21.00	275	3,681.00	175.25	13.38	.63
Feb.	21.00	350	5,162.00	245.76	14.74	.70
Mar.*	26.00	120	2,322.50	89.32	19.35	.74
1865						
Aug.*	—	25	68.50	—	2.74	—
Sept.	—	63	282.50	—	4.48	—
Oct.	—	126	492.00	—	3.90	—
Nov.	—	189	901.00	—	4.76	—
Dec.	—	190	889.50	—	4.68	—
1860*	—	276	1,341.00	—	4.85	4.85
1861	1.00/1.20	1,307	6,479.34	6,266.06	4.95	4.79
1862	1.20/2.50	2,559	12,732,65	6,370.46	4.97	2.48
1863	2.50/21.00	4,042	39,653.50	5,722.10	9.81	1.41
1864*	21.00/26.00	745	11,165.55	510.33	14.98	.68
1865*	—	593	2,633.50	—	4.44	4.44

* Totals reflect only partial months or years.

almost every night. "The bombardment is regarded with indifference by our citizens and with our boys it is a matter of both fun and profit," the *Mercury* reported on November 28. "A lad of some 12 years sold last week, a lot of brass coils from the Yankee shells."[33]

Cook also seemed to take it as a matter of course—until December 11, when one projectile struck too close to ignore. "Shelling. Hart's building struck." The S. N. Hart & Company was at 228 King, across the street and just down the block. Still, Cook's holiday business flourished as never before, so he continued working as if nothing had happened. On December 16 alone, he filled a page and a half of his account book with thirty entries and recorded gross receipts of $308.[34]

The day before, Charleston resident Emma Holmes wrote in her diary, "The Yankees have been shelling the city constantly, the Greek fire being a failure, but the shells of course injuring many houses. . . . At night it was truly terrific to hear the shells whistling all around not knowing where next they would strike."[35]

On the last day of 1863, Cook's final sale was one of his biggest of the year—$200 for matching paintings and frames of a Mr. Ketchum and his wife. Cook had six other customers that day, while the city put up with another storm of unwelcome shrapnel, some of which crashed through nearby businesses. "Shells thick. Dibble's and Marisso," Cook wrote on December 31.[36]

As 1864 began, the smattering of daily shells became a torrent. Hundreds began striking the city, day and night. Cook had noted weather observations in the margins of his account book for more than a decade, stretching back to his daguerreian days. Now Cook took note of all the sky proffered in the same concise report.

Jan. 12: Rain & shells.

Jan. 13: Rain & shelling.

Jan. 14: Rainy & shelling.[37]

Charleston, and Cook, were severely challenged by the bombardment, but not conquered. The city was not leveled, as the burned district had been in 1861, but it was shot full of holes. The explosive, bullet-shaped Parrott shells had an impact fuse on the nose, but the shells flew so fast they usually penetrated one floor before exploding. The explosion of the ten pounds of gunpowder in the shell was enough to devastate the room, but not level the building. "One shell into the owner's parlor though, was usually enough to encourage him to evacuate," writes Thomson.[38]

From a precarious perch 150 feet up the steeple of St. Michael's Church in the heart of Charleston, twenty-one-year-old Confederate Signal Corps Sgt. Augustine Thomas Smythe kept an eye on the Union forces through a telescope in 1864. He soon became used to artillery shells screaming past his post at close range, as the St. Michael's steeple was the prime target—the veritable bull's eye—in Charleston. (A shell finally punched a hole in the steeple near the clock in October 1864.) Smythe wrote on June 3, 1864, to his sister, Sarah Annie:

> I hear them coming and they all seem a matter of course, & I pay no attention to them at all. It is beautiful to see from my elevated position, these bombardments. The white smoke, puffing out in dense clouds from the batteries, then the flash & small speck of smoke, indicating the bursting shell, which gradually expands & enlarges, until it is lost among the real nebulae.[39]

No exact figures exist for the number of shells hurled into Charleston during the bombardment, but Phelps has calculated a bare minimum of 11,000, and possibly twice that many. If so, Phelps writes, "then for every two shells that the enemy threw at Fort Sumter during the siege, one was thrown at Charleston." It is unclear how many civilians were hit during the shelling; the official Confederate tally stopped in January 1864 at five killed and six wounded. There were numerous close calls, including reports that one shell "passed through a bed containing three children and exploded in the next floor" without hurting them. Another shell went through a bed between a man and his wife, without harming them, only to plunge into the cellar.[40]

Cook's business didn't appear to suffer. His account book continues uninterrupted through a busy February and into early March 1864, but comes to an end on Tuesday, March 8, when he fills the last blank page in the book.[41]

This 1863–1864 account book preserved at the Library of Congress, along with four other account books at the Valentine Richmond History Center, provide an unbroken, day-by-day, customer-by-customer chronicle of a Southern photographer's business from August 16, 1860, to March 8, 1864, and from August 12 to December 31, 1865.

When the familiar dictum of "follow the money" is applied and the transactions from 9,522 total entries in five separate Cook account books are tallied and analyzed, a remarkable picture emerges. The numbers tell the story of a Confederate businessman who had the good fortune to own a booming wartime business and who raised prices aggressively to counteract the effects of the skyrocketing inflation rate of the Confederate dollar, but who fought a futile battle. Nothing could diminish the destructive effects of inflation on Cook's business, until the war itself finally overwhelmed him and destroyed it altogether.

As with nearly all photographers, the war had been good for Cook in the beginning. Cook emerged from his deep slump in late 1860 to experience two of the biggest months of his career in April and May 1861, but business sagged again in the fall. Starting in 1862, however, the customers began to return in ever-increasing numbers (except during the usual summer drop-offs), and they continued to flock to the gallery right up to the final day of his last wartime account book on March 8, 1864.

To counter the wealth-sapping effects of inflation, as well as the higher costs of obtaining supplies, Cook instituted regular price increases during the war, eventually taking them to unprecedented levels. A sixth-plate image that cost $2.50 at Cook's gallery in 1861 skyrocketed to $20 by March 1864. In September 1863, the most common transaction at Brady's New York gallery was 12 cartes de visite for $5. That same month, in Charleston, Cook rarely sold more than a half-dozen cartes at a time, and his typical sale was three cartes for $10 to $15, or as much as a dozen times more than what Brady was charging.

Cook's price increases are reflected most dramatically in an analysis of his average gross receipts per customer. Before the war, and even through the year 1862, Cook averaged just under $5 per customer. In 1863, that average doubled to $9.81, and in the first months of 1864, it reached almost $15 per customer. (After the war, when Cook reopened his gallery in August 1865, the average dropped to $4.44 per customer, slightly less than prewar levels.)

As Cook raised prices—almost by the month—the inflation of the Confederate dollar was ravaging the Southern economy at an even faster pace. For the first five months of the war, the Confederate dollar held its ground. By the end of 1861, however, it took $1.20 in Confederate paper money to equal one dollar in gold, and by the end of 1862, with more devaluation, it took $2.50 in Confederate paper to equal a dollar of gold. Only a year later, it took $21. Clearly, the pace of inflation was far exceeding Cook's ability to keep up with it. By March 1864, although Cook was taking in an all-time high average of $19.35 per customer in gross receipts, the value of those receipts, adjusted for inflation, averaged just 74 cents per patron.[42]

Though few clues exist about Cook's business after March 8, 1864, we do know his life became filled with burdens beyond those brought on by the war. His wife Elizabeth became ill and, by the fall of 1863, was bedridden. The absence of Cook's handwriting in his account book shows he was away from the gallery February 5 through February 23, possibly because of his wife, whom he may have moved inland. After that, the threads of Cook's life seem to disappear. Gus Smythe gives a final glimpse of Cook in Charleston on October 14, 1864, when he writes to his sister of seeing "Mr. Cook" and discussing the damage to the Second Presbyterian Church, which they both attended. For the next few months, history loses George S. Cook in the fog of war.[43]

9

PHOTOGRAPHERS ON THE MARCH

With their muskets at shoulder arms, bayonets glinting in the sunlight, thousands of Yankee troops marched across two pontoon bridges on the Rapidan River at Germanna Ford on May 4, 1864, spearheading Lt. Gen. Ulysses S. Grant's campaign against the Army of Northern Virginia and Gen. Robert E. Lee. The next day, and the day after, many of them would die in the Wilderness, and the survivors would move on to Spotsylvania Court House, where they would spend the better part of two weeks embattled in desperate and bloody warfare.

Photographer Timothy O'Sullivan, working for Gardner's Gallery in Washington, climbed the south bank of the Rapidan River with his stereoscopic camera late that afternoon of May 4 to document the opening act of Grant's relentless drive toward Richmond. O'Sullivan took three, 3-D photographs of the historic crossing. Not surprisingly, two of the images can be joined together to form a sweeping panorama of the start of an eleven-month campaign that would ultimately end with the surrender of Lee and his forces. O'Sullivan was the only photographer to capture the crossing at the Rapidan. He had a knack for such occasions, having photographed the army at Franklin's Crossing in early June 1863 at the beginning of its march toward Gettysburg.[1]

The stereo views of the army crossing at the Rapidan were the only photographs O'Sullivan would take for the next two weeks. The rapid movement of the army, the confused, fluid fighting in the Wilderness and at Spotsylvania, and, finally, rainy weather all conspired to keep the lens caps secured on the cameras of the war's field photographers.[2]

Behind the Union lines, at the main Union supply depot at Belle Plain Landing on the Potomac River, cameras reappeared when good weather arrived on May 16. Three different photographers or photographic units—A. J. Russell for the military railroads, James Gardner for his brother Alexander's gallery, and Brady's photographers, possibly Berger and Woodbury or others—captured scenes that day of Confederate prisoners milling in a temporary holding area known as the "Punch Bowl."[3]

By May 18, they were all in Fredericksburg, working together at times and separately at others. Brady's men alone captured a panorama of Marye's Heights from the Union position, but Gardner joined in photographing the nearby re-

Two half-stereo negatives by Timothy O'Sullivan are combined to make a single panorama of the historic crossing of the Rapidan River at Germanna Ford on May 4, 1864, as Lt. Gen. U. S. Grant began his campaign against Robert E. Lee. Some 50,000 troops crossed these pontoon bridges that day. Eleven bloody months later, it would finally end. (Library of Congress; panorama by Michael O'Connor)

mains of houses destroyed by the Union bombardment that preceded the tragic assault. On May 19 or 20, both Gardner and Brady's men took their cameras onto Marye's Heights. The Brady operators made several memorable stereo views of wounded Union soldiers resting under the broad oaks that grew in the yard of the Marye House. Russell joined Brady's men on the nineteenth or twentieth to photograph the funeral and burial of several dead Union soldiers. With his own stereo camera, Russell took an image of one of Brady's operators aiming another stereo camera at the bodies awaiting burial, some uncovered, others concealed by blankets. Gardner, meanwhile, found his own scenes of wounded Union soldiers on May 20 at a Sanitary Commission depot set up in a brick warehouse on Charles Street.[4]

O'Sullivan, who was still in the field with the army, resumed taking photographs on May 19 at the Beverly House, field headquarters of the 5th Corps, about a mile and a quarter northeast of Spotsylvania Court House. That evening, in the final engagement of the battle of Spotsylvania, Confederate forces swung far around the federal line to probe the Union right flank. The

ensuing battle at Harris Farm produced some 2,300 casualties to the rear of O'Sullivan's location, more than a mile back up the road toward Fredericksburg.[5]

The next day, May 20, O'Sullivan backtracked to the scene of the fighting and found what he was looking for on Alsop's Farm, which was adjacent to the Harris Farm. O'Sullivan had seen dead on the battlefield at Gettysburg, but he was on his own in Spotsylvania. As his fellow photographers had done at Gettysburg, O'Sullivan used a prop. He carefully placed a musket across one body, then another to have something besides a corpse in the gruesome scene. Using his stereo camera, O'Sullivan exposed three plates of Confederate dead in the field—one plate of a group of about ten bodies lined up for burial, and two plates showing soldiers busy with the disagreeable task of collecting and burying bodies.[6]

O'Sullivan did not linger in Spotsylvania, however. He joined the army's march on May 21 as it began moving southward once more, toward another date with destiny, a place called Cold Harbor. During the next week, as Grant maneuvered south and east, O'Sullivan took several dozen images in stereo and large plate of the pontoon

Photographer Timothy O'Sullivan poses for the camera in this *carte de visite*, probably taken late in the war or just after the war. O'Sullivan took more photographs for Gardner's gallery during the war than any other photographer, including Gardner himself. (From the collection of Larry J. West)

bridges and operations along the North Anna and Pamunkey rivers. Many of these views have the same sense of immediacy and action as the photographs of the Rapidan crossing. One shows supply wagons streaming across the Pamunkey. Another shows the smoking ruins of the Chesterfield Bridge. A third shows war-weary foot soldiers taking a brief rest in a trench overlooking the bridge.[7]

None of O'Sullivan's photographs from this period were more famous or more popular than the views he took of a Union command staff meet-

ing that came to be known as "Grant's Council of War." O'Sullivan took the photographs around noon on May 21 at a crossroads sanctuary called Massaponax Church. Grant's staff had carried church pews out into the front yard and set up a temporary headquarters where Grant could confer with his generals and staff.[8]

No doubt delighted by his good fortune in coming upon the scene, O'Sullivan carried his camera and tripod up the steps to the church balcony. He set up his tripod on the final few steps to get an unobstructed view of the church yard from an upper window. Wasting no time, he exposed three stereo negatives in succession. Each scene shows a fluid tableau in the same, fixed setting; thus, the three pictures flow into one another like a rudimentary motion picture. In two scenes, the blur of moving wagon trains streaks the background, and in the third, the wagons are stopped. Horses await their riders; couriers await their orders. Grant is captured in one view sitting and smoking his ever-present cigar. In another, he is on his feet, leaning over the back of a pew studying a map with Gen. George Meade. In the third view, he is seated, writing a dispatch or a letter.[9]

O'Sullivan was fortunate to capture Grant in this candid situation; it was his first and only opportunity to photograph the commander in the field in Virginia. His boss, Alexander Gardner, was not the official photographer for Grant's headquarters command, as he had been for Hooker in 1863. Under Grant there was a switch, and the privilege and responsibility of being the official photographer for headquarters command fell instead to one M. B. Brady. His name replaced Gardner's on the newest official register of civilians doing business with the Army of the Potomac, and listed with Brady were his assistants, Berger, Woodbury, and S. T. Denney.[10]

That change became apparent in June 1864. Whereas O'Sullivan's enterprise had given him one photographic coup after another in May, Brady's unparalleled access to the Union high command provided him with the best opportu-

During one of his appearances in the field near Winchester, Virginia, M. B. Brady posed with the 15th New York Battery. Brady is in the center of the photograph, hands on hips, with his white collar just barely visible. (Courtesy of the Western Reserve Historical Society)

nities and most distinctive images the following month. While O'Sullivan took pictures of Charles City Court House (and a photograph of an execution), Brady and his operators were exposing one plate after another of Union generals and their staffs in the field, including Grant, Gen. George Meade, and others in their most recognizable campaign poses. In 1862, that privilege had belonged to Gardner. The labels on Gardner's photographs in 1864 may have billed him as "Photographer to the Army of the Potomac," but his access was not what it had been. In that respect, Brady once again had the edge.

Brady's Cold Harbor photographs were not taken until more than a week after the slaughter of June 3, when Grant hurled his army against Lee's hastily entrenched lines, losing up to 7,000

men in less than an hour. After that Union setback, both armies remained facing each other at Cold Harbor for more than a week. By June 11 or 12, the officers were willing to take time to sit for Brady's cameras. In one stereo view, Brady sat with Gen. Ambrose Burnside as Burnside read a Washington newspaper. In another, Maj. Gen. Winfield Scott Hancock sat by a tree as his division commanders—Gens. Francis C. Barlow, John Gibbon, and David B. Birney— stood behind him.[11]

As Brady and his operators did their work, Grant was refining his latest offensive. He would move farther south yet, cross the James River, and attack Petersburg, a hub for four Southern rail lines. If Grant captured Petersburg, Richmond would be cut off from the rest of the Con-

Facing page: This three-image sequence (all originally stereoscopic) of Grant and his commanders meeting in the front yard of the Massaponax Church on May 21, 1864, is one of O'Sullivan's greatest photographic accomplishments. Grant is seated between the two trees in the first image, smoking a cigar. In the second shot, he is in almost the same spot, writing a dispatch. Before O'Sullivan takes the third image, the wagon train in the rear comes to a halt, and Grant gets up to lean over Gen. George Meade as they study a map. (Library of Congress)

federacy. Again, O'Sullivan was present for part of the river crossing and captured the scene from atop a wagon that was poised near the entrance to a long pontoon bridge across the James. By June 15, Grant was outside Petersburg setting the stage for the war's final act, though it would be ten, long months before it was over.[12]

Army of the Potomac registers from 1865 and 1863 document a change among photographers attached to the command headquarters. In 1863, the official "photographist" is Alexander Gardner, with Timothy O'Sullivan also listed as "taking views on the march." In 1865, with Grant in command, M. B. Brady took over, listing S. T. Denney, Anthony Berger, and David B. Woodbury as his assistants. (From the National Archives and Records Administration)

Meanwhile, George Barnard, the former daguerreian artist who had worked with Gibson at Bull Run and Yorktown, was positioned to document the 1864 campaign against Atlanta by Maj. Gen. William T. Sherman. Barnard, after completing his work for Brady in 1862, had returned to Oswego late in the year to work temporarily at a hometown gallery. His trail is lost in 1863 until December 28, when he was hired in New York to become the photographer of the Topographical Branch of the Department of Engineers, Army of the Cumberland.[13]

After purchasing equipment, chemicals, and supplies at Anthony's establishment, Barnard traveled by train to Nashville, the primary Federal depot for the buildup to the Atlanta campaign. His primary job was to reproduce maps, but from the start, Barnard had another mandate: make photographs in the field. On February 4, Barnard traveled to Chattanooga and Lookout Mountain, returning six days later with an impressive array of negatives and several multi-plate panoramas. He also photographed Knoxville, his most ambitious effort being a seven-plate, 360-degree view from the cupola of the University of East Tennessee.[14]

As Barnard began to produce the photographs that would establish his most enduring legacy as a Civil War photographer, he followed in the footsteps of other Western theater photographers who had already created important photographic records of the conflict. Cincinnati photographers Barr and Young, who were official camp photographers based at Fort Pickering in Memphis, followed their Ohio regiments to the front at Vicksburg in 1863, where they took studio portraits and ventured into the field to make stereo views and *cartes de visite* of scenes around the Mississippi River port. One image, perhaps their most dramatic photograph, shows a huge American flag flying from the cupola of the Vicksburg courthouse after the Confederate surrender on July 4, 1863.[15]

Southern photographers in Vicksburg during Grant's siege were, like the city itself, slowly choked out of business. J. H. Fitzgibbon, a former

St. Louis daguerreian artist, had "good stock" when he moved to Vicksburg at the beginning of the war, but it eventually dwindled. The *American Journal of Photography* reported:

> Finally, with alcohol at twenty-four dollars per gallon, and many other useful things not procurable at any price, and with no money among the people to pay for pictures if he could produce them, he very properly felt that he had a call for a cooler climate. [Fitzgibbon] left Vicksburg just before its fall, tried to run the blockade, was captured, went to New Orleans, and from that city came directly to New York.[16]

Photographer William R. Pywell, an associate of Alexander Gardner, is credited with six negatives taken in and around Vicksburg in February 1864, including a view of the Big Black River battlefield. Downriver from Vicksburg, the fort at Port Hudson, Louisiana—the last Confederate bastion on the Mississippi—fell on July 8. Days afterward, Baton Rouge photographers McPherson and Oliver made a series of stereo photographs inside the wrecked fort, preserving for posterity the carnage of this Western battleground. McPherson and Oliver's business was exclusively Confederate until Union forces occupied Baton Rouge in May 1862. Like other Southern photographers in occupied cities, they quickly adapted to the new arrangement and started taking photographs of Union officers and troops.[17]

Their competitor in Baton Rouge, A. D. Lytle, also adjusted to the new regime and, like McPherson and Oliver, left his studio to take dozens of photographs in the field. Because of the demand for their services among Northern troops, Southern photographers in occupied cities were able to procure chemicals and supplies from the North with special arrangements through the military. Lytle, however, may have worked both sides of the fence. An 1892 biographical sketch based on information provided by Lytle said he "attached himself to the Confederate Signal service, with which he was connected at the fall of Port Hudson." Some reports have Lytle smuggling photographs to Confederates. His son, Howard, claimed in 1911:

Photographer George Barnard is captured by Brady's studio camera in this circa 1865 portrait. Although Barnard is best known for his Civil War photographs, he continued taking photographs almost until the turn of the century and lived until 1902. (From the collection of Larry J. West)

> [My father] used to signal with flag and lantern from the observation tower on the top of the ruins of the Baton Rouge capitol to Scott's Bluff, whence the messages were relayed to the Confederates near New Orleans; but he found this provided such a tempting target for the Federal sharpshooters that he discontinued the practice.[18]

How much of this is true is a matter of debate. What is certain is that Lytle and McPherson and Oliver continued to operate in an occupied city. They were also a few among thousands of American Civil War photographers to take the time and trouble to carry their cameras out of their studios

and into the field to visually document the sights and scenes in their small corner of the conflict.

In Chicago, several photographers made images of the Confederate prison camp, called Camp Douglas, including I. W. Crater, who took candid photographs of the raiders of John Hunt Morgan after they were captured in July 1863. Chicago photographer John Carbutt, who is best known for his photography of the Western frontier after the war, took several dozen stereo views of camps, group photographs, and panoramic landscapes during a visit to Illinois troops stationed in Columbus, Kentucky, in the summer of 1864. Carbutt, a lifelong innovator, was experimenting with dry plate negatives by mid-1864 and was burning magnesium for night or indoor photography by 1865. His war views were notable enough to be twice mentioned in the *Philadelphia Photographer* in 1864 but today are among the most rare of Civil War photographs. One of his lost views is titled "The Innocent Cause of the War," which was "another very fine and amusing stereo, made at Columbus, Kentucky by Mr. Carbutt."[19]

Barnard's advantage, allowing him to branch out from his map work and create such an extensive pictorial record of Sherman's campaign, was the unqualified support he received from the top commanders, including Sherman himself. Barnard's boss and the officer who hired him was Captain of Engineers Orlando M. Poe, whose enthusiasm for photography was well known. Poe's personal passion was collecting *cartes de visite* and getting them autographed. He arranged for Grant to sit for Barnard's camera so he could obtain an autographed likeness of the commander.[20]

On April 20, 1864, as Sherman prepared to move into Georgia, Quartermaster General Montgomery C. Meigs wrote from Washington to discuss logistics with the military railroads and supply lines. Meigs had heard about Barnard's photographs, and his curiosity and natural interest in photography led him to conclude the letter with a more personal request:

> Captain Poe, in charge of your engineer depot at Nashville, has, I am told, charge of the photographic establishment. Some very interesting photographs of the scenery about Nashville and Knoxville, I am told, have been taken. I have seen a set of Chattanooga views, which are interesting and beautiful. Can you not send me two sets of each, one for my office and one for myself? I should prefer them sent on thin paper, to be mounted here. They are less injured in the mail.[21]

Sherman's reply of April 26 underscores his support of Barnard's work. After addressing military business, Sherman wrote:

> I have sent word to Captain Poe, who will send you two copies of his photograph sketches, which are very beautiful.[22]

Poe immediately sent the prints to Meigs with the following note:

> By direction of Maj. Genl. W. T. Sherman, I have the honor of enclosing two complete setts [sic] of the Photographs, taken by my Photographer, in the vicinity of Chattanooga and also of Knoxville.
>
> I must say of the Knoxville Photographs, that they are intended more particularly to illustrate the operations of the siege of Knoxville—both attack and defense—and are therefore not so satisfactory as mere pictures as they would have been, had the views been different, and for the sole purpose of gratifying the eye. Still, they will be as high prized and as fully appreciated, by you. The deep interest you have always taken in Military Photography is well known.

Facing page: Chicago photographer John Carbutt took several dozen stereo views in and around Columbus, Kentucky, in the summer of 1864, including the upper two views. The first image is a bird's-eye image of Columbus from Fort Halleck, with soldiers of the 4th U.S. Colored Heavy Artillery changing guards. The second image, published for the first time, shows an officer's drill of the 134th Illinois Regiment. The bottom image, also previously unpublished, is a remarkable 3-D photo by Chicago photographer I. W. Crater showing some of Morgan's Raiders being held at Camp Douglas in Chicago after their capture in 1863. (From the collection of C. Wesley Cowan)

P.S. Mr. Barnard, the Photographer who made the views, desires me to say that it was done under great disadvantages of wind & cold, to which I can testify.[23]

Poe's photography department had its detractors in the military bureaucracy despite support from the top. Poe had to haggle for months to confirm a $6.75-a-day salary request for Barnard. At one point, Poe's photography account was suspended, causing him to complain that he might have to personally pay the expenses "out of the present limited salary of a Captain of Engineers."[24]

When Sherman marched into Georgia, Barnard did not follow the army. He remained in Nashville copying maps and little else, at least for part of the summer. The campaign against Atlanta began in May and ended on September 1, when the Confederates evacuated the city. Four days later, Poe telegraphed to Barnard in Nashville: "Join me at Atlanta, with Photographic Apparatus. Bring your assistants, and materials with you." By mid-September, Barnard was taking photographs in the Georgia capital in stereo and two larger formats, including a twelve-by-fifteen-inch camera.[25]

One of the first scenes Barnard photographed was the spot where popular Maj. Gen. James B. McPherson was killed. The general was surveying his lines in an area thought to be under Union control when he rode into a group of Confederate infantrymen. They shot him on his horse as he tried to flee through the woods, felling him next to a slender young tree. Barnard apparently enhanced the scene by adding some or all of the debris that appears in the photograph, including a broken artillery limber, the bleached bones of a dead horse, four artillery shells, a pair of shoes, a hat, and a leather satchel. One of these views was published as a woodcut engraving in the February 18, 1865, issue of *Harper's Weekly.*[26]

During an extensive tour of the abandoned Confederate forts and the new Union installations to the west and south of Atlanta, Barnard photographed the shell-torn Ponder Mansion

and captured the well-known images of Sherman on horseback outside the city he conquered. Perhaps Barnard's most significant work was the photographic documentation of Atlanta before, during, and after its destruction. Using mostly his stereoscopic camera, Barnard documented the city in some thirty views. One photograph showed the one hundred-room Trout House Hotel and the Masonic Hall, both of which would be destroyed upon Sherman's departure. In another view, busy train engines chug to and from the massive downtown rail car shed, and another image shows the shed after it has been destroyed, with smoke rising from a fire in the background. Boxcar roofs in one picture are empty; in the next, they are partially filled; and in a final shot, their roofs are piled high with refugee goods. Some of Barnard's final views in Atlanta show soldiers tearing up the railroad.[27]

Sherman departed Atlanta on November 15 to begin his March to the Sea, and this time Barnard went along. Barnard did not take photographs during the long daily treks of the next three weeks, probably because the army was moving too quickly to allow for proper setups. Also, despite the notoriety that the march soon attained with its sixty-mile-wide swath of destruction, it left no battlefields and probably produced little in the way of dramatic photographic opportunities.[28]

Barnard remained with Sherman's army when it occupied Savannah in December, but did not join the march into South Carolina the following month. He was dispatched to New York instead, probably to deliver negatives to Anthony and pick up supplies. The final leg of the campaign went forward without a photographer, although Samuel A. Cooley or his assistants took a few photographs of Sherman's army in camp at Beaufort, South Carolina, in January 1865.[29]

Barnard, to be sure, missed one good photographic opportunity he did have during the march through Georgia: the prison pen for Union prisoners at Millen, Georgia. Ironically, it is this lost opportunity that gives us our most revealing

When George Barnard photographed the Rebel fortifications southeast of Atlanta, his camera also captured the portable darkroom tent where he would develop this plate, as well as his wagon, other supplies, and his assistant, who is kneeling next to the tent. (From the collection of George S. Whiteley IV)

glimpse of Barnard in the field. Henry Hitchcock, Sherman's judge advocate, wrote in his diary on December 6, 1864:

Barnard, the photographer, joined us today and showed quite a number of photographic views of Atlanta, all beautifully taken, also same for stereoscope. He has negatives and when we stop will print copies. I shall send a set to my darling. Wouldn't it be gay to take them to her! Barnard went while we were at Millens the other day, to the stockade pen where our men (prisoners) were kept. It was simply a pen, surrounded or made by stockades—high posts driven into the ground close to each other—about 300 yards square; no shelter of any kind, no shed, nor tent, nor roof whatever, in any weather. He went into it and all over it and examined closely—would have photographed it (It was about 5 miles up the railroad from Millens—not at the Junction) but did now know of it time enough. There was no spring no well nor any water inside the enclosure. He saw 750 graves, no headboard nor other designation save that each 50th grave was so numbered. He heard that 5 or 6 dead bodies of our men was left there <u>unburied</u> when they removed the prisoner and <u>he saw one still lying there, unburied, himself</u>. He said, after telling about the place (at dinner this evening), "I used to be very much troubled about the burning of houses, etc., but after what I have seen I shall not be much troubled about it." If B feels so from seeing the prison pen, how do those feel who have suffered in it! The burned houses, in spite of offers, are the answer.[30]

Despite Hitchcock's description, the prison camp at Millen offered far better conditions than those at Camp Sumter, the Confederate-run,

prisoner-of-war camp at Andersonville, Georgia, some 180 miles to the west. The photographic evidence of human suffering at the prison that came to be known simply as Andersonville was captured by Confederate photographer Andrew Jackson Riddle on August 17, 1864, as Sherman was poised outside Atlanta.

Soon after the war started, Riddle opened a photographic gallery in Richmond and probably began photographing maps for the new government. In 1864, he was apparently ordered to Georgia to duplicate maps. He settled in Macon, where he billed himself as "Chief Photographer, Division of the West, Macon, Georgia." He was one of the few Southern photographers who was still active in 1864. On May 7, 1864, he was paid $112.78 by the Confederacy "for reproducing military maps of the Army Tennessee by photography."[31]

The ten or more photographs Riddle took at Andersonville, on or about August 16, 1864, included a "bird's eye view of the stockade" that showed thousands of tents that housed the more than 30,000 prisoners who swelled the twenty-six-acre stockade. Another view showed hundreds of prisoners lined up at the main gate for the ration wagon, while another showed the burial of one of 107 dead men whose corpses were logged for burial that day. (About 13,000 Union prisoners died at Andersonville.)[32]

It is unknown why the Confederate authorities allowed Riddle to take photographs that so graphically showed the degradation of Andersonville, including images of prisoners wracked by dysentery sitting at the camp latrine. During the same visit, Riddle apparently took portraits of post commander Brig. Gen. John H. Winder and camp commandant Henry Wirz, so the portraits may have been his entrée. At the time, the Union had stopped prisoner exchanges, and the Con-

federate government was seeking to resume them. Perhaps the photographs were taken in an effort to show the need for continued exchanges, though there is no record they were used in this manner. In any event, Riddle sold his Andersonville photographs to the public, each print mounted on a four-by-five-inch card with the printed label: "Union Prisoners of War At Camp Sumpter, Andersonville, Ga." Each label included Riddle's name, the apparent wrong date of August 17, 1864, and a notice of "copyright secured."[33]

Prisoner Robert Kellogg saw Riddle moving around the compound, taking photographs from four different guard posts. Kellogg's diary entry of August 16 dripped with sarcasm. "Some artists from Macon have been taking pictures of our misery from posts around the stockade. They will probably adorn the parlor of some chivalrous sons of the South." After the war, Riddle went to New York to market the images, apparently without great success. By the mid-1880s, however, the Andersonville photos were among the most sought after by Northern veterans.[34]

Most of the work that Riddle, Barnard, and dozens of other photographers in the North and South did for their governments was the tedious, repetitive printing of photographic maps, an obscure but significant aspect of the topological and photographic history of the war. Maps were engraved and lithographed when possible, but in the field, in a pinch, and when daily modifications might need to be made, the photographic map was easier and much faster to duplicate.[35]

Alexander Gardner was busy during much of 1862 making photographic map copies for the Army of the Potomac in his work with Allan Pinkerton's new Secret Service Department. It has been written that Gardner used photography for espionage, but there is no credible docu-

Facing page: Among the nine photographs of Andersonville prison by Macon photographer A. J. Riddle, the top image shows prisoners gathering near the north gate as the daily ration of corn bread is distributed to the sergeants of the various messes. In the lower view, behind the prison latrine, the skimpy shelters of Union prisoners stretch to the stockade's south wall, which is topped by guard towers. (Courtesy of the Western Reserve Historical Society)

mentation to support that contention. Gardner and Pinkerton were friends, and Gardner was affiliated with or attached to the Secret Service. The most overt result of that connection, however, was the inordinate number of photographs of Union spies (known then as "scouts and guides"), especially of Pinkerton himself, who had the alias "Maj. E. J. Allen." Pinkerton's son William recalled in 1909 that Gardner "was utilized by the Government for photographing maps and other articles of that kind which were prepared by the secret service. I used to travel around with Gardner a good deal while he was taking these views and saw many of them made."[36]

When in need of a map, one Union commander did not hesitate to dragoon the camp photographer. Maj. Gen. W. S. Rosecrans reported to Secretary of War Edwin Stanton from Corinth, Mississippi, on October 22, 1862:

> Destitute of engineers or topographical engineers, groping our way through an unknown wooded and hostile country, we have been obliged to resort to every possible device to obtain and diffuse information among commanders of troops. Having no copyists, when we get a map we have to resort to an improvised photographer, who, taking likenesses, was required to provide himself with the means of copying maps as the tax for the privilege of staying in camp."[37]

No comprehensive numbers exist as to how often Union military leaders used photographs or photographic maps in their campaigns, but more than forty Union reports published in the *Official Records* were submitted with photographs, spoke of the use of photographs, or referred to photographic maps. One glimpse of how frequently photographic maps were used is evident in the 1863 annual report that Secretary of War Stanton provided to President Lincoln. That year, the War Department produced for military purposes "an aggregate of 8,841 maps, of which 6,927 were engraved and lithographed and 1,914 were photographed." During Grant's 1864 campaign in Virginia in which he was cross-

ing the Rapidan from May 4 through July 30, the army topographical department produced more than 1,600 photographic maps.[38]

The Confederates also used photographic maps and documents, although to a far lesser extent. The demand for maps by Confederate commanders prompted Capt. Albert Campbell to institute a photographic copying process after he was appointed Chief of the Topographical Office in June 1862. No hard figures exist for the number of Rebel maps that were photographs, but of the 101 maps that Jed Hotchkiss and other Confederate topographical engineers in the Shenandoah Valley created during the campaign of 1864, twenty-three were produced with photography.[39]

As the war dragged on, photography was used in all manner of ways by the federal government. The navy photographed hundreds of Union vessels. The Treasury Department, the Coast Survey Office, and the Patent Office all had photographic operations. Photographer William Bell operated a Washington studio, but he also took photographs for the Army Medical Museum of "shattered bones, broken skulls, and living subjects, before and after surgical operations [had] been performed upon them," *The Philadelphia Photographer* reported in July 1866. "Of course all these subjects were created by the war." Four hundred of these images, which were often graphic, are preserved today at the National Museum of Health and Medicine.[40]

Abner Doubleday had hinted at the possible connection of photography to spying during George S. Cook's visit to Fort Sumter in 1861, but two years later, the concern about photographic espionage became very real on a small island in San Francisco Bay called Alcatraz. Long before the small rock outcropping was turned into a maximum-security prison, it bristled with gun emplacements; and by 1863, more than one hundred pieces of heavy artillery. Its commander, Capt. William Winder, was justifiably proud of his fortress, and he decided to commission a photographic record. He hired San Francisco photographers Bradley and Rulofson, who went to

This large-plate image by one of Gardner's photographers shows the winter quarters of the photographers at Petersburg in March 1865. They were attached to the engineering corps, as evidenced by the large map copying stand, including a camera with a special lens for copying and the board on which the maps were placed for photographic reproduction. (Library of Congress)

work exposing 2,000 negatives to produce a set of fifty choice prints that showed every detail of the island's fortification. The $400 that Winder paid was less than a third of the $1,500 requested by the photographers, but Winder agreed to let them make up the difference by selling prints to the public.[41]

One of Winder's engineers dutifully forwarded a detailed report on the projects at the fort to the War Department in Washington, taking the trouble to enclose prints of two of the photographs. His conscientiousness ignited a firestorm. The entire chain of command was horrified. What better way to aid the enemy? It didn't help Winder's cause that his father John was the Confederate general in charge of Andersonville and other prisoner camps in the South. Secretary of War Stanton personally ordered the photos seized. A party of armed soldiers arrived at the Bradley and Rulofson studio on Montgomery Street in San Francisco at 4:00 p.m. on August 2, 1864, and seized all negatives, prints, correspondence, and the names of all customers who had ordered prints, no doubt with the mission to destroy all traces of the images. Winder, in disgrace, requested and received a transfer to a tiny, inconsequential artillery post.

In 1990, San Francisco historian John A. Martini identified eight original albumen prints as long-lost copies of the Alcatraz Island photographs. A Union soldier posted at Alcatraz during the war had owned the prints. They had somehow slipped through the cracks and were passed down through the family before being donated to the Sacramento History Center, where they languished as anonymous war images until Martini identified them. The other forty-two images remain lost, not to mention the 1,950 additional negatives.[42]

This image by San Francisco photographers Bradley and Rulofson showing the South Battery of the Union fort on Alcatraz Island was one of two photographs that caused controversy in Washington in early 1864. Capt. William Winder's ambitious program to photograph the growth and expansion of the fort prompted one of his engineers to forward this and another image to the War Department, where authorities considered the photographic project to be a major security breach. (Courtesy of the Florence Markofer Collection, Sacramento Archives and Museum Collection Center)

In January 1865, Secretary of State Seward received a warning about the use of photography for the transmission of hidden messages. R. J. Kimball, U.S. consular agent in Toronto, submitted a report on spying that said Rebels in Canada could trade dispatches with Richmond in fourteen days, relying on couriers who used various tricks to hide them. "These messengers wear metal buttons, which upon the inside dispatches are most minutely photographed, not perceptible to the naked eye, but are easily read by the aid of a powerful lens."[43]

If mankind's ingenuity led to new ways to tap into photography's vast potential, then all-too-human inclinations led to the occasional uniting of photography and lawlessness. Of the 75,962 Union Army general court-martials, eight involved photography, including the theft of photo cases, alcohol, other supplies, or money from camp photographers. One drunk private was drummed out of the service after he refused to leave an ambrotype saloon before having his picture taken, and after he punched the corporal who dragged him out.[44]

One case was rooted in the question of whether a soldier should pose with his firearm while having a picture taken. Many thousands did, posing with guns, swords, bowie knives, and sometimes all three. Scores of others preferred to simply pose in uniform. Though it was a matter of personal taste, the question nonetheless sparked an ugly incident inside the photograph saloon operated by William Moon at Camp Hamilton, Virginia, on August 25, 1862. It led to the court-martial of Pvt. Harry McCauley of the 11th Pennsylvania Cavalry. McCauley, who sometimes drank a bit too much, went with Sgt. James Whitman, Pvt. Samuel Greenwalt, and another private to have their pictures taken. When Greenwalt posed with his sword, McCauley scoffed, "It's folly to have your picture taken with arms on."

"Don't meddle with him," Sgt. Whitman told McCauley. "The man can have his picture taken any way he chooses."

"He can do so, but it's childish to have it taken that way," McCauley said. He wouldn't let up. The sergeant told him to shut his mouth, but McCauley kept talking.

"You shut your mouth, or I'll make you do it," Whitman said.

"How are you going to make me?" McCauley replied.

"I'll kick your damn guts out!" the sergeant said, rising from a chair.

The private fearfully shrunk back into a corner, drew his pistol, and told Whitman: "Now make me shut my chops. I'll shoot anyone who comes near me!"

Further strife was prevented when the officer of the day, Capt. E. F. M. Fachts, burst into Moon's gallery, stomped up to the private, and jerked the pistol out of his hand. Charged with "conduct prejudicial to good order and discipline," McCauley was acquitted by a panel of seven officers after they ruled that he had not aimed the pistol at Fachts as accused.[45]

Pornography made a lone appearance in the military legal system when a long list of charges was filed against Lt. Col. Arthur F. Reed, the white commander of the 40th U.S. Colored Infantry, that included "conduct unbecoming of an officer and a gentleman" for allegedly showing an obscene photograph to a lady on a train trip.

It was one of thirty-two offenses that Reed was accused of, including being absent multiple times without leave, neglecting his command, failing to drill his troops, stealing from prisoners, staying out all night, and altering the regimental register. Reed was also charged with "utter incompetence" for ordering the African American troops under his command to perform impossible movements during the only battalion drill he ever commanded. Reed ordered the troops to wheel into line from "column closed in mass, without taking wheeling distance," according to the formal charges. One can only imagine soldiers crashing into one another trying to execute the command.[46]

In the eyes of society, however, botching the movement of troops paled in comparison to making advances upon a married woman. On March 13, 1865, Reed boarded the train from Gallatin, Tennessee, to Nashville, sat down next to the wife of a fellow officer, and, with her permission, began a conversation. As they chatted, Reed pulled out some *carte de visite* photographs. He showed the woman an image of a drawing of George Washington and his wife. Apparently encouraged, Reed also showed the woman an image titled "The Couch" that showed "a young lady in a nude state retired," according to Maj. William H. Wade, who was also aboard the train. Wade gave testimony at the trial:

Q: Did you see that photograph, was it shown you by Lt. Col. Reed, and was it a decent one, such as a gentleman would show a lady?

A: Lt. Col Reed showed me the photograph and it was not a decent picture."

The woman's reaction went unrecorded, though Reed was said to have used rude language as well, "compelling her to appeal to other passengers for protection," according to the charges. (Reed later told Wade he didn't know "The Couch" was among his photographs.) During the commotion, Reed allegedly refused to leave the car and was removed by armed soldiers and kept under guard until the train reached Nashville. In June 1865, after four days of testimony, Reed

Pornography during the Civil War came in the form of *cartes de visite* and stereo views. The *carte* at left is of French origin and is considerable less graphic than some examples. At right, the English *carte* with the title "Crinoline Advantages" is an example of a less explicit image—an R-rated Civil War image in today's movie rating terminology. (From the collection of Michael J. McAfee)

was found guilty of nearly every charge against him and cashiered out of the service. For unexplained reasons, he was acquitted of all charges related to the obscene photograph.[47]

Photography also played a crucial role in one of the most controversial incidents of the war. When Col. Ulric Dahlgren was killed in a failed cavalry raid to free Union prisoners in Richmond on March 2, 1864, the Confederates were shocked to find documents on his body that called for Richmond to be burned and Confederate President Jefferson Davis to be killed. One document that carried his signature said, "We will cross the James River into Richmond, destroying the bridges after us and exhorting the released prisoners to destroy and burn the hateful city; and do not allow the rebel leader Davis and his traitorous crew to escape."[48]

Robert E. Lee made a formal inquiry of Gen. George M. Meade as to Union motives. "To enable you to understand the subject fully I have the honor to enclose photographic copies of the papers referred to," Lee wrote. Brigadier General Judson Kilpatrick, the raid's commanding officer, agreed that the "photographic papers referred to are true copies of the papers approved by me," except for the part about killing Davis and burning the city, leaving the implication that the Rebels had forged the terrorist threats onto the papers and starting a debate that continues to this day.[49]

Historian Stephen Sears is convinced the papers were genuine and that the terror plot may have gone as far up the chain of command as Edwin Stanton, citing the secretary of war's order in late 1865 that demanded he be given all

This image from Gardner's *Sketch Book of the Civil War*, titled "Studying the Art of War," shows Capt. Ulric Dahlgren (standing), other Union officers, and a visiting Prussian count at the army headquarters near Fairfax Court House in June 1863. The war would take its toll soon after the image was taken. The following month, at Gettysburg, Lt. Col. Joseph Dickinson, wearing the straw hat, would suffer a career-ending wound at Gettysburg, and Dahlgren would suffer a foot wound and lose his leg in a post-Gettysburg cavalry fight. In 1864, Dahlgren lost his life in what became known as "the Dahlgren Affair," and photography played a role in documenting the incident.

original documents and Confederate records of the affair. These written records promptly disappeared, but a Confederate government set of faded photographic copies of the incriminating documents did survive and are preserved today at the National Archives.[50]

If Stanton felt bedeviled by photography in 1864 after the uproar over the Alcatraz images and the fact that Lee used photographs to establish the authenticity of Dahlgren's evil-minded documents, it would only get worse for him in 1865. As the war ended and peace finally returned, Stanton would become embroiled in more than one debacle over photography. He would ban the sale of one image, censor another, and confiscate yet another in a frenzy of media control in the wake of the assassination of President Abraham Lincoln.

10

THE END FINALLY COMES

When Sherman started his March to the Sea, Confederate Gen. John Bell Hood turned toward Tennessee, intent on diverting the Yankees from their destructive mission in Georgia. Hood's army of some 30,000 Rebels suffered more than 6,000 casualties in reckless frontal assaults against Union forces under Gen. John Schofield on November 30, 1864, in Franklin, Tennessee. Undaunted, Hood pushed on toward Nashville, the crucial Union supply base since early 1862, and spread his lines out facing the city on December 2 and 3. Gen. George H. Thomas was slow to attack the overextended Confederates, but when he finally did on December 15 and 16, the Confederate Army was shattered, and Hood resigned.[1]

As Thomas's Union forces attacked Hood south of the city on December 15, photographer Jacob F. Coonley set up his tripod and stereo camera on Capitol Hill and aimed it toward the distant rumble of battle. One scene, a two-plate panorama, shows seven spectators peering toward the hazy distance at what may be battle smoke. In another image, the crowd has swelled to more than thirty people, nearly half of them having decided to sit and stay a spell. The next day, Coonley ventured out toward the battlefield and made three stereo images along the Federal outer line.[2]

Coonley is the rare exception among Civil War photographers; he actually wrote of his memories. Coonley left two short articles about his experiences: one published in 1882 and another in 1907. Born in 1832, Coonley was a painter whose landscape career evaporated during the Panic of 1857. He learned photography from George Barnard, briefly ran his own gallery in Syracuse, and was hired by Edward Anthony in 1858 to manage the Anthonys' new, stereoscopic printing shop. In 1860, Coonley moved behind the camera, taking scenic stereo negatives for Anthony until the war started. He then went to Washington with Barnard to shoot field and camp portraits for Brady's gallery. "I was assisted in this work by Mr. T. O'Sullivan during a part of the time, and, when not along, I had the help of Mr. David Woodbury," Coonley wrote. "My work extended to Annapolis, Fortress Monroe and Harper's Ferry in 1861 and 1862." He returned to New York, married, briefly ran galleries in Philadelphia and New York, and in 1864 resumed taking stereo views for Anthony. Coonley's 1907 narrative picks up at this point:

A panorama created from two stereo half-negatives by photographer Jacob F. Coonley shows citizens watching the Battle of Nashville from below the Tennessee State Capitol on December 15, 1864. Coonley's original negatives are rich with detail, and the background has been darkened to bring out distant features. The spectators face southwest toward the battlefield, and what may be battle smoke rises at left center between the most distant hill and the darker ridge ahead of it. (Library of Congress; panorama by John J. Richter)

"Returning to New York, I was informed that a contract had been awarded me by the Quartermaster-General [Montgomery C. Meigs] for photographic work along the lines of the railroads in possession of and used by the War Department, extending from Nashville to Chattanooga, Knoxville, Johnsonville, Tenn.; Atlanta, Ga., and Decatur and Huntsville, Ala. This work called for negative 9 × 13 inches, and Messrs. Anthony & Co. contracted to take all the stereoscopic negatives I could make on the trip at five dollars each. On arriving at Nashville the military authorities had a box-car equipped for my work, and this, with an engine, was placed at my disposal with authority to go over the territory. The work had many interruptions, owing to the destruction of bridges or being chased by cavalry or similar causes. On returning to Nashville, just before the battle of that name, we had to run the gauntlet twice to escape capture by Hood's cavalry. Arriving safely at Nashville we awaited the coming battle between Hood and Thomas. As soon as the battle was well under

way I had an ambulance with drivers take me as near as possible to make negatives of everything in sight, two days being given to this work. Then the rain came and continued for several days, so that I left there several days after the retreat of Gen. Hood.[3]

Coonley was following the accepted practice of simultaneously working for the government and a private concern, such as Anthony. Barnard worked for Poe and the army engineers, but he also supplied stereo views to Anthony. Photographer Thomas C. Roche worked for Meigs but sold stereo negatives to Anthony as well. Meigs also supervised A. J. Russell at times and contracted with Samuel Cooley, E. G. Fowx, and possibly others.[4]

The E. & H. T. Anthony & Company had quickly and aggressively become the country's largest producer of original stereo views after entering the business in 1858, but the company's performance during the Civil War seems inconsistent. One thing is clear: the shrewd, opportunistic Anthonys nearly always had their hands in what was on the market. In 1861 and 1862, the Anthonys produced several dozen views in a rather modest, loosely connected, ongoing series titled "War Views" and, later, "Camp Scenes." After Rebel cavalry burned Chambersburg, Pennsylvania, in July 1864, they issued a small series of scenes of the gutted city named "Feats of the Chivalry." The company's primary role during the war, however, was serving as the exclusive wholesale agents for the burgeoning series of war views being produced by Brady's Gallery, and, after the Brady/Gardner split, the views by Gardner's Gallery. Fully one-third (five of fifteen pages) of the celebrity *cartes de visite* and other card photographs in the Anthony November 1862 catalog was devoted to a listing of more than 300 Brady war photographs.[5]

When Gardner split from Brady in 1863, he began issuing his own catalogs and sold his own views directly, but he continued to use Anthony as his wholesale agent. The transition appears to have been smooth and successful. Brady, however, apparently was unable to continue his wholesale relationship with Anthony. A December 1864 Anthony advertisement promotes only Gardner views, describing the Gardner "Photographic Incidents of the War" series, having grown to well over 500 views by then, as "the largest and finest collection of War Views ever made."[6]

Even as that advertisement was published, the Anthonys were assembling what would become the largest individual series of stereo views ever issued, and the Anthony wholesale arrangement with Gardner was about to end. That same December, Barnard was busy in Georgia taking stereo views for Anthony. Coonley was doing the same in Tennessee, as was Thomas C. Roche in Virginia. From Brady would come the 1861 and 1862 stereo views he retained after the split with Gardner, as well as his Gettysburg views from 1863 and most or all of his Virginia stereo images from 1864.[7]

Published here for the first time, this *carte de visite* image from the Coonley family nineteenth-century photograph album shows Jacob F. Coonley, the enterprising photographer who captured the battle of Nashville while under contract to Quartermaster General M. C. Meigs. Coonley was just over thirty when this photograph was taken. He was originally a painter who learned photography from another great Civil War photographer, George N. Barnard. (From the collection of Larry J. West)

Brady's Washington gallery had gone into a tailspin after Gardner's departure in late 1862 or early 1863. While Gardner was in charge, the Washington gallery had brought in about $12,000 a year, with Brady netting another $4,000 from the sale of negatives to Anthony. After Gardner left, the Washington gallery's net profits shrunk to $4,860 in the twelve months between August 1863 and August 1864, and business with Anthony withered to $276.[8]

The downturn did not stop Brady and his operators from venturing to Gettysburg in 1863 and returning to the field in Virginia in 1864 when Brady became the official photographer of

Grant's headquarters command. In June 1864, Brady issued "Brady & Co.'s Catalogue of Photographs and Stereoscopes of Lt. Gen. Grant's Late Campaign," an ambitious, six-page printed listing of 231 different photographs in four different formats. Brady seems to have issued little else than the catalog, the only known copy of which is at the Library of Congress. Original prints from this series are rare, if they exist at all. (I have never encountered an original Brady stereo view from this series, nor has photo historian William A. Frassanito.) To manage his flagging Washington gallery after Gardner departed, Brady hired James Gibson, the veteran photographer of the Peninsular Campaign. Brady also renewed his Anthony relationship, reaching an agreement to provide his collection of war stereo views for the extensive, new, Anthony "Photographic History: The War for the Union" series.[9]

The Anthony "War for the Union" series of more than 1,100, 3-D, Civil War photographs was one of the largest series of stereo views ever issued. It was not published until the end of the war, and its debut came in the face of a controversial "sun picture" tax instituted by the Office of Internal Revenue in August 1864. Northern photographic studios and many other businesses were already obligated, beginning in September 1862, to purchase an annual license. Now, photographers had to purchase revenue stamps as well, which were sold to the customer, pasted on the backs of pictures, and cancelled by the photographer. Stereo views and *cartes de visite* that had cost 25 cents now cost 27 cents, including the two-cent tax stamp. Fifty-cent photographs were now 53 cents, including the three-cent stamp. The rates rose from there to 25 cents in tax for a large, five-dollar print.[10]

Despite the potential adverse effects of the tax, the Anthony Company went ahead with the new "War for the Union" series, issuing views on stylish, bright yellow mounts with the lettering "The War for the Union" on one side and "Photographic History" on the other. The series was reviewed in August 1865 in one of the early issues

of *The Nation*, a new weekly periodical that debuted that summer. The views "bring up vividly some of the most prominent scenes in the drama of the late rebellion," said *The Nation*. "Here are alike the instruments of ruin and the ruin itself—views from the cradle and views from the grave of secession." The review describes ten of the photos and devotes a full sentence to one of the most intriguing views in the entire series: an image taken during the construction of the Dutch Gap Canal that purports to show the smoke from one of the 9,000 shells that the Confederates lobbed into the work zone during the months it was being built. "A shell, dropping into the water of the Dutch Gap Canal, has raised a mist which is preserved for us on paper long after it has evaporated from the living air."[11]

Questions persist about whether the scene actually shows smoke from an enemy shell, as the caption claims. The subject is at least obliquely referred to in one of the best-known narratives of a Civil War photographer at work. In 1882, A. J. Russell looked back across the span of almost two decades and recalled the early spring night of April 1, 1865, in the final days of the siege of Petersburg, when T. C. Roche, the contract photographer for the government and Anthony, visited Russell's tent at City Point, Virginia. Roche told Russell:

> Cap., I am in for repairs and want to get things ready for the grand move, for the army is sure to move to-night or tomorrow night. The negatives on hand I wish to send North with some letters, prepare my glass and chemicals; in fact, get everything ready for the grand move, for this is the final one, and the Rebellion is broken, or we go home and commence over again.

Russell sat up with Roche until the "wee sma'" hours, as he put his equipment and chemicals in order, and then they had a few rare moments to relax and reminisce. Russell recalled:

> We sat smoking and talking of adventures, etc., etc., and among others of Dutch Gap Canal, and of the pictures taken there under

Presented together for the first time, the Anthony "War for the Union" stereo view that purports to show the smoke of an exploded Confederate shell is displayed with the image taken at around the same time. The same officer stands in place in both images. The caption on the back of the second view says: "The mist arising against the bank is caused by a Rebel shell, which exploded just as this view was being photographed." The drawing (left) accompanied an 1882 article by Capt. A. J. Russell in which he recounts talking with T. C. Roche about being under fire while taking photographs at Dutch Gap.

difficulties a few days before, of which a friend of mine had been an eye-witness. The enemy [was] bombarding the works from Howlett's Point, throwing immense shells every few minutes, tearing up the ground and raising a small earthquake every time one of them exploded. He had taken a number of views and had but one more to make to finish up the most interesting points, and this one was to be from the most exposed position. He was within a few rods of the place when down came with the roar of a whirlwind a ten-inch shell, which exploded, throwing the dirt in all directions; but nothing daunted, and shaking the dust from his head and camera he quickly moved to the spot, and placing it over the pit made by the explosion, exposed his plate as coolly as if there was no danger, and as if working in a country barnyard. The work finished he quickly folded his tripod and returned to cover. I asked him if he was scared. "Scared?" he said, "two shots never fell in the same place."

At this moment the heavy boom of cannons were heard in the direction of Petersburg. Roche jumped to his feet, and rushing to the door, said, "Cap., the ball has opened; I must be off," calling to his assistant. In the next quarter of an hour two horses were harnessed, everything snugly packed, and shaking my hand, with a "we will meet to-morrow at the front," said "good-bye," and the wagon rattled off into the darkness of midnight toward that doomed city above which was such another display of pyrotechnics as few photos have ever witnessed—shells flying in all directions, leaving their trails of fire and fading away only to be replaced by others. This was not all. The whole world seemed alive; every road was teeming and the call to arms seemed to find a response from every foot of the ground; the rumbling of artillery, the clatter of cavalry, the tramp of infantry, the shrieking of locomotives, calling men to their posts, plainly told that the time had come—that the destiny of a nation hung in the balance.

In the morning [actually April 3] Petersburg was ours. I found Mr. Roche on the ramparts with scores of negatives taken where the fight had been the thickest and where the harvest of death had indeed been gathered—pictures that will in truth teach coming generations that war is a terrible reality.

A few minutes later I saw his van flying toward the war-stricken city, and in the wake of a fleeing enemy. Many were the records he preserved that day that will last while history endures, to relate the eventful story of a victory sorely won.[12]

Roche took about fifty stereo photographs in the days after Petersburg fell, including twenty-two stereo negatives of dead Confederates within Fort Mahone on the day after bitter fighting there. The Confederates had held the fort at the end of the battle, but abandoned it when Lee withdrew from Petersburg. As Roche set up his tripod in the fort, Lee was on his way to a date with destiny at Appomattox. Surrender was only six days away.[13]

Roche's images of the dead of Petersburg marked the seventh and last time a Civil War photographer captured the dead of battle in the field before their burial. Most of the images show individual dead Confederates, but the lack of numbers is more than made up for by their graphic grittiness: faces of death are sharp, clear, and all too close. Some are obviously only teenagers. One face is crushed, another streaked with blood. Nearly all of the dead lie spattered with mud in the knee-deep degradation of the mud-filled trenches. Aside from the graphic display of death itself, Roche's Petersburg images are most evocative in showing how entrenched the Civil War had become, the scenes in these troughs of hell being little different than what photographers of World War I would find in the trenches of Europe. Roche's images were part of the "War for the Union" series, and while no sales figures exist, they surely were among the best-selling images in the series as they are among the most common war views encountered today.[14]

As Roche exposed one stereo plate after another of soldiers who fell less than a week before the end, the Federal cavalry was dashing into Richmond. Much of the city was in flames from fires set by the fleeing Rebels. President Lincoln visited the conquered capital on April 4, while the ashes were still smoldering. The next day Alexander Gardner began shooting photographs. It was Gardner's first appearance behind a camera in the field since Gettysburg, and he spent almost a week roaming the city and the vast area of destruction known as the Burnt District. Brady and his operators were there by April 7, along with sketch artists for *Harper's Weekly* and *Frank Leslie's Illustrated.*[15]

Brady took a side trip to City Point to fulfill his official duties and photograph Grant and his commanders before they departed for Washington or other fronts. He then returned to Richmond and scored another major coup by photographing Robert E. Lee on the back porch of his home after Lee's return from the field. When Brady first asked the defeated general to sit for the camera, Lee is said to have replied, "It is utterly impossible. How can I sit for a photograph with the eyes of the world upon me as they are today?" With encouragement from Mrs. Lee, and probably with an appeal to history, Brady managed to get a stone-faced Lee to comply. Brady departed Lee's home with several of the most popular and most recognizable photographs of Lee ever taken.[16]

Jacob F. Coonley, meanwhile, had returned to New York after Hood's defeat, but the moment the war ended, he was back on the road again for Anthony. He took the first steamer leaving New York for the South and arrived in Charleston in time for the ceremonial raising of the American flag back above Fort Sumter by Robert Anderson, now a general. The fort had been reduced to rubble, but the parade ground was cleared, an elaborate flagpole was set up, and rows of benches were constructed for the visiting dignitaries. Coonley recalled:

> I made thirty-one negatives of the Charleston celebration, all made with a drop shutter. . . . The day was bright, there was a strong breeze blowing, and the harbor was gay with a great fleet of steamers and excursion boats, all decorated, with their flags standing straight out in the wind. The impressive sight and the great crowds of spectators will never be forgotten by those who were present. This was on the 14th of April.[17]

That night, William Child, the New Hampshire surgeon who had been photographed in front of his tent at Smoketown Hospital in 1862, was in Washington, D.C., passing through the capital on his way back to the field after a furlough. Working with bone saws, chloroform, splints, and a cast-iron stomach, Child had seen the worst of the war with the oft-bloodied 5th New Hampshire. He had been at Chancellorsville, where "the bullets rattled like hail in the oak trees," and on the field at Gettysburg, where he "never was under such terrific shelling." A visit to the front lines at Cold Harbor in 1864 gave him "a good taste of shells and musket balls," and he hunkered down in his own hole in the ground at Petersburg.[18]

Now Child arrived in Washington in time to see Gen. Grant in person ("his pictures do not do him justice") and to see the exuberant celebrations that swept through the city in the wake of Lee's surrender. Child wrote his wife on the afternoon of April 14, "The City celebrated the surrender of Gen. Lee last evening by illumination, fire-works—and one grand drunk." Then he set his pen aside and prepared for the evening's entertainment—a visit to Ford's Theater to see a performance of *Our American Cousin*. Child returned to his hotel room in utter shock and penned another letter to his wife:[19]

> Wild dreams and real facts are but brothers. This night I have seen the murder of the President of the United States.
>
> Early in the evening I went to Fords Theater. After a little time the President entered—was greeted with cheers. The play went on for about an hour. Just at the close of an interesting scene a sharp quick report of a pistol was heard and instantly a man jumped from the box in which was the President, to the stage—and rushing across the stage made his escape. This I saw and heard. I was in the theatre—and sat opposite the President's box. The murderer assassin exclaimed as he leaped "Sic Semper Tyrannis"—"Thus always to tyrants."
>
> I never saw such a wild scene as followed! I have no words to describe it.
>
> Sect. Seward was also wounded by a knife about the same minute. The city is now wild with

excitement. The affair occurred only an hour since.

Are we living in the days of the French Revolution? Will peace ever come again to our dear land? Are we to rush on to wild ruin?

It seems all a dream—a wild dream. I cannot realize it though I know I saw it only an hour since.

W.C.

In the four years, one month, and ten days of his presidency, Abraham Lincoln had forged a legacy that made him an American icon. He had also become the most photographed chief executive in the nation's history. As president, Lincoln had been in the lenses of at least ten different photographers for at least sixty-eight different images. Brady and operators Anthony Berger and Thomas Le Mere had captured at least twenty-five photographs of Lincoln on seven different occasions. Alexander Gardner had taken the most—at least thirty-two studio portraits or photographs in the field, including a series of at least eight images at Lincoln's second inauguration.[20]

In the wake of Lincoln's assassination, photography became even more pervasive as a way of not only documenting events but also influencing them. In bold print, Secretary of War Stanton placed his name at the bottom of "wanted" posters created with the photographs of assassin John Wilkes Booth and suspected accomplices John Surratt and David E. Herold. Copies of Booth's image were spread among the officers leading the relentless manhunt. On April 25, the day before Booth was trapped and killed, Lt. Edward Doherty of the 16th New York Cavalry spoke to local residents near the Garrett farm south of the Rappahannock in Virginia and, a report said, "after exhibiting the photographs, [they] concluded that [they] were on the right track."[21]

Photographers for both Brady and Gardner photographed Ford's Theater, and Anthony added stereo images of the president's box and chair to its soon-to-be-released "War for the Union" stereoscopic series. Gardner himself photographed Lincoln's funeral parade in Washington before the funeral train set out for Illinois with plans to stop in every city Lincoln had visited on his way to Washington in 1861.

On April 24, as the train arrived in New York, photographer Jeremiah Gurney set up his tripod above the Governor's Room in City Hall and took two test photographs of the mourning draperies hanging over the spot where the casket of President Lincoln would be placed. Gurney had been M. B. Brady's chief rival on Broadway for nearly twenty years, stretching back to the early daguerreian era of the mid-1840s. During the war, however, Gurney had remained in his studio in New York, making steady money off portrait work, while Brady, having thrown financial caution to the wind, went into the field.

Now Gurney had a remarkable opportunity. He had secured permission to photograph the assassinated president in his coffin. This would be nothing garish or crude, it was to be a postmortem photograph in the best of taste. Gurney was forty feet from the resting place and twenty feet above it. After the casket was placed in the hushed room, two people stepped forward to be part of the pictures. Admiral Charles H. Davis stood near the head of the casket. At the foot of the casket, arms folded, stood Gen. Edward D. Townsend, who had been personally designated by Stanton to tend to Lincoln's funeral. Gurney took two photographs, one of which was with a multiple-lens camera. Late the following night, Townsend received a telegram from his boss that must have chilled his innards.

WAR DEPARTMENT,
Washington City, April 25, 1865—11.40 p.m.
Brigadier-General TOWNSEND,
Adjutant-General, New York:

I see by the New York papers this evening that a photograph of the corpse of President Lincoln was allowed to be taken yesterday in New York. I cannot sufficiently express my surprise and disapproval of such an act while the body was in your charge. You will report what officers of the funeral escort were or ought to have been on duty at the time this was

Among the greatest photographs of the Civil War are M. B. Brady's classic images of Robert E. Lee at the back door of his home in Richmond, both alone and with his aides, less than a week after his surrender at Appomattox. Brady used his longtime acquaintance with Lee and his considerable persuasive powers to convince the defeated commander to sit for photographs. Lee dressed in his Confederate uniform for Brady's camera and posed, in the words of historian Douglas Southhall Freeman, "before the fire of battle had faded from his eyes." (Library of Congress)

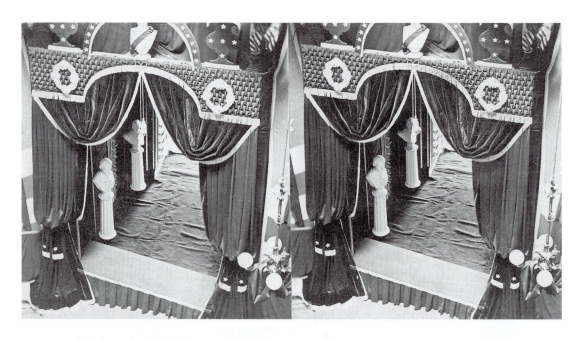

done, and immediately relieve them and order them to Washington. You will direct the provost-marshal to go to the photographer, seize and destroy the plates and any pictures or engravings that may have been made, and consider yourself responsible if the offense is repeated.

EDWIN M. STANTON,
Secretary of War.

Major ECKERT:
Please order this telegram to be delivered to-night, and if the escort has left New York order it to be forwarded to Albany.[22]

At 10:40 a.m. the next day, a contrite Townsend responded to Stanton: "I regret your disapproval, but it did not strike me as objectionable under the circumstances as it was done. I have telegraphed General [John A.] Dix your orders about seizing the plates." He asked Stanton who should take command in his place.

Stanton had no one to relieve Townsend. Two hours later, he wired back: "Continue in charge of the remains. The taking of a photograph was expressly forbidden by Mrs. Lincoln, and I am apprehensive that her feelings and the feelings of the family will be greatly wounded."[23]

Townsend, however, would not let the matter rest. That evening he wired Stanton: "It seemed to me the picture would be gratifying, a grand view of what thousands saw and thousands could not see." A short time later, he sent another wire, this time appealing on behalf of Gen. Dix, who also wanted to save the photograph and "suggest that I should explain to you how the photograph was taken." Townsend said Gurney's camera was discreetly tucked in a gallery forty feet from the casket. "Admiral Davis stood at the head and I at the foot of the coffin. No one else

was in view. The effect of the picture would be general, taking in the whole scene, but not giving the features of the corpse." Dix sent a print of one of the images from the four-lens plate so Stanton could see the image for himself.[24]

This was followed at 7:10 p.m. by a wire from leading abolitionist Henry Ward Beecher, on behalf of Gurney, asking Stanton to modify his order about destroying the negatives and "hold them without breaking until Gurney can present to you the facts in the case. They do not intend to have the face represented." Ninety minutes later, Stanton received yet another appeal, this one from *New York Times* owner Henry J. Raymond, who joined in Beecher's request "that General Dix may postpone destroying the negatives of President Lincoln taken by Gurney & Son till they can see you." Finally, that same night, Gurney appealed to Assistant Secretary of War Charles A. Dana: "Can you not assist us?"[25]

Stanton was unmoved. The Lincoln family had not given consent, in fact, had expressly forbidden it. The plates and prints were destroyed, except for a single print that would remain hidden for almost a century. Gurney's loss was compounded by a scathing commentary published the following month in *Humphrey's Journal*. Gurney's exclusive access to the Governor's Room struck a raw nerve with other New York photographers. One report said it was disgruntled photographers who had alerted Stanton. The anonymous correspondent found it particularly galling that Gurney was the photographer who had gained access to the casket because Gurney was a Copperhead who was bitterly opposed to the president.

Had not Mr. Gurney during President Lincoln's four years administration, sufficiently exhausted

---

Facing page: After Jeremiah Gurney's photograph of the body of Abraham Lincoln lying in state in New York City Hall was confiscated by Secretary of War Edwin Stanton, Gurney was left only with images of the empty bier, which he photographed from at least two vantage points, including this stereo view from a high angle, which has never been previously published. The sole surviving print of Gurney's photograph with Lincoln in his casket was rediscovered in the papers of Lincoln's secretary John Nicolay in 1952 by fourteen-year-old Lincoln researcher Ronald Rietveld. (*Top*: from the collection of John J. Richter; *bottom*: courtesy of the Abraham Lincoln Presidential Library and Museum)

his vial of wrath and vengeance against him, that he must now disturb the repose of the dead, and insult and injure the bereaved family and true friends of the departed? The whole scheme was a disgraceful outrage upon humanity, and deserves the execration of every American citizen.[26]

Stanton no sooner had dealt with one photographic controversy when another touchy photographic matter developed. The body of John Wilkes Booth was brought back to Washington and taken aboard the monitor USS *Montauk*, where the surgeon general conducted an autopsy on April 27. The *New York Tribune* reported the next day that a photographic view of Booth's body had been taken before it was removed from the *Montauk*. Among those present during the procedure were Alexander Gardner and Timothy O'Sullivan, who had taken the picture. The photograph, however, has never surfaced.[27]

In 1896, while searching for the lost Booth autopsy photograph, historian Osborn H. Oldroyd interviewed former government detective James A. Wardell, who had been assigned to stay with Gardner that day in 1865. Wardell gave a statement describing his role:

> Under no circumstances was I to allow him or his assistant out of my sight until they had taken a picture and made the print, and then I was to bring the print and the glass back to the War Department and give it only to Col. [L. C.] Baker [chief of the secret service] or Secretary of War Stanton. . . . [Gardner] was told that only one plate was to be made and it was to have only one print made and both were to be given to me when finished. I was told that the plate and print was to be brought to the War Department and given to either Col Baker or Secretary Stanton.
>
> Gardner took the plate and then gave it to the assistant and told him to take it and develop it and to make one print. I went with him and even went into the dark room. About 4:00 in the afternoon I got the plate and the print from the assistant and took it to the War Department. I went in to the outer office and Col. Baker was just coming out of the War Office. I gave him the plate and print and he stepped to one side and pulled it from the envelope. He looked at it and then dismissed me. I hope that you are able to find the plate but I doubt that you will. The War Department was very determined to make sure that Booth was not made a hero and some rebel would give a good price for one of those pictures of the plate.

The concern that photos could be used to glorify the conspirators was underscored on May 2, 1865, in Baltimore when Gen. Lew Wallace issued an order forbidding "the sale of portraits of any rebel officer or soldier or of J. Wilkes Booth, the murderer of President Lincoln." Stanton rescinded the order on May 27.[28]

Though Gardner was unable to preserve his photograph of the Booth autopsy, he was given exclusive, unfettered access to make and sell multiple photographs of the eight other conspirators, or suspected conspirators, who had been rounded up and brought on board the *Montauk* or USS *Saugus*. Gardner's images, taken head-on and in profile, include a resolute Lewis Payne, who had savaged Secretary of State Seward in a knife attack, and a bewildered David E. Herold, who had been yanked out of the burning Garrett barn before Booth was killed.[29]

Although the war was over, Washington was still busy with war-related events. On May 23 and 24, the Union armies paraded down Pennsylvania Avenue in a final march known as the Grand Review. The group of photographers gathered on the steps of the Treasury Building, their cameras aimed down the broad avenue, may have looked like an early version of a press photographers' bullpen as they exposed one plate after another of the regiments and units marching toward them. Gardner or an associate photographer was present, as was a Brady operator, and J. F. Coonley was there shooting stereo negatives for Anthony.

"I shall never forget that great pageant, as for two days a formidable host of hardy veterans marched through the nation's capital under the eyes of their commanders," Coonley recalled. He photographed the event "with the assistance of Mr. David Woodbury, the plates being exposed

This large-plate image by Alexander Gardner, one of a series of the hanging of the Lincoln conspirators on July 7, 1865, is the clearest view of the condemned in their last moments. At right, an agitated George Atzerodt appears to recoil as the noose is looped around his neck. Next to Atzerodt, David E. Herold peers toward the ground and the five-foot drop that awaits him. Lewis Payne, standing erect, has already had his hood placed over his head, while at far left, Mary E. Surratt is seated as her noose is adjusted. (Library of Congress)

with a drop shutter, this being the nearest approach to an instantaneous exposure with a wet plate."[30]

Brady may have had superior access in the field in Virginia, but it was Gardner who ruled in Washington. He had gained exclusive access to the Booth autopsy to make a photograph for Stanton and was the only photographer to make images of the prisoners after they were rounded up. Brady had to settle for studio portraits of

Sgt. Boston Corbett, the Union soldier who had shot Booth. More notably, on July 7, Gardner's gallery was the only photographic studio admitted to the Old Arsenal Prison to photograph the hanging of the Lincoln conspirators.

Gardner was issued his pass on July 5 and may have scouted the execution site ahead of time. He and his assistants were well experienced in making pictures under pressure and shooting news events on short notice, as they

As the gathered soldiers chanted, "Wirz, remember Andersonville!" Capt. Henry Wirz was hanged at Old Capitol Prison almost in the shadow of the new dome of the U.S. Capitol building. This image shows the reading of the death warrant to the condemned commander of Andersonville prison. Alexander Gardner not only photographed the hanging, he also photographed the autopsy. But unlike his censored photo of the autopsy of John Wilkes Booth, Gardner was allowed to keep and print the Wirz autopsy negative. (*Top*: Library of Congress; *left*: Courtesy of the Western Reserve Historical Society)

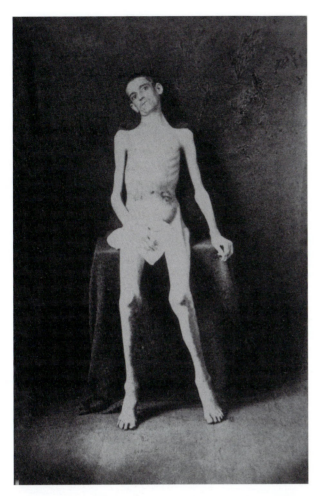

When the Confederates began releasing sick and dying prisoners in 1864, Northern caretakers immediately summoned photographers to document their emaciated condition, including the unfortunate man shown here. The images infuriated Southerners, who believed the goodwill gesture was being exploited. The photos "are designed to inflame the evil passions of the North; to keep up the war spirit among their own people; to represent the South as acting under the dominion of a spirit of cruelty, inhumanity, and interested malice, and thus to vilify her people in the eyes of all on whom these publications can work," a joint committee of the Confederate Congress complained. (Library of Congress)

had done at Lincoln's second inaugural. For the hanging, they equipped themselves with two cameras, a stereoscopic camera and a large-plate camera, and exposed as many plates as they could during the hanging of Herold, Payne, George Atzerodt, and Mrs. Mary Surratt.[31]

That day the *Washington Star* reported:

> At 12 o'clock the click of a hammer was heard in the upper story of the old workshop of Penitentiary days, in the centre of the prison yard, and the eyes of all were turned in that direction. Presently a window was raised, and forthwith was seen protruding the familiar snout of the camera, showing that the inevitable photographer was on hand. Gardner's good-humored face presently was seen over the camera, as he took "a sight" at the gallows, to see that it was focused properly.[32]

One hour later, the condemned emerged and mounted the scaffold. In the next twenty minutes, Gardner and his assistants exposed four large plates and four stereo plates, recording almost moment by moment the sequence of events: their arrival, the reading of the death warrant, the adjustment of the nooses, and, finally, a 3-D photo titled "The Drop" that showed the blurred bodies swinging at the end of their ropes. Without question, these were the most dramatic photographs to emerge from the assassination and its aftereffects, and Gardner took full advantage, selling folio prints on imprinted mounts, *cartes de visite*, and stereo views.[33]

On November 10, Capt. Henry Wirz, commandant of Andersonville prison, was executed at Old Capitol Prison in Washington. Gardner had exclusive access to this hanging as well, and he again took a series of photographs of the execution, some with the U.S. Capitol building looming in the background. Afterwards, Gardner photographed the Wirz autopsy; this time, however, the photograph survived. The Wirz hanging assuaged some of the outrage over Andersonville that spread through the North in part because of the photographs taken of the returning prisoners, who appeared barely able to support their emaciated bodies to sit and pose for the camera.

The indignation in the North fueled an equally virulent reaction in the South.[34]

A joint committee of the Confederate Congress bitterly complained about photographs taken of Union prisoners, who were released as part of a humanitarian exchange, as being unrepresentative of the general prisoner population.

> Men in the last stages of emaciation, suffering not only with excessive debility, but with "nostalgia," or homesickness, whose cases were regarded as desperate, and who could not live if they remained. . . . Yet these are the cases which, with hideous violation of decency, the Northern committee have paraded in pictures and photographs. They have taken their own sick and enfeebled soldiers; have stripped them naked; have exposed them before a daguerreian apparatus; have pictured every shrunken limb and muscle—and all for the purpose, not of relieving their sufferings, but of bringing a false and slanderous charge against the South.

In these images and others taken at the end of the war, photography touched nerves and stirred passions more deeply and in more ways than ever before.[35]

11

THE YEARS AFTER THE WAR

The war was finally over, and though it had been profitable for photographers, they welcomed the return to unrestricted business and commerce. "As fast as communication can be opened by mail, we shall send greeting to our old friends," the *American Journal of Photography* announced on April 15, 1865, having lost a third of its subscribers after the fall of Fort Sumter. "The insane rebellion . . . has received its mortal wound. We are in the dawn of a new era of peace and progress."[1]

In Shepherdstown, West Virginia, ex-Confederate Major Henry Kyd Douglas, who had served on Stonewall Jackson's staff, doubtless would not have shared that same sentiment after he made the mistake of visiting Thomas Darnell's gallery with a female friend on May 5, 1865, to have photographs taken in his Confederate uniform. Douglas had arrived wearing a civilian coat and his uniform pants, but he walked back to his hotel room in full uniform, complete with a star on his collar. The next morning, a Federal cavalry company pounded into town with a gaudy show of force, raided the photo gallery, confiscated the negatives, and hauled Douglas off to solitary confinement at nearby Martinsburg.[2]

The yearning for a photographic keepsake led to criminal charges against Douglas, and he became the only Confederate tried for treason after the war was over. He was charged not for being photographed in uniform but for wearing the Rebel gray on the street afterward. Douglas explained in his defense that he had departed from the gallery in uniform only because "after the negative was taken, the room and antechambers was so occupied by ladies as to make it impractible [*sic*] and indelicate for me to change my dress."[3]

Five days after his offense, Douglas went on trial before a three-member military commission. "Seldom even in these strange times has so small an act been so grossly misconstrued; so light an offense so greatly exaggerated; so trivial a fault so grievously answerable," Douglas wrote in a statement to the court. He was acquitted of treason, but convicted of violating military orders. His two-month sentence at the military prison at Fort Delaware on Pea Patch Island in the middle of Delaware Bay was, Douglas said, more like a two-month summer vacation at a summer resort. He was one of only two prisoners and was granted all the liberty he desired.[4]

This previously unpublished Royan Linn stereo view (*at top*) shows the interior of the Linn studio at Gallery Point Lookout atop Lookout Mountain, with photographs on display on the back wall, some including Civil War officers and soldiers posing at the point. The second image, a panorama from two stereo half-negatives, shows Linn's gallery and the point. (*Stereo view*: from the collection of Jeffrey Kraus; *panorama*: from the collection of George S. Whiteley IV)

Facing page: Photographer Richard Wearn of Columbia, South Carolina, was among the very few Southern photographers who took pictures throughout the war. Temporarily sidelined when Columbia (and his studio) burned in February 1865, Wearn saved his equipment and used his camera in the spring or summer of 1865 to record nineteen *cartes de visite* of the damage. The first image shows Wearn with his portable developing outfit in front of the remains of the Palmetto Armory. The second shows Main Street of gutted Columbia, looking south from the front of the State House. (Courtesy of the South Caroliniana Library, University of South Carolina, Columbia)

In Charleston, South Carolina, the photographic gallery of George S. Cook came back to life on August 12, 1865, after apparently being closed for more than a year. No hard documentation exists to establish precisely when Cook had to close his doors and flee the chaos of the bombardment, but his 1863–1864 account book does provide some information.

Cook had fared better than most Southerners during the war's first thirty-six months, taking in more income than ever before during his career. Despite the bombardment and the ravages of the ever-increasing inflation of Confederate paper money, Cook's business was thriving until at least March 8, 1864, the final business day recorded in his 1863–1864 account book. That happened to be the day when Cook reached the last blank page in his account book, and he filled it quickly. Twenty-one customers came through the gallery doors on that busy Tuesday, purchasing thirty-seven images in four different formats and spending a total of $360.50. Cook noted the usual requests: some customers wanted cases, some didn't. Many wanted their pictures hand-tinted, and Cook knew that his tinting artist, a man named Mathias, would be busy.

It must be assumed that business continued uninterrupted the following day and for some time afterward and that Cook opened a new account book to record the entries for March 9 and all subsequent dates. If so, that book is missing. The 1863–1864 account book, however, includes not only daily customer entries but records of investments and expenses. Cook continued recording his expenses in this book until the end of March 1864. On March 19 and 26, he noted the payment of a weekly salary of $75 to his assistant, "Wilson," thus documenting that his gallery was open at least until the end of the month.[5]

At some point, Cook may have moved his gallery out of the range of the Union guns. The expense records in Cook's 1863–1864 book show that on January 7, 1864, Cook paid his landlord $137.50 to cover his rent in full and noted:

"2 months not chgd." Cook also wrote an additional notation: "Room given up." If Cook did give up his room, however, it does not appear to have happened on or about January 7, because his daily customer log shows no disruption of business around that date. Furthermore, during the following week, Cook noted "shelling" on three consecutive days, suggesting he was still in the line of fire at his King Street gallery. There is also no indication where Cook might have moved.

The account book, so precise and comprehensive as a business chronicle, leaves the story of Cook's final days in Charleston shrouded in mystery. When did he finally have to close his gallery's doors? When did he flee the city? These questions cannot be answered with the information available today. It is possible, however, that he remained in Charleston through much of 1864. As mentioned previously, Cook was sighted in the city as late as October 1864. He also continued recording dividends and interest payments in his account book through late 1864, with notations in September, October, and November.

The Confederate States of America might have been coming apart at the seams in late 1864, but Cook was still reaping the rewards of his canny wartime decision to invest in blockade runners. On September 10, 1864, he recorded the receipt of $500 as a dividend on one share of "Cobia" stock (Henry Cobia was a Charleston merchant). And on November 29, 1864, Cook recorded the receipt of $8,000 as a "dividend on 10 shares of Chicora stock." The fact that this is the largest amount of money recorded in any single entry in all of Cook's wartime account books is tinged with the irony that this is the last business transaction Cook is known to have recorded during the Civil War.[6]

Some time in 1864, according to several works, Cook closed his business, fled Charleston, and relocated in Columbia, assuming that Gen. William Tecumseh Sherman's ever-advancing army would target the "Cradle of Secession" and move on Charleston. Sherman, however, bypassed the coast and occupied Columbia on February 17.

The steep-gabled home of Charleston photographer George S. Cook appears as the center of the three homes in this April 1865 photograph taken on South Bay (now South Battery) in Charleston. The mansion at right served as the headquarters of Union Gen. John P. Hatch after the city fell. All three homes are draped in black mourning cloth in the wake of Lincoln's assassination, and Cook's home is shuttered and apparently vacant, awaiting the return of its owner. These homes were undamaged in the bombardment, but others further down the Battery were destroyed. (Library of Congress)

That night, in what E. B. Long calls "the epic depredation of the war," the capital city of South Carolina burned. The flames are said to have consumed Cook's temporary studio in Columbia and destroyed his thousands of photographic negatives. Unfortunately, no hard documentation exists to establish exactly what happened to one of the most extensive negative collections ever created of Southern Civil War personages.[7]

Whether Cook's negatives cracked and melted in the flames of Columbia or whether they were destroyed in some other calamity, nearly all of them were indeed destroyed. This loss is revealed with stark certitude to anyone who examines the Cook Collection of photographs and negatives at the Valentine Richmond History Center. The researcher assumes otherwise at first, be-cause the Cook Collection negative catalog lists a stunning collection of 563 portraits of Confederate generals, officers, and other notables, seemingly the very essence of Cook's studio work. An examination of the images themselves discloses the sad truth: each and every one is a copy negative from another negative or an albumen print, and most of the images are the work of others, leaving only a handful of copy negatives from Cook's own *carte de visite* prints. That Cook went to such great lengths to resurrect a comprehensive negative collection of Confederate notables indicates how profoundly affected he was by the loss of his own portrait negatives. Cook's most notable portraits, those of Maj. Robert Anderson and his officers, were gone, too. Twenty years after the war, the Anderson image was still in demand, and Cook filled that demand. But the circa 1880s cabinet card that he sold with his imprint was affixed with a copy print of a pathetic-looking original albumen print, so wrinkled it appeared to have been retrieved from a waste can after having been wadded up and thrown away. Apparently, it was the only remaining print of Anderson that Cook had.[8]

Fortunately, not all was lost. The original negatives of several dozen of Cook's most important Civil War photographs survive at the Valentine. Among them are thirteen negatives from Castle Pinckney in 1862 and the thirteen negatives taken on September 8, 1863, at Fort Sumter, including the combat action images of the Federal ironclads affixed side by side on a separate glass plate for the convenient printing of stereoscopic views. The likely explanation for the survival of Cook's most important negatives from the field is that he considered them so valuable he kept them among his personal possessions and apart from his vast collection of commercial portrait negatives.[9]

Though he lost his portrait negatives and probably most of his equipment to the ravages of war, Cook retained a good bit of his wealth. His house on the battery survived the bombardment with little or no damage. In May 1865, Cook was able to send his seventeen-year-old son, George LaGrange Cook, north to Newark, New Jersey. The son's diary documents that his father joined him and other family members in New Jersey in mid-August 1865. Apparently this happened immediately after Cook arranged with an assistant to reopen his Charleston studio on August 12, 1865. Lacking a proper blank ledger book, Cook's assistant used a blank "Sunday-School Receiving Book" attendance log from the 1840s for recording the daily parade of customers. He logged three customers and $7.50 in sales on that August 12. The gallery struggled at first, and it took a full week before enough customers came in to fill a single page of the new account book. The entire month of September 1865 yielded $282.50 in gross receipts—far less

than the $360.50 (in inflated Confederate dollars) that Cook had grossed on that single day of March 8, 1864, when his previous account book came to an end.[10]

By mid-October, Cook and his children were back in Charleston, and Cook had returned to work at the gallery, his familiar handwriting once again filling the pages of the account book. Though most sales continued to be studio portraits of civilians, each month's list of customers that autumn included the names of a dozen or more Union officers. The account book also documents nineteen transactions for war photographs during the final four months of 1865, including five sales of Cook's 1863 Fort Sumter views. Business was picking up—November gross receipts totaled $901—and part of the boost was coming from the continuing demand for Civil War photographs.[11]

The notion that the public's interest in Civil War photographs dwindled at the end of the war because people were tired of the bad news has no basis in fact. The public's interest in war photographs, both gruesome and bucolic, remained strong after the war. Sales of Civil War photographs, particularly stereo views, probably did not even peak until *after* the war was over. Gen. Ulysses S. Grant was in greater demand than ever among photographers and was sought out for sittings in every city he visited. In May came the excitement of the Grand Review of the Union armies; June brought the dedication of the first battlefield monument at Bull Run; and July's hot sun saw the Lincoln conspirators swinging from the gallows. It was a heady time, and photographers responded, offering the North souvenirs of the great Union triumph.[12]

During the summer of 1865, E. & H. T. Anthony & Company began advertising and selling its ambitious "Photographic History: The War for the Union" series of stereoscopic views, forging ahead despite the annoying federal "sun tax." On July 6, 1865, the Anthony Company advertised the new stereo series in the inaugural issue of the magazine, *The Nation*. Five issues later, the Anthonys doubled the size of the ad and continued running it through the rest of the year.[13]

"The War for the Union" series appears to have been quite successful. The Anthonys marketed the views for eight years, publishing two distinct editions: the first, beginning in 1865, on yellow mounts and the second, in the late 1860s, on orange. The later, orange-mount views seem to be as common, if not more common, than yellow-mount views, indicating that views from the second edition probably sold as well as the first and that the popularity of the series continued through the 1860s and possibly into the early 1870s. Today, more original Anthony "The War for the Union" stereo view cards appear for sale on Internet auction sites and at Civil War and antique photo shows than any other type of Civil War stereo view.[14]

The Anthony Company's pricing structure for the series further suggests that the views continued to find buyers long after the war was over. When they were first issued in 1865, "The War for the Union" views were among the most expensive stereo cards in the Anthony catalog, selling at $5 a dozen ($7 a dozen for hand-colored versions). Most other views in the 1865 catalog were $3 a dozen, including all of the instantaneous views. That premium price of $5 a dozen for war views did not change for three years. In 1868, as part of a 50-cent, across-the-board price cut for Anthony stereos, "The War for the Union" views were reduced to $4.50 a dozen, and most other views dropped to $2.50 a dozen. The following year, the series fell to $4 a dozen, while prices on most other views remained the same. Ultimately, an undated Anthony catalog, either from 1870 or 1871, advertised the series at $3.50 a dozen. Apparently, after the financial depression of 1873, the Anthony Company finally lost its market for war views and put the negatives in storage.[15]

Alexander Gardner also continued selling stereo views and large photographs. Some of the images he took in Richmond in April 1865 were labeled with a new title: "Memories of the War."

Gardner, however, did not use the Anthony Company as his wholesale agent for his 1865 photographs, as he had with most of the stereo views in his extensive "Photographic Incidents of the War" series. Instead, Gardner used the Washington publishing company of Philp & Solomons as the exclusive publisher and wholesale agent, and it cost him dearly. Whereas the Anthony views sold briskly, Gardner's "Memories" and his other 1865 views sat on the shelves, if they ever even reached the booksellers and photo galleries that marketed stereo views. Copies from the "Memories" series are rare, appearing today at a fraction of the frequency of Gardner's "Incidents."[16]

Gardner devoted much time in 1865 and 1866 to the creation and production of his Civil War photography masterwork, the elaborate and expensive, two-volume *Gardner's Photographic Sketch Book of the War.* From his vast inventory of some 1,000 large-plate negatives, Gardner selected one hundred of the best, including "Lincoln at Antietam," "A Harvest of Death" and "A Sharpshooter's Last Sleep" at Gettysburg, and "A Burial Party on the Battlefield of Cold Harbor." Every image in each book was a custom-printed, seven-by-nine-inch, albumen print glued to paper almost as thick as *carte de visite* card stock. The thickness of the pages limited each volume to fifty images.[17]

Gardner wrote the following in the introduction:

As mementoes of the fearful struggle through which the country has just passed, it is confidently hoped that the following pages will possess an enduring interest. . . . Localities that would scarcely have been known, and probably never remembered, save in their immediate vicinity, have become celebrated. . . . Verbal representations of such places, or scenes, may or may not have the merit of accuracy; but photographic presentments of them will be accepted by posterity with an undoubting faith.[18]

Each photograph was accompanied by a facing page of descriptive text by Gardner, who was obviously enamored with the flowery language popular at the time. Gardner wrote his most extensive discourse about the war in the *Sketch Book*, but his writing focused on the war itself and offered few insights into his photographic work. Through Philp & Solomons, Gardner published 200 *Sketch Books*. The relatively small number has been cited to support the myth that Civil War photos did not sell after the war. In fact, the *Sketch Book* price of $150 (the equivalent of about $2,000 in 2005 dollars) was out of the reach of nearly everyone but the wealthy, and the book was offered by subscription only. The $150 price tag "may seem a large price for a book; but it is put within very reasonable limits for such a work as this," reported the *Philadelphia Press*. "The price comes to $1.50 for each mere photograph—mounting, letter-press, lithographed title-pages, and rich binding, being thrown in for nothing. Thus, this really is a remarkably low-priced work." Among Gardner's first customers was Quartermaster General Montgomery C. Meigs, who received the two-volume set for his approval on March 6, 1866, and two days later approved payment to the publisher.[19]

On March 7, 1866, photographer George Barnard penned a letter to Gen. Orlando Poe, his boss during the war, and described his desire to produce what would become Barnard's answer to Gardner's *Sketch Book*, a one-volume book with sixty-one albumen prints and titled *Photographic Views of Sherman's Campaign*:

I am just now thinking of getting up a set of Photographic views illustrating Gen. Sherman's operations and Grand March through Ga. commencing at Chattanooga . . . [but] I would also like your advice in the matter. . . . To make it a profitable matter, I will want one hundred subscribers but I will commence the work with fifty.

Barnard said he would need to revisit some of the more notable locations in Chattanooga and Georgia to make a complete photographic record of the campaign. All of the images, both new and wartime, would be from the huge twelve-by-fifteen-inch negatives from his largest cam-

era. They would be more than twice the size of Gardner's *Sketch Book* prints.[20]

Poe responded enthusiastically, and Sherman endorsed the project as well. On April 3, working through the Anthony Company, Barnard had a formal prospectus printed for potential subscribers. A few days later he left for Tennessee with assistant James W. Campbell, and they spent the next two months retracing Sherman's campaign and taking more photographs. By the end of July, he was back in New York.

Barnard wrote to Poe on July 29:

I have got nearly half done printing the one hundred copies and will continue to print until I get another hundred off. The first lot is nearly all spoken for and there [are] many that do not know that I am getting it up. I know [they] will want copies.[21]

It is unknown whether Barnard printed and sold all 200 copies he spoke of, or whether he stopped at 100 or at a number in between. If he needed 50 to break even and sold 100, Barnard obviously made a tidy profit for himself and for the ever-opportunistic Anthony, who seems to have helped Barnard produce and distribute the book. Barnard's super-size, parlor table masterpiece was bestowed with the same enthusiastic reviews Gardner's *Sketch Book* received, but when Barnard's book was placed beside Gardner's, it was like looking, in today's world, at high-definition versus regular television. Not only were Barnard's prints more than twice as large as Gardner's, they were also crisper, clearer, and more vivid in contrast. Both photographers printed on albumen paper, but the tones in Barnard's prints were far closer to black and white than Gardner's, whose prints had the sepia tones more commonly seen in wartime albumen prints. Barnard's prints had another feature that made them almost breathtaking—skies filled with big, puffy, sun-drenched, cumulus clouds that imbued the atmosphere with a visual acuity, making the landscapes more striking than ever.

Clouds were not visible in most wet plate negatives because the proper exposure needed for

This view of Confederate fortifications at the end of Peachtree Street in Atlanta, with the heavily damaged Ponder family mansion at right center, is one of the classic images by George Barnard in his *Photographic Views of Sherman's Campaign*. The image is one of the more vivid examples of Barnard's technique of double-printing each print, adding sun-bathed clouds to what would have printed as an otherwise plain sky. (From the collection of George S. Whiteley IV)

the landscape usually overexposed the sky. Barnard, however, made a number of separate plates of the cloud-filled skies over Georgia during his 1866 trip, and then double-printed about twenty of the sixty prints in each book, sun-printing the landscape and the clouds at separate times. He had to mask the negatives with precision to achieve a clean horizon line and carefully monitor the printing processes to achieve tonal consistency in the two separate printing sessions. Barnard used his cloud negatives interchangeably, but only through a careful examination of different copies of Barnard's book can an observer notice that the same array of clouds in the sunlit sky over Nashville in one copy of the book might appear over Atlanta in another copy.[22]

In terms of presenting actual Civil War photographs, Barnard's work was less authentic than Gardner's *Sketch Book*. Photohistorian Harvey S. Teal has noted, "Of the sixty-one photographs included in Barnard's 1866 book, only fourteen were clearly documented as being produced during the Civil War," while another eleven were produced in either 1864 or 1866. Whereas less than 40 percent of Barnard's images were taken during the war itself, more than 75 percent of Gardner's images (at least 77 of 100) were taken before hostilities ceased, and none later than June 1865.[23]

The books of war photographs produced by Gardner and Barnard were, in essence, their own memoirs of the conflict. Each was their own Grand Review—their way of encapsulating the essence of their wartime careers in a single, cohesive work, capping the greatest adventure of their lives. Gardner's *Sketch Book*, with the image of "Lincoln at Antietam" and the highly prized Gettysburg images, is today worth at least $100,000, and Barnard's book would easily command $50,000 or more. Only a few intact copies of either book still exist. The bindings for their heavy pages could not stand much wear. As copies of the books fell apart, they were entirely disassembled so prints could be sold individually. Today, a single print from either book often commands $1,000 and up, but lesser known, original albumen prints from the *Sketch Book*—each nonetheless a 140-year-old, antique photographic print created by the sun through direct contact with the original glass plate negative—still sell on occasion for $200 to $300, which is about the same price as a mass-produced lithograph crafted by a modern Civil War artist.[24]

For some photographers, the Civil War had not been adventure enough. Timothy O'Sullivan, Alexander Gardner, and Andrew J. Russell, among others, still felt the spirit in their feet and headed West to visually document America's great frontier expansion. Some of O'Sullivan's most memorable images come from Virginia City, Nevada, in 1868, where he descended into the silver mines to capture some of the first photographs using artificial light. Holding a piece of burning magnesium, O'Sullivan bathed the dank mineshafts with a hot light that illuminated the craggy faces of the miners as he exposed each plate. Gardner made several trips West, recording history with his camera at every opportunity. None of his Western images would be more important and historic than the images of Native Americans taken in the field and in his studio. Arguably, the greatest triumph of all were the photographs taken by Russell on May 10, 1869, at Promontory Point, Utah, when the eastern and western rail crews met to drive the final "golden" spike, completing the transcontinental railroad.[25]

Life went on for Civil War photographers, and the war became an ever-receding memory, whether they were traipsing through the West or staying close to home. Charleston may have been shot full of holes, but its charm, albeit a bit bedraggled, still seduced Barnard and Coonley. The latter photographer worked there in 1867 and 1868 as the manager of the gallery belonging to longtime Charleston photographer Charles J. Quinby. Barnard had visited with his camera in the spring of 1865 and had moved to Charleston in 1868 to become partners with Quinby. Barnard's

Lee's Headquarters, at the Junction of Plank Road and Wilford's Furnace Road.

On the Plank Road in the woods around Chancellorsville, Union veterans study a map near the site of the headquarters of Robert E. Lee during the May 1863 battle. This image was taken in the mid-1880s by an experienced but unknown photographer who returned to the sites of his wartime adventures with fellow veterans and family.

South Carolina connection lasted, with few breaks, until 1880. The most significant interruption came in 1871, when he moved to Chicago at the urging of his family. It was an unfortunate choice; the city's Great Fire in October 1871 wiped out his new gallery. As Barnard and an assistant endeavored to rescue his equipment, the relentless flames are said to have driven them eastward toward Lake Michigan and finally into the cold water itself, where they stood holding the most valuable lenses and cameras above the waterline as they watched the city burn. Barnard quickly replaced lost supplies and was one of many photographers to produce stereo views

of the ruins. He returned to Charleston in mid-1873, opened a gallery on King Street, and produced many photographs and stereo views, but he lost everything to another fire in 1875. Undaunted, he rebuilt and reopened his business. In 1880, at age sixty, Barnard left Charleston and once again moved North, this time to a suburb of Rochester, New York. After a photography career of more than forty years, Barnard retired in 1888.[26]

George S. Cook, meanwhile, remained in business in Charleston until 1880, when he saw greater potential for prosperity in Richmond and established a studio there, leaving the Charleston

Scene of the charge by the Eighth Penna. Cavalry, near Hazel Grove.

This striking image from the Chancellorsville battlefield was taken in the 1880s by the same photographer who took the image on the preceding page. Here, one veteran poses with his young family at the scene of a desperate charge by the 8th Pennsylvania Cavalry on May 2, 1862, against the main column of Stonewall Jackson's corps, which occurred at a loss of thirty men and eighty horses.

gallery under the charge of his son George LaGrange Cook. Ten years later, the Cooks closed the Charleston establishment, and George L. joined his father in the former Confederate capital, allowing the elder Cook to go into semi-retirement.[27]

Brady, after hiring James Gibson as his Washington gallery manager in 1863, sold half of the studio to him in 1864, hoping the veteran photographer would turn the business around. Instead, it went under around 1867, and Brady and Gibson blamed each other. Brady declared bankruptcy and repurchased his Washington business in July 1868 for $7,600. By 1873, the capital gallery was thriving again under a new manager, Andrew Burgess, but Brady was declared bankrupt in New York. Before the authorities could act on the judgment, Brady conspired with City of New York Sheriff Matthew T. Brennan, a leader of the corrupt Democratic city's "Tammany Hall" and an ally of William Marcy "Boss" Tweed, to remove nineteen cartloads of equipment, supplies, and goods from his New York gallery. Brady had them shipped to Washington. He then moved there permanently in 1873. More financial problems forced Brady to close his own gallery for good in 1881, but the grand old man of American photography continued taking pictures for others, including his nephew, Levin C. Handy, into the 1890s.[28]

Edward Anthony remained behind his desk in New York, constantly extending the tentacles of a company that he and his brother had built into the largest, most profitable photographic business in the country. In the early 1870s, as the company's stereo view business waned, Anthony turned his attention to building a publishing powerhouse that ultimately produced nearly every significant American book on photography for the next thirty years. The company also began developing and marketing a wide array of studio furniture. The Anthony camera and supply business thrived as well, and the company prided itself on its frequent innovations with camera shutters, lenses, accessories, and other supplies. No employee was more valued as an inventor and creator of new products than Civil War photographer T. C. Roche. In the years after the war, Roche obtained numerous patents for his innovations and helped the Anthony Company stay on top as the industry began to focus on pre-prepared, dry-plate technology and to market to the burgeoning numbers of amateur photographers. Roche had also continued as an Anthony photographer after the war, traveling West for the company in 1870 and 1871 to shoot stereo photographs of the Yosemite Valley. By 1884, the Anthonys were no longer making or selling stereo views, but Roche had become so valuable to them as a creator of new technology that they honored him with a sumptuous banquet, where he was given elaborate tributes and a gold watch. Roche continued to work and that same year invented a new enlarging camera for his employers.[29]

Time took its toll, and on January 14, 1882, Timothy O'Sullivan, the youngest of the great war photographers, succumbed to tuberculosis and died at age forty-two. Gardner, the Scotsman for all seasons, retired from photography in 1879 to devote his life to philanthropy. When he died on December 10, 1882, at age sixty-one, after

During an attack on Confederate lines outside Petersburg, Virginia, on June 18, 1864, Private Alfred A. Stratton of the 147th New York Volunteers was struck by a solid shot that shattered his arms, both of which were amputated above the elbows. Stratton eventually recovered and worked at the Treasury Department in Washington, possibly as a watchman. Stratton, who died in 1874 from pulmonary complications from his wounds, was photographed by several commercial photographers and personally sold copies of his images. This *carte de visite* was by Fredericks & Co. of New York.

an illness of about two weeks, the *Philadelphia Photographer* said, "He was one of our veterans—one of photography's staunchest friends."[30]

Henry T. Anthony's life came to an end at age seventy-one in October 1884, a few days after he was run down by a passing wagon on a busy

New York Street. Business at the Anthony Company continued, of course, and when Edward Anthony died of heart failure at age sixty-nine on December 14, 1888, the company he had founded was still the leading photography company in the United States; yet, even that was changing. Around 1880, the shrewd Anthony had seen promise in the dry plate glass negatives created by an enterprising, twenty-six-year-old Rochester bookkeeper, George Eastman, and he had given the young man his big break by agreeing to market Eastman's plate. Soon Eastman started his own company and became a spirited competitor. In 1889, the year after Edward Anthony died, Eastman began to market his inexpensive, handheld, "Kodak" camera, selling 13,000 in less than nine months. That same year, one of Eastman's chemists developed flexible film. The die was thus cast for a new leader in the American photography business. Though the change happened over the course of many years, just as the nineteenth century had been dominated by E. & H. T. Anthony & Company, the American photographic giant of the twentieth century was the Eastman Kodak Company.[31]

Of the old-time daguerreians who became leading Civil War photographers, only Barnard and Cook lived to see the twentieth century. Brady died in 1896, a year after having an accident similar to Henry Anthony's, when he was struck by a horse car on a Washington street and received a broken leg. Chronically fraught with financial woes, Brady spent much of his later life living in memories, clinging to the legacy of his Civil War accomplishments and wearing his past as his persona like an old general wears his medals. "They all came to me, and I can see them in my mind's eye, like a procession of ghosts, passing in review," Brady told a newspaper reporter a few years before his death, recalling the hundreds of celebrities who had sat for his camera. To Washington stenographer Lydia Mantle Fox, Brady was "the sad little man" who haunted the Riggs Hotel office where she provided services for Congressmen who had no staff of their own. Brady would bitterly complain of his misfortunes, or in his better moods mesmerize her with the stories of his past. Occasionally he would beg her to prepare petitions to congressmen in his never-ending campaign to promote his war photographs. Six years after Brady's passing, Barnard died in February 1902 in Syracuse, New York. Ten months later, Cook breathed his last in Richmond, perhaps comforted that the venerable Southern photographic studio he started in those lazy antebellum days in Charleston, and which was operated by his two sons, George and Huestis, was still a thriving business in Richmond. If Cook had been able or so inclined, one can only wonder what his final entry would have been in his meticulously kept account book.[32]

12

THE JOURNEY OF THE NEGATIVES

As the adventures of America's photographic pioneers faded into the past, the story of their legacy began. It is a story fraught with drama and mystery and populated with characters of every stripe—all with their own motives— all united in a single belief that something important happened, both in front of the camera lens and behind the viewfinder, on those American battlefields.

That single belief aside, not all of the motives were as altruistic as we might hope. There was, of course, the desire for riches, or as in M. B. Brady's case, the need to keep one's head above water. Brady, probably spurred as much by the need for money as by the urge to preserve history, was the first to solicit a public institution to buy his negatives. He tried without success, in 1866, to convince the New York Historical Society to purchase his collection. Next, he turned to the government. On February 17, 1869, Massachusetts Sen. Henry Wilson submitted a petition on behalf of Brady asking Congress to appropriate money to purchase Brady's collection of war negatives. Though only four years had passed since the end of the war, "many of the prominent personages [were] dead," the petition argued.

The fortifications are in ruins, the bridges . . . have been destroyed, the picturesque military camps have been broken up, and the battlefields wear a changed appearance. The preservations of all this rich historical materials becomes, therefore, a matter of National importance. It is too precious to remain in the hands of any private citizen.[1]

Four days later, on February 21, Kansas Senator Samuel C. Pomeroy submitted a similar petition on behalf of Alexander Gardner—a petition Gardner had written in his own hand. The photographer noted that he possessed the only photographs from Antietam, Gettysburg, and Spotsylvania taken "immediately after the battle." Gardner said he had "always regarded them as having a National character and has long indulged the hope that they would someday belong to the Nation. They [were] beyond the reach of private enterprise in both their value and importance."[2]

Much has been made of Gardner's statement that he "conceived the idea" to photograph the war versus Brady's assertion that he "organized, at great expense, an efficient corps of Artists for the production of photographic views." The argument is that the statements reflect each

The presence of Alexander Gardner's portable photographic wagon at right center is unmistakable in this detail from Gardner's stereoscopic negative of Main Street in Sharpsburg, Maryland, near the Antietam battlefield. Hanging from the rear of the wagon is the long tarp that the operator used to seal himself into a sunlight-proof environment in the back of the wagon to prepare and develop plates. A different wagon in other Antietam images, which has also been identified as Gardner's photo wagon, may be a second photo wagon or a supply wagon. (Library of Congress)

man's desire to claim that he alone came up with the idea of photographing the war. Aside from the fact that the two assertions are not really in conflict, the argument is spurious. Both men clearly had seminal roles in the photography of the war, along with many other photographers. The notion that one photographer alone had an epiphany is unreasoned.

Congress took no action on either petition. Gardner apparently did not pursue the matter further, but Brady could not afford to be complacent. Though a congressional committee in 1871 recommended the purchase of 2,000 Brady portrait negatives, again no action was taken. In 1874, a New York warehouse owner sold Brady's stored property at public auction, including some 2,250 Civil War negatives. An agent for Secretary of War William W. Belknap purchased the negatives for $2,500, the cost of the unpaid storage bill.[3]

An enraged Brady accosted Belknap in a New York hotel and accused him of buying the collection out from under him at a fraction of its worth. Belknap defended his action but agreed to support Brady's effort to convince Congress, once and for all, to buy his collection. The House and Senate finally acceded, and in 1875 appropriated $25,000 to purchase the remainder of Brady's Civil War collection, which amounted to 3,467 negatives, consisting of portraits and about 750 war scenes. Ultimately, the government found itself in possession of 5,995 Brady negatives, most of them portraits. The keepers of Brady's legacy, however, reported the breakage of at least several hundred plates during the next twenty years. Damage occurred most often when the negatives were actively used to make prints and were sometimes mishandled. This collection of "Brady War Photographs" formed the backbone of the Civil War photographic negative collection that was kept for years at the War Department Library.

In 1897, the library published a single catalog of all of its images, combining into one large group the 5,876 negatives of the Brady collection and the more than 1,000 images from the Quartermaster's Department, which represented the core of Russell's images and those of other government contract photographers. This included approximately fifty Barnard negatives from Atlanta (the photographer was allowed to keep a portion of his plates, now presumably lost), several hundred other miscellaneous images, and 153 stereoscopic view cards by Sam Cooley. In time, all of the images in this group came to be known, at least informally, as Brady photographs, and the mischaracterization of his role and influence in Civil War photography grew. In 1940, the National Archives took possession of this collection, and today it is kept at Archives II in College Park, Maryland.[4]

Gardner's more than 2,000 wartime negatives and over 1,100 negatives from Anthony's huge "The War for the Union" stereoscopic series had a more adventurous ride before being preserved by the federal government. John C. Taylor, a war veteran and commander of the Grand Army of the Republic chapter in Hartford, Connecticut, was drawn to the photographs of the war and sought to learn more about them, find them, and preserve them. His interest was no doubt heightened after meeting Brady several times. The old photographer once told him dramatically, "No one will ever know what I went through in securing those negatives. The world can never appreciate it. It changed the whole course of my life."[5]

Around 1879, Taylor found about 7,000 negatives being "stored in an old garret" maintained by the Anthony Company, along with a huge cache of leftover Anthony orange-mount stereo view cards. The collection apparently included all of Gardner's negatives from the field, "The War for the Union" negatives, and several thousand portrait negatives. (It is unknown how and when Gardner's negatives came to be grouped with the Anthony "War for the Union" negatives.) Taylor purchased all rights to the view cards and began selling them, pasting his own label on the reverse of each card. As for the negatives, he arranged for their purchase by Gen. Albert Ordway and Col. Arnold Rand on behalf of the Massachusetts command of the Military Order of the Loyal Legion of the United States (MOLLUS), a Civil War officers' veteran organization. Ordway and Rand had started collecting wartime photographs before the war ended, and they soon came to believe it was one of the most important tasks of their organization. With Ordway in Washington and Rand in Massachusetts, they began scouring the country, North and South, for images of officers, both Union and Confederate, as well as scenes taken in the field. Clearly, Taylor's find was their greatest coup.[6]

Beginning in 1882, the two veterans began assembling albums of Civil War photographic prints. They also actively encouraged other MOLLUS units, or "commanderies" to assemble their own collections by custom-ordering volumes from them. Ordway and Rand furnished a detailed catalog of available images from their negative collection, retaining the numbering systems used by Gardner and Anthony. Several other commanderies agreed to assemble collections, including those in Philadelphia, New York, and elsewhere.[7]

Ordway and Rand, however, took several hamhanded steps that undercut the quality of their core collection—the albums of prints. As they assembled the albums, they added pictures so haphazardly that one can only conclude they pasted new images onto the pages in the order in which the images arrived in the mail, giving no thought whatsoever to a cohesive presentation. The sole key to making any sense of the collection, which eventually filled 135 albums, was their index card catalog of subjects and

War veteran and sketch artist James E. Taylor of New York City sits among his vast collection of relics, which included three scrapbooks of Civil War photographs, in this circa 1880s photograph. Taylor was an enthusiastic and effective locator of photographs for Gen. Albert Ordway as Ordway assembled the vast collection of Civil War images in the 1880s under the auspices of the Massachusetts commandery of the Military Order of the Loyal Legion of the United States (MOLLUS). (Courtesy of the West Point Museum)

persons, which fortunately survives today. When they received *cartes de visite* as outright gifts, they separated the prints from the cards (by soaking them in water), pasted the albumens into their albums, and discarded the cards, thus destroying any record of who took the image. In instances where they made a copy negative of a loaned *carte de visite* before returning it to its owner, Ordway and Rand likewise did not record the original photographer's name. They also cannibalized virtually all stereo views they received into half stereos, banishing the magic of the 3-D image from their collection. W. F. Porter was one of several Ordway correspondents who objected. He complained, "I was of the opinion that they were to be mounted as regular stereoscopic views. . . . I think it brings out the pictures much better. . . . I much prefer the stereoscopic views."[8]

Ordway's letter file from 1885 and 1886 reveals a lively correspondence from a wide array of Civil War photography enthusiasts. The son of the late Gen. George Meade was an avid collector who ordered a number of photographs. Like so many others, he was captivated by the Andersonville photographs by A. J. Riddle. "They are specially interesting," he wrote to Ordway.[9]

Ordway had a number of photograph "pickers," or searchers, beating the bushes for rare images, including one collector, W. P. Hopkins, who had developed a thick skin for rejection. Hopkins wrote on January 31, 1886, "You may be sure I am looking for what cannot be had. I have been in this hunting business more than twenty years [and] have had many refusals to comply with my wishes." One of Ordway's most enthusiastic and successful searchers was James E. Taylor, a former Union soldier and wartime sketch artist (not related to the aforementioned John C. Taylor). Taylor found many photographs for Ordway and Rand. At the same time, he assembled three personal scrapbooks of war images and clips. These scrapbooks, preserved at the Huntington Library in San Marino, California, are filled with half-stereo and larger images. More than a few of the photos, pasted onto the scrapbook pages, are extraordinarily obscure and rare, and some are possibly one-of-a-kind prints that do not appear in the MOLLUS collection.[10]

In handwriting so sloppy it belied him as an artist, Taylor gave the impression in one letter that A. J. Russell had not been particularly cooperative. "I accidentally stumbled over Capt. Russell today & he's coming up to see me. He did have a number of valuable negatives and prints, as he hinted to me years ago, but would not let me or any one see them—it may be that he has them yet!" No follow-up letter exists.[11]

While Ordway and Rand were still actively seeking new images, they also sought to convince the government to purchase the vast collection of original negatives. As they noted in their petition, "It is apparent that the Government's collection and our own are each incom-

plete" without each other. Indeed, almost no duplication existed between the negatives the government already owned, including the Brady collection, and the negatives owned by Ordway and Rand. The government, nevertheless, turned a blind eye.[12]

Failing in that effort, Ordway and Rand found a ready buyer in John C. Taylor, the veteran who had brought them the negatives in the first place. While selling the excess orange-mount stereo view cards from the same cache, Taylor had discovered that an eager market once again existed for Civil War stereo views. The veterans of the war, reaching middle age, had embraced their past with a passion, and memorials were being erected at battlefields across the country and the town squares throughout the North and South. To expand his business, Taylor found a partner and around 1890 formed Taylor and Huntington (later the War Photograph and Exhibition Company) to produce its own select series of Civil War stereo views from the original negatives, and more. That year, their "War Memories" catalog offered a selection of 228 stereo views culled from the Gardner and Anthony negatives groups and 200 images from Gardner large-plate negatives. They devoted nearly half the catalog (eleven of twenty-four pages) to an ambitious, national marketing program for stereopticon slide shows of the war and museum exhibitions of prints. For $248, a deluxe "double outfit" consisted of two stereopticon projectors lit by gas or oil, as well as sixty-eight glass slides, black and white and colored, and even 2,000 admission tickets.[13]

Based on the frequency with which the various formats are encountered today, the stereo views sold well, the large-plate views not as well, and the stereopticon program was a complete failure. Taylor and Huntington glass slides are extremely rare, and large-plate views are scarce, but stereo views are common and appear almost as frequently as Anthony's "The War for the Union" views. Even the stereo views, however, were not as successful as expected. A large number of Taylor and Huntington cards in mint condition continue to be available on today's market. They represent, perhaps, as much as a quarter of the overall available pool. They were part of a large cache of unsold stock rediscovered in New England in the 1970s.[14]

In 1894, the Taylor and Huntington negative collection was used to produce the first photo-engraved book of Civil War photography, the *Memorial War Book.* The single volume's 610, gold-edged pages present about 2,000 photographs (though none in stereo) by "U.S. Government photographers, M. B. Brady and Alexander Gardner." Here, at least, Gardner's credits were equal to Brady's. The negatives then apparently went back into storage until Edward B. Eaton, president of *Connecticut Magazine,* became captivated by their historical significance. In 1906 or 1907, Eaton purchased the collection from Taylor, who apparently was only willing to sell with the stipulation that the images be made available once again to the public in published works. Eaton stored his collection, "valued at $150,000," in a fire-proof vault and began publishing the photos through Phelps Publishing Co. in Hartford. This time, however, whether or not the photograph was stereo or large-format, all of the images were published as single, non-stereo images. The actual legacy of the photographs became skewed in another way, too. Though Gardner's name was listed on the title page of Eaton's first published book of war photos, Brady's name predominated the text. By then, not only were the government's five thousand-plus negatives collectively known as the "Brady" photographs, but Eaton's collection, including all of Gardner's work, became "the 7,000 Brady negatives."[15]

Under Eaton's ownership, the negatives were used to help produce the groundbreaking, ten-volume *Photographic History of the Civil War,* published in 1911 on the fiftieth anniversary of the war, when interest once again peaked. The text was riddled with factual errors, and not a single image was presented in 3-D, but the series still reigns today as the greatest assemblage of Civil War photographs ever presented on the printed page.

Once again, interest waned, and the "Brady" negatives went back into storage. Eaton still owned them in 1934 when the *Hartford Courant* published a section-front feature about his collection, still safely stored in a fireproof vault. Eaton told the paper that owning and publishing the images had been the greatest event of his life. In 1942, the same year Eaton died, Thomas Norrell, a railroad history buff, stumbled across the negatives, still in storage, while looking through the Phelps Publishing archives for a daguerreotype of a locomotive known only from an engraving. Norrell notified the National Archives, which contacted the Library of Congress. On January 13, 1944, in the midst of World War II, the library finally saved the core collections of Civil War negatives taken in the field, paying Phelps Publishing Co. $6,900 for the entire lot, or about a dollar a negative. The Library of Congress initially incorporated the priceless photographic record into its archives as the "Brady Collection."[16]

Thus, ultimately, the largest and most comprehensive collections of Civil War negatives came to be saved for future generations. Many smaller collections were lost, such as the negatives by Osborn and Durbec, but prints survived. With all that was saved, breakage inevitably occurred over the years, even after the National Archives and Library of Congress took possession. One difference from the past, at least at the Library of Congress, was that, when a plate was broken, it was not thrown out but carefully preserved, with every shattered piece receiving its own archival sleeve.[17]

And what of the intriguing tales of the mass destruction of thousands of negatives? It has been reported, for example, that thousands of war negatives were scraped clean to salvage the silver from the emulsion and to recycle the glass plates, with some of the plates ultimately being used to provide the eyepieces for gas masks worn by American Doughboys in World War I.

The original Civil War wet plate negatives of Alexander Gardner and other photographers are kept at the Library of Congress. At *right* is a selection of original Civil War stereoscopic wet plate negatives illuminated on a light table. In the *bottom left* image, a photoduplication technician holds one of the original plates. The nineteenth-century paper sleeves at *bottom right* were used to hold the negatives until around the turn of the twenty-first century. The library has preserved the old paper sleeves. (Photographs by Paul Hogroian)

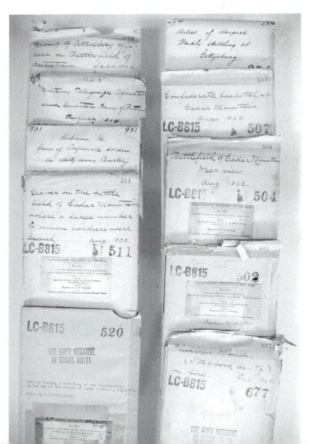

Another account asserts that "hundreds, if not thousands, of the glass negatives were sold to gardeners [and] used as panes in greenhouses, the sun slowly erasing any memory of the images they once held." If true, this would be the ultimate irony: the same radiating sunlight that had created the images on the glass plates burning them off.[18]

In this instance, however, irony falls short, and truth wins out. In fact, there are no major collections of negatives from the field that cannot be accounted for, though all have suffered losses. Anthony's "The War for the Union" series is in the best shape. Of 1,120 images, negatives exist for 1,058, nearly all in their full stereoscopic format. Only 113 are damaged. The Gardner negatives show greater losses but also are still largely intact. Of 1,234 documented stereo negatives by Gardner, glass plates still exist for 1,074 (with 953 full-stereo examples). Two hundred and sixty-three of the existing plates are damaged. Only 160 are missing entirely. The greatest losses are in Gardner's more fragile, easily breakable, seven-by-nine-inch large plates. Of 948 negatives that Gardner was known to have produced, 195 are missing. Of the 753 that survive, 207 are damaged. The greatest loss, unfortunately, are with the negatives that produced Gardner's greatest work. Of the one hundred plates of his *Sketch Book*, only sixteen negatives survive.[19]

Two other huge collections of portrait negatives have been preserved at other federal archives. In 1902, collector Frederick Hill Meserve purchased more than 5,000 Civil War glass plate negatives from yet another cache found at the Anthony & Scovill Co., successors to E. & H. T. Anthony & Company. The Meserve Collection, consisting almost entirely of portraits, is preserved today at the Smithsonian Institution's National Portrait Gallery. In 1954, Alice H. Cox and Mary H. Evans, two elderly descendants of M. B. Brady, sold their father Levin C. Handy's collection of glass negatives to the Library of Congress. Handy had spent many years in the late nineteenth century working with Brady, who

was his uncle, and had preserved about 10,000 original, duplicate, and copy negatives. Nearly all are studio portraits, and nearly all were taken after the war.[20]

Before the library secured what is known today as the Brady-Handy Collection, the elderly owners had lent Roy Meredith, author of the then celebrated Brady biography, *Mr. Lincoln's Cameraman*, a number of items, including several glass plate negatives. When Meredith finally answered the library's request for the return of the materials, he sent only some of the items. Of what he returned, two priceless glass negatives—one showing Ford's Theater and the other depicting Edwin Stanton and Robert Lincoln—"were broken as a result of improper packing," an irate library official wrote to Meredith in January 1956, adding, "The light cardboard box and wrapping paper [was] not sufficient."[21]

The second half of the twentieth century became an age of rediscovery in Civil War photography. One of the most dramatic finds was made by a fourteen-year-old, budding Lincoln scholar, Ronald Rietveld, on July 20, 1952. While browsing through file "X:14" of the Nicolay-Hay Collection at the Illinois State Historical Library in Springfield (John Nicolay and John Hay were White House secretaries during the Lincoln administration), Rietveld came across an envelope that contained a letter and a blank, folded sheet of stationary that held within it a single, small, unmounted albumen print. It was one of Gurney's banned photographs of Lincoln in his coffin. Rietveld recalls:

> Then I opened up the folded sheet of plain stationary and there lay a faded brown photograph. I thought it was sepia tone at first, and then I saw what it was immediately. I knew Lincoln photography fairly well at 14 and knew that this picture, if it was indeed a photograph, did not exist. . . . So I knew where it was taken—it was New York City, and when it was taken—April 24, 1865, and I picked it up and ran and said [to his host, Illinois State Historian Harry Pratt], "Harry, look at what I just found! This is a picture of Lincoln in his coffin taken in New York City at the time of the funeral!"

About two months later, when the photograph's authenticity was verified, Rietveld's find became a national news story. The letter that was contained in the same envelope as the photograph revealed the origin of the sole surviving print of Gurney's controversial photograph. The letter was written in 1887 to John Nicolay by Edwin Stanton's son, Lewis, who explained that he had found the photograph in his father's papers and thought Nicolay might have a use for it. Nicolay apparently did nothing with the image other than to keep it.[22]

Three years after Rietveld's find, another important but far less dramatic event occurred that would ultimately have a profound effect on the modern study of Civil War photography. When the September 12, 1955, issue of *Life* magazine arrived in the mail at the Long Island home of Americo and Edythe Frassanito, it changed their young son's life as surely as Edward Anthony's visit to the daguerreotype exhibition in 1840 had changed his. William A. Frassanito, who was just shy of nine years old, became captivated by the photographs presented in an article on the Civil War. Soon he was studying Civil War photos in books, and at age eleven he was poring over the ten volumes of Miller's *Photographic History*.[23]

The Gettysburg photographs in particular caught his interest, but the more he studied them, the more confusing things became. By 1962, when Frassanito turned sixteen, he had figured out that about ten Gardner photographs of the dead of Gettysburg showed the same group of bodies, even though different books and publications located them in four different places. Frassanito began searching for the actual location, eventually setting his sights on finding a distinctive split boulder that appeared in the background of one of the images. For years he searched fruitlessly. He enrolled in Gettysburg College in 1964 and, while in attendance, passed the rigorous test to become a licensed battlefield guide, yet he still could not find the elusive broken boulder. On February 1, 1967, after discovering the original spot where a Gardner "Slaughter Pen" photo had been taken, Frassanito recalled that he was "so pumped up, I vowed that now I would make an all-out effort to scour the battlefield and find that split rock." For the next five weeks, he conducted his most intensive field investigation yet, systematically examining and eliminating areas of the battlefield as possible locations. He knew that two of Gardner's images showed a distant ridgeline with fairly open land in between, so he began looking for similar areas, deciding to work backward from

In the summer of 1966, before his junior year at Gettysburg College, nineteen-year-old William A. Frassanito posed with four of his fellow licensed battlefield guides—men who had been guiding since the 1920s and taken actual veterans of the Civil War around the battlefield. From left are Lloyd Hartman, Charlie Rosensteel, Herb Oyler, and Bob Sheads. (Courtesy of William A. Frassanito)

This half-stereo, cropped version of an Alexander Gardner image of the dead on the Gettysburg battlefield includes a distinctive split boulder in the background. This rock proved to be the all-important geological feature used by William A. Frassanito to discover actual camera locations and to establish that this and nine other Gardner images were taken near the Rose Farm on the southern portion of the battlefield. In the modern image (taken from a spot just in front of the distant group of bodies), the split rock remains in place, and the afternoon sun casts light across it the same way it did more than 140 years ago. (Library of Congress; modern photograph by John Richter)

The same skylight that George S. Cook used to illuminate Confederate officers and his other photographic subjects still bathes the third floor of the original studio building, now occupied by the architectural and engineering firm of Cummings & McCrady, Inc. At left is John Crouch. (Photograph by Charles Rhoden)

the ridgeline. On March 10, 1967, he went to the southern extension of Seminary Ridge, turned toward the battlefield, and began walking across the fields. He crossed Emmitsburg Road, came onto the Rose Farm, and after walking about half a mile, reached a tree line. Just inside the wood line, there sat the distinctive split rock. Suddenly, it all came together, and he could see the scene as if through Gardner's camera, from all the various camera positions. Now Frassanito alone knew where that location was, and it was not any of the four places he had read about. He felt a connection to the battlefield like never before, and with it came an overwhelming feeling of elation. "It was like I had discovered the Rosetta Stone," he recalls. One hundred and one years earlier, in his *Sketch Book* preface, Gardner had written how his photographs had brought fame to "localities that would scarcely have been known, and probably never remembered." The Rose Farm images were never forgotten, but the knowledge of their actual location had died with the photographers. It took more than five years of detective work by the grandson of Italian immigrants to bring full veracity to Gardner's statement.[24]

These discoveries led Frassanito to conduct

more research and, in 1975, publish his first book, *Gettysburg: A Journey in Time*, redefining the study of Civil War photography. Since the publication of *Journey*, it has become routine to differentiate between Brady photographs and those by Gardner, O'Sullivan, Barnard, Cook, and the other photographers of the Civil War. Frassanito's "then-and-now" style of presentation, with vintage images presented next to modern photographs taken from the original camera position, is widely duplicated. Meanwhile, stereoscopic history enthusiasts have resurrected the 3-D perspective of literally hundreds of war images that, for two generations, were presented only in a two-dimensional perspective.

Modern technology has simplified research beyond measure and made the negative collections far more accessible. In 2001, the Library of Congress launched a two-year digitizing project of its entire collection of more than 12,000 Civil War photographic negatives. Completed in 2003, this groundbreaking project has made the detailed study of Civil War photographs possible for anyone with access to the Internet. Thousands of images that were previously difficult to see or obtain are now visible with a few clicks of the mouse.

Previously, for hundreds of stereoscopic images, only one of the twin negatives was available to the public. Now, virtually all of the full stereo negatives are available online. Even those broken negatives, so carefully preserved with an individual sleeve for each piece, were scanned after having been reassembled like a puzzle. Negatives that had turned dark were scanned as well, including some that were barely visible. These, too, are available online, and with sophisticated photo restoration software, researchers can now recover usable images from negatives that just a few years ago would have been considered hopelessly ruined.

The library scanned the negatives at high resolution, and most of the images with online digital files available for download allow the researcher to conduct intimate examinations of all the minute detail contained on the original glass plates. In 2003, antique photo collector John J. Richter was exploring the background of Gettysburg images for previously unseen details when he discovered M. B. Brady himself in the deep background of a Gettysburg image, sitting on the back steps of the John Burns house a few feet from where Brady's portable developing outfit sat on its tripod.

Today, the attics and basements of America still yield new Civil War photographic treasures from time to time. As 2005 began, for instance, only nine of Chicago photographer John Carbutt's Civil War stereo views were known to exist. In mid-February, a treasure trove of forty-nine Carbutt views (once owned by the colonel of the regiment Carbutt photographed), including thirty-nine previously unknown wartime images, suddenly surfaced on an Internet auction site. (They sold for $12,650 to collector and dealer Jeffrey Kraus.) With this, more than three-dozen new windows into the history of the Civil War opened. Thus, in a very real way, the study of Civil War photography is still a developing field. Our understanding of the work of America's pioneer war photographers is being constantly reevaluated as we reassemble the history made with their cameras, one image at a time.

NOTES

CHAPTER 1. THE ERA OF THE AMERICAN DAGUERREOTYPE

1. Merry A. Foresta and John Wood, *Secrets of the Dark Chamber: The Art of the American Daguerreotype* (Washington, DC: Smithsonian Institution Press, 1995), p. 15.

2. Ibid.

3. The nineteenth-century definition of photography was specific to a negative/positive image-making process; the widely accepted definition today includes all forms of still pictures recorded by cameras on light-sensitive material or by electronic means.

4. William Welling, *Photography in America: The Formative Years, 1839–1900, A Documentary History* (New York: Thomas Y. Crowell Company, 1978), p. 20.

5. Brady was born in Warren County, New York, in 1823 or 1824—the exact date is lost to history. He referred to himself as "M. B. Brady," a fact that has helped generate modern debate over how he spelled his first name. The commonly accepted form is "Mathew" with one "t," although Alan Johanson discovered a case that includes a circa 1844–1845 printed label with the name "Matthew B. Brady" (see Alan Johanson, "Another Brady Case?" *The Daguerreian Annual 1998* [Pittsburgh, PA: The Daguerreian Society, 1998], pp. 241–245). "War Time Pictures," *Chicago Evening Post*, 11 February 1893, says Brady learned the process from Morse in 1840.

6. William Marder and Estelle Marder, with Sally Pierce, "Philip Haas: Lithographer, Print Publisher, and Daguerreotypist," *The Daguerreian Annual 1995* (Pittsburgh, PA: The Daguerreian Society, 1995), pp. 21–22.

7. Jack C. Ramsay Jr., *Photographer . . . Under Fire: The Story of George S. Cook* (Minneapolis, MN: Bolger Publications, 1994), pp. 9–13, 16–17.

8. These numbers were provided in an e-mail of 20 September 2004 from John S. Craig to the author. For a listing of more than 9,400 American daguerreian artists and assistants of the nineteenth century, see John S. Craig, *Craig's Daguerreian Registry*, rev. ed. (Torrington, CT: John S. Craig, 2003), accessible online in 2005 at http://www.daguerreotype.com/.

9. George Alfred Townsend, "Still Taking Pictures," *New York World*, 12 April 1891, p. 26.

10. See, for example, "The Cave of Chauvet-Pont-D'Arc," accessible online in 2005 at http://www.culture.gouv.fr/culture/arcnat/chauvet/en/.

11. See "Camera Obscura History," accessible online in 2005 from *Historic Camera* at http://www.historiccamera.com/cgi-bin/librarium/pm.cgi?action5display&login5camera_obscura.

12. "The First Photograph," online exhibition, Harry Ransom Humanities Research Center, University of Texas at Austin, accessible in 2005 at http://www.hrc.utexas.edu/exhibitions/permanent/wfp/.

13. Welling, *Photography in America*, p. 7.

14. "The First Photograph," online exhibition.

15. Mary Warner Marien, *Photography: A Cultural History* (London: Laurence King Publishing Ltd., 2002), pp. 12–13.

16. William Marder and Estelle Marder, *Anthony: The Man, the Company, the Cameras* (Plantation, FL: Pine Ridge Pub. Co., 1982), p. 14. Monetary conversions are based on figures provided by the Federal Reserve Bank of Minneapolis, accessible online in 2005 at http://minneapolisfed.org/research/data/us/calc/.

17. Beaumont Newhall, *The Daguerreotype in America*, 3d rev. ed. (New York: Dover Publications, Inc., 1976), p. 15.

18. Robert Taft, *Photography and the American Scene* (New York: MacMillan Company, 1942), p. 11.

19. Newhall, *Daguerreotype in America*, p. 152; a South Carolina professor, Francis Lieber, gave a detailed description of the creation of a daguerreotype in New York City on Sept. 21, 1839, in a letter written the next day to his son. See Harvey S. Teal, *Partners with the Sun: South Carolina Photographers 1840–1940* (Columbia, SC: University of South Carolina Press, 2001), pp. 9–10; Craig's *Daguerreian Registry* says that Seager went to Mexico in about 1857 as an economic adviser to the government and was there at least through 1867.

20. Gail Buckland, *First Photographs* (New York: MacMillan Publishing Co., Inc., 1980), p. 229.

21. Floyd Rinhart and Marion Rinhart, *The American Daguerreotype* (Athens, GA: The University of Georgia Press, 1981), p. 46.

22. Rinhart and Rinhart, *American Daguerreotype*, p. 48; "Photography in the United States," *The Photographic Art-Journal* (reprinted from the *New York Daily Tribune*), June 1853, p. 339.

23. Welling, *Photography in America*, p. 17; Buckland, *First Photographs*, p. 165.

24. Marder and Marder, *Anthony*, pp. 19–20; Welling, *Photography in America*, p. 35.

25. James D. Horan, *Mathew Brady: Historian with a Camera* (New York: Crown Publishers, Inc., 1955), p. 9; Marder and Marder, *Anthony*, pp. 25–26.

26. Marder, Marder, and Pierce, "Haas," pp. 21–27.

27. Marder and Marder, *Anthony*, pp. 22–23, 31–32.

28. Ibid., 34–35.

29. Welling, *Photography in America*, pp. 44–46; C. Edwards Lester, "M. B. Brady and the Photographic Art," *The Photographic Art-Journal*, January 1851, p. 38; Townsend, "Still Taking Pictures," p. 26.

30. Various sources provide different dates for Cook's arrival in New Orleans, ranging from late 1837 to 1843. In the earliest account, the Rev. A. D. Cohen, author of "George S. Cook and the Daguerreian Art," in *The Photographic Art-Journal* of May 1851 (pp. 285–287), wrote that Cook "became intimately acquainted with several artists" and daguerreotypists while visiting New Orleans in 1843 and learned the art at that time. Cook's travels and work as an itinerant daguerreotypist are documented in his 1845–1850 account book in the George S. Cook Collection, Manuscripts Division, Library of Congress.

31. Michael L. Carlebach, *The Origins of Photojournalism in America* (Washington, DC: Smithsonian Institution Press, 1992), pp. 37–39.

32. Martha A. Sandweiss, Rick Stewart, and Ben W. Huseman, *Eyewitness to War: Prints and Daguerreotypes of the Mexican War, 1846–1848* (Washington, DC: Smithsonian Institution Press, 1989), p. 3.

33. Foresta and Wood, *Dark Chamber*, p. 146; "Sacramento Squatter's Riot—G. H. Johnson Captured the Scene," *The Daguerreian Annual 1990*, pp. 19–20; *The Photographic Art-Journal*, February 1853, pp. 126–127.

34. *The Photographic Art-Journal*, March 1853, p. 141.

35. See Getty Center, accessible online in 2005 at http://www.getty.edu/art/collections/bio/a2841-1.html.

36. T. W. Kriner, *Journeys to the Brink of Doom* (Buffalo, NY: J&J Publishing, 1997), p. 107.

37. George W. Holby, *The Falls of Niagara* (New York: A. C. Armstrong & Son, 1883), p. 118; Richard Rudisill, *Mirror Image: The Influence of the Daguerreotype on American Society* (Albuquerque, NM: University of New Mexico Press), p. 163; "Frightful Accident at Niagara Falls—Three Men Swept over the Falls—Dreadful Scene," *New-York Daily Times*, 20 July 1853.

38. Holby, *Falls of Niagara*, pp. 118–119.

39. *New-York Daily Times*, 20 July 1853.

40. Holby, *Falls of Niagara*, p. 119; Gordon Donaldson, *Niagara! The Eternal Circus* (Toronto: Doubleday Canada Limited, 1979), p. 237; documentation on three copies of "Avery Stranded" is in *E Photo Newsletter*, Issue One, 25 April 1999, accessible online in 2005 at http://www.iphotocentral.com/news/issue_view.php/1/1. The Library of Congress also owns a copy.

41. Keith F. Davis, *George N. Barnard: Photographer of Sherman's Campaign* (Kansas City, MO: Hallmark Cards, Inc., 1990), pp. 28–29.

42. Davis, *George N. Barnard*, pp. 38, 48; see "Platt Babbitt" entry in Craig's *Daguerreian Registry*.

43. Ross J. Kelbaugh, "The Swedish Nightingale and the Baltimore Daguerreians," *The Daguerreian Annual 1991* (Pittsburgh, PA: The Daguerreian Society, 1991), pp. 155–159; *The Daguerreian Journal*, 15 November 1850.

44. *The Daguerreian Journal*, 15 November 1850; *The Daguerreian Journal*, 1 November 1850, pp 14–15; *The Daguerreian Journal*, 15 February 1851; Buckland, *First Photographs*, pp. 36, 144, 150, 237.

45. H. E. Insley, "The Nineteenth Century," *The Daguerreian Journal*, 15 May 1851.

46. Wm. B. Becker, "Are These the World's First Color Photographs?" *American Heritage*, June–July 1980, pp. 4–7; and "The Enduring Mystery of Levi L. Hill," *Camera Arts*, January–February 1981, pp. 4, 6, 28–31, 125–127; George Gilbert, "The Twentieth Century's First Natural Color Daguerreotypist," *The Daguerreian Annual 1999* (Pittsburgh, PA: The Daguerreian Society, 1999), pp. 17–27.

47. *The Photographic Art-Journal*, September 1851, p. 171; Ramsay, *Photographer*, pp. 31–32; The *Daguerreian Journal*, 1 July 1851 and 1 August 1851. Ramsay (p. 36) suggests that Cook's purchase of Harrison's gallery, while operating for Brady, caused a rift that prompted Cook to leave New York abruptly and return to Charleston.

48. Welling, *Photography in America*, pp. 81, 211.

CHAPTER 2. THE ROOTS OF CELEBRITY

1. Harold Holzer, *Lincoln at Cooper Union* (New York: Simon & Schuster, 2004), p. 82.

2. Charles Hamilton and Lloyd Ostendorf, *Lincoln in Photographs: An Album of Every Known Pose* (Dayton, OH: Morningside, 1985), pp. 6–31; Holzer, *Lincoln at Cooper*, p. 90; Townsend, "Still Taking Pictures," p. 26.

3. Holzer, *Lincoln at Cooper*, p. 93.

4. Ibid., 5.

5. Marder and Marder, *Anthony*, p. 114; *The Photographic and Fine Art Journal*, November 1858, p. 346, and January 1854, pp. 6–7.

6. *The Photographic and Fine Art Journal*, November 1858, pp. 346, 350.

7. *American Journal of Photography*, 15 December 1858, p. 225; *Humphrey's Journal*, 15 June 1853, pp. 73–74. (The "extravagances" noted are from a description of Brady's downtown gallery written five years earlier.)

8. Josephine Cobb, "Mathew B. Brady's Photographic Gallery in Washington," *Columbia Historical Society Records* (Washington, DC: Columbia Historical Society, 1955), 53–56:20–21.

9. Jeana K. Foley, "Recollecting the Past: A Collection Chronicle of Mathew Brady's Photographs," in *Mathew Brady and the Image of History*, ed. Mary Panzer (Washington, DC: Smithsonian Institution Press, 1997), p. 190.

10. D. Mark Katz, *Witness to an Era: The Life and Photographs of Alexander Gardner* (New York: Viking, 1991), pp. 3–7.

11. *Photographic and Fine Art Journal*, April 1858, p. 128; Townsend, "Still Taking Pictures," p. 26.

12. Articles covering Cutting's patent dispute may be found in various contemporary photographic journals published from 1855 to 1857, particularly the *Photographic and Fine Art Journal*, January, March, April, October 1856, and February 1857.

13. *Humphrey's Journal*, 15 December 1861.

14. William C. Darrah, *The World of Stereographs* (Gettysburg, PA: Darrah, 1977), p. 2.

15. Oliver Wendell Holmes, *Soundings from the Atlantic* (Boston: Ticknor and Fields, 1864), p. 148.

16. Darrah, *Stereographs*, p. 21.

17. Marder and Marder, *Anthony*, pp. 52–53, 115.

18. Ibid., 113, 114, 126; Jacob F. Coonley, "Pages from a Veteran's Note-Book," *Wilson's Photographic Magazine*, March 1907, p. 105.

19. Marder and Marder, *Anthony*, p. 110, documents a stereo catalog from 1860: "New Catalogue of Card Photographs, Published and Sold by E. & H. T. Anthony," November 1862.

20. Darrah, *Stereographs*, p. 2; e-mail from Harold Holzer to the author, 21 December 2004.

21. Marder and Marder, *Anthony*, pp. 116–117; Darrah, *Stereographs*, pp. 4, 23.

22. Marder and Marder, *Anthony*, pp. 116–117; Henry Fox Talbot, "On the Production of Instantaneous Photographic Images," *Humphrey's Journal*, 15 April 1852, pp. 1–4 (reprinted from *Foreign Journal*); Welling, *Photography in America*, pp. 81, 140.

23. Holmes, *Soundings*, pp. 176, 181.

24. Marder and Marder, *Anthony*, pp. 110–111.

25. "Destructive Conflagration," *New York Times*, 30 December 1859, p. 1.

26. Welling, *Photography in America*, p. 145; Author's interview with Rob Gibson, 12 November 2004.

27. William A. Frassanito, *Antietam: The Photographic Legacy of America's Bloodiest Day* (New York: Charles Scribner's Sons, 1978), p. 26.

28. *American Journal of Photography*, 15 December 1860, pp. 223–224.

29. George S. Cook Account Book, 16 August 1860–14 March 1862, George Smith Cook Papers, Valentine Richmond History Center, Richmond, VA. It should be noted that before confining his work to Charleston in late 1860, Cook was active in other cities as well. He was affiliated with Marcus A. Root in Philadelphia and may have lived there for a time. Cook advertised a gallery at one Chestnut Street address in Philadelphia in 1857 and at another in 1859. Cook also entered into a studio partnership in Chicago in 1857 with Samuel A. Fassett, who on October 4, 1859, took a photograph of a beardless Abraham Lincoln that was said to be the best likeness Mary Lincoln had ever seen of her husband. See Teal, *Partners with the Sun*, p. 43; and entries for Cook, Root, and Fassett in *Craig's Daguerreian Registry*.

30. *American Journal of Photography*, 15 December 1860, p. 224.

31. Frassanito, *Antietam*, pp. 19–23.

32. More information on Fenton's Crimean War photographs and 263 images are available online at the Library of Congress Web site at http://lcweb2.loc.gov/pp/ftncnwquery.html.

33. "Photographs from Sebastopol," *Humphrey's Journal*, 15 November 1855, p. 224 (reprinted from *London Art Journal*, October 1855); Roger Fenton, Esq., "Narrative of a Photographic Trip to the Seat of War in the Crimea," *Humphrey's Journal*, 1 March 1856, pp. 329–336.

34. See Fenton images on Library of Congress Web site, and Fenton, "Narrative of a Photographic"; William A. Frassanito letter to the author, 21 July 2004; Frassanito, *Antietam*, p. 22.

CHAPTER 3. THE REBELS SHOOT FIRST

1. A. W. McCormick letter to George S. Cook, 2 January 1861, The George Smith Cook Collection, Manuscript Division, Library of Congress (LC), Washington, DC

2. J. B. Van der Weyde letter to Cook, 19 January 1861, Cook Collection, LC.

3. Walter Dinmore letter to Cook, 11 January 1861, Cook Collection, LC.

4. "Major Anderson Captured—Another Triumph of Gun-Cotton," *American Journal of Photography*, 1 March 1861, pp. 298–300.

5. "Major Anderson Taken," *Charleston Daily Courier*, 11 February 1861; Cook Account Book, 1860–1862 (see expense report), Valentine.

6. "Major Anderson Captured," *American Journal of Photography*, pp. 299–300.

7. Ibid., 300.

8. "Major Anderson Taken," *Charleston Courier*; Cook Account Book, 1860–1862, Valentine; "Major Anderson Captured," *American Journal of Photography*, p. 299.

9. S. W. Crawford letter to George S. Cook, 14 February 1861, George Smith Cook Papers, Valentine Richmond History Center, Richmond, VA. The address of Cook's gallery at 235 King Street is taken from his newspaper advertisements of April 1861. The *Census for the City of Charleston, S.C. for the Year 1861* (Charleston: Evans & Cogswell, 1861) lists Cook at 265 King Street. For the sake of consistency, this narrative will use the 235 King Street address.

10. Steward Sifakis, *Who Was Who in the Civil War* (New York: Facts on File Publications, 1988), pp. 150–151; Robert Hendrickson, *Sumter: The First Day of the Civil War* (New York: Dell Publishing, 1990), p. 41; Crawford to Cook, 14 February 1861, Cook Papers, Valentine.

11. Crawford to Cook, 26 February 1861, Cook Papers, Valentine.

12. Ibid.

13. Crawford to Cook, 3 March 1861, Cook Papers, Valentine.

14. Abner Doubleday, *Reminiscences of Forts Sumter and Moultrie in 1860–1861* (New York: Harper & Brothers, 1876), p. 123.

15. Crawford to Cook, 12 March 1861, Cook Papers, Valentine.

16. Crawford to Cook, 16 March 1861, Cook Papers, Valentine.

17. Cook Account Book, 1860–1862, Valentine.

18. Crawford to Cook, 3 March 1861; Crawford to Cook, 12 March 1861, Cook Papers, Valentine.

19. Crawford to Cook, 20 March 1861, Cook Papers, Valentine.

20. Hendrickson, *Sumter: The First Day*, p. 168; Crawford to Cook, 26 March 1861, Cook Papers, Valentine.

21. Crawford to Cook, 1 April 1861, Cook Papers, Valentine.

22. Cook Account Book, 1860–1862, Valentine.

23. Teal, *Partners with the Sun*, p. 90.

24. Samuel W. Crawford, *The History of the Fall of Fort Sumpter* (New York: Francis P. Harper, 1896), p. 383; Teal, *Partners with the Sun*, p. 90; Doubleday, *Reminiscences*, p. 119.

25. E. B. Long with Barbara Long, *The Civil War Day by Day: An Almanac 1861–1865* (New York: Doubleday & Company, Inc., 1971), pp. 55–56; Cook Account Book, 1860–1862, Valentine.

26. Ibid.

27. "Splendid Pyrotechnic Exhibition," *The Charleston Mercury*, 13 April 1861, p. 1.

28. Hendrickson, *Sumter: The First Day*, p. 192.

29. Cook's 1860–1862 account book documents no trip to Fort Sumter after the surrender.

30. Hendrickson, *Sumter: The First Day*, pp. 215–216; Long, *Day by Day*, p. 57.

31. Doubleday, *Reminiscences*, pp. 157–158.

32. Hendrickson, *Sumter: The First Day*, p. 227.

33. Teal, *Partners with the Sun*, p. 96.

34. *Charleston Daily Courier*, 16 April 1861; *Charleston Mercury*, 16 April 1861.

35. *Charleston Mercury*, 16 April 1861, and 25 April 1861.

36. *Charleston Courier*, 19 April 1861, and 22 April 1861.

37. William C. Davis, ed., *The Image of War 1861–1865, Volume 1: Shadows of the Storm* (New York: Doubleday & Company, Inc., 1981), pp. 100–104; Teal, *Partners with the Sun*, p. 96.

38. *Charleston Courier*, 23 April 1861.

39. *Charleston Courier*, 3 May 1861.

40. Davis, *Shadows of the Storm*, pp. 106–107.

41. Statistics, information, and descriptions regarding Osborn & Durbec war views in this paragraph and the previous paragraph are from author's records of examination of extant prints in various public and private collections.

42. The South Caroliniana Library, University of South Carolina, has a contemporary display-piece, discovered by Harvey S. Teal. Several multi-plate panoramas of Fort Sumter after the surrender were fashioned from numerous half-stereo, albumen prints by Osborn & Durbec.

43. Cook Account Book, 1860–1862, Valentine.

44. As an example, see Cook ad in *Charleston Mercury*, 25 April 1861.

45. Cook Account Book, 1860–1862, Valentine.

46. "Anderson Captured," *American Journal of Photography*, p. 299.

CHAPTER 4. BRADY AT BULL RUN

1. Long and Long, *Day by Day*, p. 61; Erich Langsdorf, "Jim Lane and the Frontier Guard," *Kansas Historical Quarterly*, February 1940, p. 16; Dale R. Niesen, with Robert Coch and William Munday, "Wolverines: A Photographic Study of Men from the Great Lakes State in the War of the Rebellion," *Military Images*, November–December 1994, p. 6; William C. Davis, ed., *The Image of War 1861–1865*, vol. 2: *The Guns of '62* (Garden City, NY: Doubleday & Company, Inc., 1981), p. 166.

2. Leslie D. Jensen, "Photographer of the Confederacy: J. D. Edwards," in *Image of War*, vol. 1, Davis, ed., pp. 344–363.

3. Ibid., 344–347; Francis Trevelyan Miller, ed., *The Photographic History of the Civil War*, vol. 6: *The Navies* (New York: Review of Reviews Company, 1911), p. 17.

4. Bob Zeller, *The Civil War in Depth*, vol. 2 (San Francisco: Chronicle Books, 2000), p. 27 (shows example from collection of Robin Stanford).

5. "In Memoriam—M. B. Brady," *Wilson's Photographic Magazine* 33 (1896): 121–123; "Tribute to M. B. Brady's Memory," *New York Daily Tribune*, 18 January 1896, p. 4. See other examples of "Illustrations of Camp Life" portraits from the collection of Michael J. McAfee in *Military Images*, November–December 1994 and March–April 2000.

6. Davis, *Barnard*, p. 53; J. F. Coonley, "Photographic Reminiscences of the Late War, No. 2," *Anthony's Photographic Bulletin*, September 1882, p. 311, and "Pages from a Veteran's Note-Book," *Wilson's Photographic Magazine*, pp. 105–106.

7. Davis, *Barnard*, pp. 46, 52.

8. Coonley, "Photographic Reminiscences," p. 311. That Coonley worked at Brady's gallery while employed by Anthony is illustrative of the close business relationships and agreements that Anthony had with Brady, Alexander Gardner, other photographers, and the Union Army throughout the war. These interrelationships sometimes make it difficult to determine who was doing what work for whom.

9. An Anthony *carte de visite* of "Gymnastic Field Sports" (also issued as a stereo view) from the William Gladstone collection credits G. N. Barnard and C. O. Bostwick as the photographers, establishing them as the likely photographers of other Anthony views from Camp Cameron.

10. Coonley, "Photographic Reminiscences," p. 311. Listings of Anthony's war views and other stereo views can be found in "New Catalogue of Stereoscopes and Views Manufactured and Published by E. & H. T. Anthony & Co." A copy of the 1869 catalogue, with a complete listing of all Anthony war views, is available at the Oliver Wendell Holmes Stereoscopic Research Library, 3665 Erie Avenue, Cincinnati, OH 45208.

11. Long and Long, *Day by Day*, pp. 90–96.

12. From the handwritten inscription on the reverse of an original *carte de visite* in the collection of Michael J. McAfee.

13. Long and Long, *Day by Day*, pp. 96–97.

14. Louis M. Starr, *Bohemian Brigade: Civil War Newsmen in Action* (New York: Alfred A. Knopf, 1954), pp. 43–44.

15. "George N. Barnard" (obituary), *Anthony's Photographic Bulletin*, April 1902, p. 127.

16. Townsend, "Still Taking Pictures," p. 26.

17. Ibid.

18. Starr, *Bohemian Brigade*, p. 45.

19. "Photographs of the War," *New York Times*, 17 August 1861.

20. William A. Croffut, *An American Procession 1855–1914: A Personal Chronicle of Famous Men* (Boston: Little, Brown, and Company, 1931), pp. 49–50.

21. Roy Meredith, *Mr. Lincoln's Camera Man: Mathew B. Brady* (New York: Charles Scribner's Sons, 1946), pp. 10–11.

22. Ibid., 51–52.

23. Ibid.

24. Horan, *Mathew Brady*, p. 40.

25. Ibid. The Fairfax Court House view is among the lowest numbered of all Civil War stereo views issued by the Anthony Company, the lowest being No. 813. This is the only instance where a contemporary account describing a photograph related to the First Bull Run campaign can be linked to a known image.

26. "Photographs of War Scenes," *Humphrey's Journal*, 15 August 1861, p. 133.

27. Ibid.

28. Ibid.

29. Horan, *Mathew Brady*, pp. 230–231.

30. "Catalogue of Card Photographs Published and Sold by E. & H. T. Anthony," November 1862, pp. 13–17. A so-called Brady photograph that surfaced in 1954 purported to show Confederate dead on Mathews Hill but proved to be a staged image, as was established by Frassanito in 1974 and revealed on page 31 of *Antietam*.

31. Cook Account Book, 1860–1862, Valentine.

32. Ibid.

33. Ibid.; *List of Taxpayers of the City of Charleston for 1860* (Charleston: Evans & Cogswell, 1861), entry for G. S. Cook (who also paid a $20 tax for his carriage and $10 for a horse).

34. W. A. Swanberg, *First Blood: The Story of Fort Sumter* (New York: Charles Scribner's Sons, 1957), p. 107; "A Chronology of Castle Pinckney," a Web page of the South Carolina State Ports Authority, accessible in 2005 at http://www.port-of-charleston.com/Community/history1.asp; Miller, *Photographic History of the Civil War*, 1:107.

35. Cook Account Book, 1860–1862, Valentine.

36. Sifakis, *Who Was Who*, p. 101; "Chronology of Castle Pinckney," Web page.

37. Miller, *Photographic History*, 7:25, 27.

38. Cook Account Book, 1860–1862, Valentine; Miller, *Photographic History*, 1:89, 107; 3:171; 7:4, 25, 27, 59, 157.

39. Alexander Gardner, *Catalogue of Photographic Incidents of the War* (Washington, DC: H. Polkinhorn, September 1863), pp. 3, 8–9. Most of these images are available online from the Library of Congress, accessible in 2005 at http://lcweb2.loc.gov/pp/cwpquery.html.

CHAPTER 5. GARDNER AT ANTIETAM

1. "Telegrams Collected by the Office of the Secretary of War (Unbound), 1860–1870, National Archives and Records Administration (hereafter NARA), Washington, DC, Record Group 107, Microfilm No. M 504 (in alphabetical order by sender).

2. "Brady's Photographs: Pictures of the Dead at Antietam," *New York Times*, 20 October 1862.

3. Gardner, *Catalogue*, pp. 10–11; see image LC–B811–349 online in 2005 at http://lcweb2.loc.gov/pp/cwpquery.html.

4. Thomas Waldsmith, "James F. Gibson: Out from the Shadows," *Stereo World*, January–February 1976, pp. 1, 5, 6; Josephine Cobb, "Alexander Gardner," *Image*, June 1958, p. 132.

5. Gardner, *Catalogue*, pp. 11–16.

6. Ibid. Images available online in 2005 at http://lcweb2.loc.gov/pp/cwpquery.html.

7. Davis, ed., *Image of War*, vol. 2, pp. 140–143; *Official Records of the Union and Confederate Armies, War of the Rebellio*n (Washington, DC: Government Printing Office, 1880–1901), Series 3, vol. 3, part 1, pp. 252–319. Citations are from online version available in 2005 using search engine at http://www.ehistory.com/uscw/library/or/.

8. Buckland, *First Photographs*, pp. 26–27; "Aerial Photography," *Humphrey's Journal*, 1 September 1860, p. 132, and 1 November 1860, p. 195.

9. *Official Records*, Series 3, vol. 3, part 1, pp. 269, 278.

10. "American Photographs," *Photographic Notes* (London), 1 October 1862, pp. 242–244 (reprinted from the *Times*).

11. *Harper's New Monthly Magazine*, 25 November 1862, pp. 852–853. Digital image of original negative, LC–B815–491, accessible online in 2005 at http://lcweb2.loc.gov/cgi-bin/query.

12. Davis, ed., *Image of War*, vol. 6, pp. 122–145; Long and Long, *Day by Day*, p. 200.

13. See LC–B815–510 and LC–B815–511.

14. Frassanito, *Antietam*, p. 36; Gardner, *Catalogue*.

15. Frederic Ray, "Rare Photographs Identified. Show Rebel and Yankee Troops in Frederick," *Civil War Times Illustrated*, April 1965, pp. 22–24.

16. Frassanito, *Antietam*, p. 35; Miller, *Photographic History*, 8:23; Cobb, "Alexander Gardner," p. 132.

17. "Telegrams, Secretary of War," NARA (wording has been slightly modified for clarity).

18. *New York Times*, 17 September 1862.

19. Letters of H. Lansdale Boardman, 1862, Manuscripts and Archives Division, Humanities and Social Sciences Library, New York Public Library.

20. *New York World*, 18 September 1862; *New York Herald*, 18 September 1862.

21. Frederic Ray, "No Finer Picture of an Engagement?" *Civil War Times Illustrated*, February 1963, pp. 10–13.

22. Edwin Forbes, *Thirty Years After: An Artist's Memoir of the Civil War* (Baton Rouge, LA: Louisiana State University Press, 1993), p. 258.

23. Kathleen A. Ernst, *Too Afraid to Cry: Maryland Civilians in the Antietam Campaign* (Mechanicsburg, PA: Stackpole Books, 1999), p. 165.

24. Horan, *Mathew Brady*, p. 42; Meredith, *Lincoln's Camera Man*, p. 127.

25. John W. Schildt, *Drums along the Antietam* (Parsons, WV: McClain Printing Company, 1972), p. 286; "The Dunker Church," Job Corps Brochure, National Park Service, U.S. Department of the Interior.

26. Gardner, *Catalogue*, p. 3. "Imperial Carte" is documented by the Brady ad reproduced herein. After Gardner separated from Brady, Gardner did not offer Imperial Cartes.

27. Gardner, *Catalogue*, pp. 20–21; Frassanito, *Antietam*, pp. 93–96

28. Frassanito, *Antietam*, pp. 160–170. The September 19 date of the photograph of Knap's Battery has come into question since the publication of Frassanito's *Antietam*, which established that the Twelfth Corps, to which the battery was attached, departed the battlefield some time before noon on September 19. However, the diary of Sgt. David Nichol of the battery, preserved at the Army Heritage and Education Center in Carlisle, PA, includes an entry dated Saturday, September 20, that says: "We were about to go off the battlefield when we were halted by an artist to take our picture." Curiously, Nichol's 1862 diary entries are handwritten in an 1863 diary book, raising questions about when he actually wrote the 1862 entries and whether he might have erred on the September 20 date.

29. Miller, *Photographic History*, 1:46; Author's interview with Rob Gibson, 12 November 2004.

30. Author's interview with Rob Gibson, 12 November 2004.

31. Ibid.

32. Author's interview with Mark Osterman of Scully & Osterman, 27 March 2005.

33. Roger Fenton, "Narrative of a Photographic Trip to the Seat of War in the Crimea," *Humphrey's Journal*, 1 March 1856, p. 334.

34. Author's interview with Rob Gibson, 12 November 2004.

35. Ernst, *Too Afraid to Cry*, p. 165.

36. Author's interview with Rob Gibson, 12 November 2004.

37. "Telegrams, Secretary of War," NARA (wording has been slightly modified for clarity).

38. Davis, ed., *Image of War*, 1:423. Image with Woodbury handwritten caption is presently in author's collection.

39. Calculations are based on author's review of all known images, captions, and other information.

40. The image and portfolio cover are in the author's collection.

41. Gardner, *Catalogue*, p. 20.

42. Oliver Wendell Holmes, "Doings of the Sunbeam," *Atlantic Monthly*, July 1863, p. 11; Frassanito, *Antietam*, pp. 22–23.

43. *New York Times*, 20 October 1862.

44. *Harper's Weekly*, 18 October 1862, pp. 663–665.

45. Holmes, "Doings of the Sunbeam," pp. 11–12.

CHAPTER 6. EMBEDDED WITH THE TROOPS

1. William Child, M.D., *Letters from a Civil War Surgeon* (Solon, ME: Polar Bear & Company, 2001), pp. 33–34.

2. Ibid.; William Child, M.D., *History of the Fifth New Hampshire Volunteers* (1893; reprinted, Gaithersburg, MD: Ron R. Van Sickle Military Books, 1988), p. 310; Long and Long, *Day by Day*, p. 717.

3. Child, *Letters*, pp. 45, 47 (letter of 7 October 1862).

4. Child, *Letters*, p. 43 (letter of 4 October 1862).

5. George Washington Adams, *Doctors in Blue* (New York: Collier Books, 1961), pp. 71–73.

6. Child, *Letters*, p. 45 (5 October 1862 postscript to letter of 4 October 1862), p. 49 (letter of 14 October 1862).

7. Ibid., 60.

8. Bob Zeller, "Lost Photos of Antietam Hospital," *Civil War Times Illustrated*, May 1996, pp. 36–43.

9. Bob Zeller, "Rare Photos of the Naval Academy," *Civil War Times Illustrated*, May 1997, pp. 36–39.

10. Child, *Letters*, p. 67.

11. William A. Frassanito identified Brown as the photographer from a copy at the Library of Congress with Brown's name on the copyright line; had Brown not marketed the images, the copyright line would have been unnecessary. See Taber illustrations in *American Heritage Century Collection of Civil War Art* (New York: American Heritage Publishing Company, Inc., 1974), pp. 146, 334; first book publication of Corinth photographs in George F. Williams, *Memorial War Book* (New York: Judge Publishing Company, 1894), p. 339.

12. Gardner, *Catalogue*, pp. 5, 24–25.

13. Child, *Letters*, p. 71; Child, *5th New Hampshire*, pp. 162–163.

14. Gardner, *Catalogue*, pp. 25–26.

15. Horan, *Brady*, pp. 22, 314, 315, 319. (Horan's books contain many inaccuracies but also much reliable primary source material.)

16. James D. Horan, *Timothy O'Sullivan: America's Forgotten Photographer* (New York: Bonanza Books, 1966), pp. 313–318.

17. "Prisoners, Agents, Sutlers," Army of the Potomac Register No. 77, Record Group 393, Part I, Entry 4075, 3 of 13 volumes, NARA.

18. Ibid.

19. "List of Permits (import) as Granted by Maj. Gen. Benj. Butler," Record Group 393, part 1, Entry 5199, vol. 229. NARA; "Capt. Andrew J. Russell, 141st New York Regiment," Military Service Records, NARA.

20. "Distribution of Photographs of Construction and Transportation Departments," Record Group 92, Box 815, Quartermaster General's Consolidated Correspondence File, "Photography" subfiles, NARA.

21. Susan E. Williams, "Richmond Taken Again," *Virginia Magazine of History and Biography*, 2002, vol. 110, no. 4, pp. 437, 444.

22. For more information and photographs of Haupt's work, see "War on Rails" chapter, *Image of War: 1861–1865*, vol. 2: *The Guns of '62*, Davis, ed., pp. 399–445.

23. Letter of 24 February 1864 by J. H. Devereux to Col. D. C. McCallum, Record Group 92, Box 815, Quartermaster General's Consolidated Correspondence File, "Photography" subfiles, NARA.

24. Ibid.

25. "Distribution of Photographs" list, NARA.

26. Ibid.

27. Ibid.

28. Ibid.; John Kelley, "Embedded with the Troops," slide lecture manuscript, p. 1.

29. Kelley, "Embedded," p. 14. (Susan E. Williams claims E. G. Fowx took these images.)

30. Williams, "Richmond Taken Again," p. 446.

31. "Telegrams Collected by the Office of the Secretary of War," NARA.

32. Kelley, "Embedded," p. 43.

33. See image in Civil War Oversize II, Folder 179, Places: Virginia: Fredericksburg: Views; Western Reserve Historical Society (hereafter WRHS), Cleveland, OH.

34. See image in Civil War Oversize II, Folder 178, Places: Virginia: Fredericksburg: Views, WRHS.

35. See image in Civil War Oversize II, Folder 180, Places: Virginia: Fredericksburg: Views, WRHS.

36. See image in Civil War Oversize II, Folder 182, Places: Virginia: Fredericksburg: Views, WRHS.

37. The image was one of twenty-five Addis Civil War photographs in lot 460, Cowan's Historic Americana Auction, Spring 2004. The lot brought $3,737.50, including buyer's premium.

CHAPTER 7. GETTYSBURG

1. Katz, *Witness to an Era: Gardner*, p. 51.

2. Brady and Gardner remained together at least through Gardner's photographs of Burnside at Warrenton, Virginia, in November 1862; the author has an electronic reproduction of a mounted print of Burnside with Gardner's name imprinted as photographer and Brady as publisher.

3. These numbers are based on the author's review of original stereo views, as well as on Gardner's 1863 *Catalogue* and Anthony's 1869 "Catalogue of Stereoscopes and Views."

4. Civil War–era copyright records, U.S. District Court, District of Columbia, are on microfilm at the United States Copyright Office, Madison Building, LC.

5. Ibid.

6. Holmes, *Atlantic Monthly*, July 1863, p. 11; *Harper's Weekly*, 18 October 1862, pp. 663, 665; *New York Times*, 20 October 1862.

7. William A. Frassanito, *Gettysburg: A Journey in Time* (New York: Charles Scribner's Sons, 1975), pp. 31, 37; Mary Panzer, *Brady and the Image of History*, writes on page 109 that Brady's "nearly empty landscapes provided a screen on which [viewers] could project a private vision of the battle."

8. Frassanito, *Journey in Time*, pp. 162–163, explains that atmospheric conditions may have prevented Gardner, O'Sullivan, and Gibson from taking panoramic views from Little Round Top that, like Brady's views, showed the distant landscape.

9. Frassanito, *Journey in Time*, p. 40.

10. Gardner, *Catalogue*, p. 27, no. 228; William A. Frassanito, *Early Photography at Gettysburg* (Gettysburg, PA: Thomas Publications, 1995), pp. 25, 408.

11. Frassanito, *Early Photography*, p. 21.

12. Garry E. Adelman and Timothy H. Smith, *Devil's Den: A History and Guide* (Gettysburg, PA: Thomas Publications, 1997), pp. 18–19.

13. Frassanito, *Early Photography*, pp. 20–26.

14. See chronological listing of Gettysburg photographs in Alexander Gardner, *Catalogue*; "A Numerical Compilation from Known Sources by Bob Zeller," published by the Center for Civil War Photography, 2003. The sole exception to this pattern is No. 277, a Gettysburg view that follows Virginia negatives designated with Nos. 275 and 276.

15. Frassanito, *Early Photography*, p. 318.

16. Frassanito, *Journey in Time*, pp. 198–221.

17. Frassanito, *Journey in Time*, pp. 186–192, and *Early Photography*, pp. 268–273.

18. Frassanito, *Journey in Time*, pp. 172–181, 158–169, and *Early Photography*, pp. 25, 148, 98–99. Gardner's *Catalogue* lists both a stereo negative by Gardner and a large plate by O'Sullivan of this scene, but Frassanito reports that the large plate is an enlargement of the stereo negative.

19. Katz, *Witness to an Era: Gardner*, p. 63.

20. "Telegrams," NARA RG 107, Microfilm M 504 (by name of sender). The Gardner telegrams from the field were first uncovered by researcher Marie Melchiori and first published by Katz, *Witness to an Era: Gardner*.

21. Frassanito, *Early Photography*, pp. 22–23.

22. Ibid., 25–28.

23. "The Daguerreian Art—Its Origin and Present State," *Photographic Art-Journal*, March 1851, p. 138.

24. Numbers are based on author's review of all known sources of information about the photographs.

25. *Harper's Weekly*, 22 August 1863, pp. 532–533.

26. Copyright records, LC.

27. Frassanito, *Early Photography*, pp. 33, 50, 160.

28. Philip Van Doren Stern, ed., *Soldier Life in the Union and Confederate Armies* [includes *Hardtack and Coffee*, by John D. Billings], (Bloomington, IN: Indiana University Press, 1961), p. 236.

29. "Having Your Photograph Taken," *American Journal of Photography*, 1 January 1863, p. 292.

30. "Photography in the Army," *Humphrey's Journal*, 15 February 1862, p. 319.

31. Mark H. Dunkelman, *Gettysburg's Unknown Soldier: The Life, Death and Celebrity of Amos Humiston* (Westport, CT: Praeger Publishers, 1999), p. 104.

32. Ibid., 1, 7, 14, 32, 39, 48, 52.

33. Ibid., 57, 71, 72, 86, 103, 108.

34. Ibid., 118–119.

35. Ibid., 119–120, 130–131.

36. Ibid., 130–133.

37. Ibid., 138–140, 150–151, 161–163.

38. Ibid., 133, 157, 179; e-mail communication 21 January 2005 from Mark H. Dunkelman to author.

39. Dunkelman, *Gettysburg's Unknown Soldier*, pp. 183, 194–195.

40. Ibid., 201–203.

41. Ibid., 203–204.

42. Ibid., 206, 208.

CHAPTER 8. THE DAWN OF COMBAT PHOTOGRAPHY

1. Milton Kaplan, "The Case of the Missing Photographers Haas & Peale," *A Century of Photographs 1846–1946* (Washington, DC: Library of Congress, 1980), p. 54–55; Marder, Marder, and Pierce, *Haas*, p. 31.

2. Teal, *Partners with the Sun*, pp. 119–120.

3. Keith F. Davis, "A Terrible Distinctness: Photography of the Civil War Era," *Photography in Nineteenth Century America*, Martha A. Sandweiss, ed., p. 165; W. Jeffrey Bolster and Hilary Anderson, *Soldiers, Sailors, Slaves, and Ships: The Civil War Photographs of Henry P. Moore* (Concord, NH: 1999).

4. "Editorial Department," *American Journal of Photography*, 1 January 1863, p. 312.

5. Cook Account Book, 1860–1862, Valentine; Cook Account Book, 1863–1864, Cook Collection, LC.

6. George S. Cook stock sales, Cook Account Book, 1860–1862, Valentine; Cook Account Book, 1863–1864, Cook Collection, LC.

7. Cook Account Book, 1863–1864, Cook Collection, LC.

8. John Johnson, *The Defense of Charleston Harbor* (1890; reprinted, Germantown, TN: Guild Bindery Press, 1994), p. 143.

9. W. Chris Phelps, *The Bombardment of Charleston 1863–1865* (Gretna, LA: Pelican Publishing Company, 1999), p. 27; Cook Account Book, 1863–1864, Cook Collection, LC.

10. Phelps, *Bombardment*, pp. 2, 34–35.

11. *Official Records of the Union and Confederate Navies in the War of the Rebellion* (Washington, DC: Government Printing Office, 1902), Series 1, vol. 14, part 1: 549–550.

12. Miller, ed., *Photographic History*, 1:100; "The Ironsides and Two Monitors Taken," *Charleston Courier*, 12 September 1863; "Photographing Fort Sumter under Difficulties," *Providence Daily Journal*, 20 October 1863; *Official Records of the Navies*, Series 1, vol. 14, part 1, Daily log of Cmdr. John Lee Davis, USS *Montauk*, p. 563.

13. *Charleston Courier*, 12 September 1863.

14. *Official Records of the Navies*, Series 1, vol. 14, part 1, p. 575; Johnson, *Defense of Charleston Harbor*, p. 158.

15. Johnson, *Defense of Charleston Harbor*, pp. 157–159; *Official Records of the Navies*, Series 1, vol. 14, part 1, p. 550.

16. Ibid., 551, 575; letter of 8 September 1863 from Stephen Elliott to "Hal," copy in author's files, courtesy of David Ruth.

17. "Photographing under Difficulties," *Providence Daily Journal*, 20 October 1863. The article was reprinted from the *Mobile Advertiser*, making Cook's feat news in both the North and South.

18. *Charleston Courier*, 12 September 1863.

19. *Official Records of the Navies*, Series 1, vol. 14, part 1: 550, 551, 556.

20. Johnson, *Defense of Charleston Harbor*, pp. 161–163.

21. Cook Account Book, 1863–1864, Cook Collection, LC.

22. No wartime prints of the ironclads in action are known to exist, but several ca. 1880 copies have surfaced that were part of a small series, "Charleston during the War," issued by Cook's son, George LaGrange.

23. To see images, type Haas in the search field at http://lcweb2.loc.gov/pp/cwpquery.html.

24. LC call number for battle image is LC–B8156–79.

25. Jack Thomson, *Charleston at War: The Photographic Record 1860–1865* (Gettysburg, PA: Thomas Publications, 2000), pp. 74–79.

26. LC call number for this image is LC–B8156–78.

27. "Timothy O'Sullivan," *Photography Speaks II*, Brooks Johnson, ed. (New York: Aperture, 1995), p. 36.

28. Johnson, *Defense of Charleston Harbor*, pp. 170, 184; Phelps, *Bombardment*, p. 57.

29. Phelps, *Bombardment*, p. 11; Cook Account Book, 1863–1864, Cook Collection, LC.

30. See Charleston historical timeline at http://barns.ill.fr/hewat/Charleston-Timeline.html; Thomson, *Charleston at War*, pp. x, 31–33.

31. Phelps, *Bombardment*, pp. 62, 66; Thomson, *Charleston at War*, p. x.

32. Cook Account Book, 1863–1864, Cook Collection, LC.

33. Phelps, *Bombardment*, p. 61; *Charleston Courier*, 30 November 1863; *Charleston Mercury*, 28 November 1863.

34. Cook Account Book, 1863–1864, Cook Collection, LC.

35. John F. Marszalek, ed., *The Diary of Miss Emma Holmes* (Baton Rouge, LA: Louisiana State University Press, 1979), p. 327.

36. Cook Account Book, 1863–1864, Cook Collection, LC.

37. Ibid.

38. Thomson, *Charleston at War*, p. 168.

39. Ibid., 162.

40. Phelps, *Bombardment*, pp. 150, 151; E. Milby Burton, *The Siege of Charleston 1861–1865* (Columbia, SC: University of South Carolina Press, 1970), p. 259.

41. Cook Account Book, 1863–1864, Cook Collection, LC.

42. Ibid.; see September 1863 entries in Mathew Brady registers, 1863–1865, Manuscript collection, Humanities and Social Sciences Library, New York Public Library. Cook's 1863 prices varied widely for undetermined reasons. He frequently logged three or four different prices on the same day for the same item. Inflation figures for the Confederate dollar are compiled and published in Official Publication #13, Richmond Civil War Centennial Committee, available online in 2005 at http://www.mdgorman.com and http://www.inflationdata.com.

43. Ramsay, *Photographer*, p. 69; Cook Account Book, 1863–1864, Cook Collection, LC; Thomson, *Charleston at War*, p. 196.

CHAPTER 9. PHOTOGRAPHERS ON THE MARCH

1. See LC–B811–700, LC–B815–701, and LC–B811–702 at http://lcweb2.loc.gov/pp/cwpquery.html; Kelley, "Embedded," pp. 97, 98, 108, 110, 111, 112, establishes that *Gardner's Photographic Sketchbook of the Civil War*, Plate 32, mislabeled as having been taken in May 1863, was actually taken in early June.

2. William A. Frassanito, *Grant and Lee: The Virginia Campaigns 1864–1865* (New York: Charles Scribner's Sons, 1983), pp. 99–101.

3. Ibid., 50.

4. Ibid., 61–98.

5. Ibid., 99–108.

6. Ibid.

7. Ibid., 127–149; specific photos cited are on pp. 149, 133, and 137.

8. Ibid., 116–121.

9. See LC–B811–730, LC–B815–731, and LC–B815–732 at http://lcweb2.loc.gov/pp/cwpquery.html.

10. "Register of the Names and Employment of Citizens other than Sutlers, Agents and Purveyors Doing Business with the Army of the Potomac," Record Group 393, Part I, Entry 4075, Book 83.

11. Frassanito, *Grant and Lee*, pp. 174–193; specific photos cited are LC–B811–2432 and LC–B811–2433.

12. Ibid., 207–215; specific photo cited is LC–B815–781.

13. Davis, *Barnard*, p. 63.

14. Ibid., 63–75.

15. Zeller, *Civil War in Depth*, pp. 80–81; digital reproduction of courthouse image in author's files, original sold 13 December 2001 for $637.99 on eBay internet auction site.

16. "Editorial Department," *American Journal of Photography*, 15 September 1863, p. 143.

17. Big Black River battlefield image is LC–B815–1056. All images accessible through "Pywell" word search at http://lcweb2.loc.gov/pp/cwpquery.html; William C. Davis, ed., *Image of War 1861–1865*, vol. 4: *Fighting for Time* (Garden City, NY: Doubleday & Company, Inc., 1983), pp. 61–80.

18. Charles East, "A Yankee in Dixie: Baton Rouge Photographer A. D. Lytle," *Touched by Fire: A Photographic Portrait of the Civil War*, vol. 1, William C. Davis, ed. (Boston: Little, Brown and Company, 1985), pp. 197–232; Miller, *Photographic History of the Civil War*, 1:44.

19. Wes Cowan owned in 2005 two I. W. Crater views of "Morgan's Raiders at Camp Douglas;" digital copies in author's files; *Philadelphia Photographer*, July 1865, p. 116; William Brey, *John Carbutt: On the Frontiers of Photography* (Cherry Hill, NJ: Willowdale Press, 1984), p. 38; *Philadelphia Photographer*, September 1864, p. 175.

20. Davis, *Barnard*, pp. 63, 65.

21. OR, Series I, vol. 32, part 3, p. 434.

22. Ibid., 504.

23. O. M. Poe letter of 26 April 1864 to M. C. Meigs, "Photography" subfile, Quartermaster General's Consolidated Correspondence File, RG 92, Box 815, NARA.

24. Davis, *Barnard*, p. 75.

25. Ibid., 78

26. Ibid., 78–79.

27. Images available from "Atlanta" word search at http://lcweb2.loc.gov/cgi-bin/query; specific images cited are LC–B811–3581, 3665, 2715, 2718, 2712, 3671, 3611, 3630.

28. Davis, *Barnard*, p. 89.

29. Davis, *Barnard*, p. 93; Teal, *Partners with the Sun*, p. 84.

30. Henry Hitchcock Diary, entry for 6 December 1864, Manuscript Division, LC.

31. "Our Art in Rebeldom—The Latest News from Dixie," *American Journal of Photography*, 1 May 1864, pp. 502–503; "Confederate Papers Relating to Citizens or Business Firms," Microfilm M 346 (arranged in alphabetical order by surname of citizen or business), NARA; Anne J. Bailey and Walter J. Fraser Jr., *Portraits of Conflict: A Photographic History of Georgia in the Civil War* (Fayetteville, AR: University of Arkansas Press, 1996), pp. 3–4.

32. William Marvel, "The Andersonville Artist: The A. J. Riddle Photographs of August 1864," *Blue & Gray*, August 1993, pp. 18–23. The Andersonville images are widely reproduced. See also Davis, ed., *Image of War, Fighting for Time*, pp. 433–437; or Miller, *Photographic History*, 7:175–180.

33. Marvel, "Andersonville Artist," p. 18. Marvel suggests images were taken August 16, not August 17, because of the accuracy of Kellogg's diary in dating other Andersonville events.

34. Ibid. The images were among the most requested by correspondents of Civil War photograph collector Albert Ordway in 1885–1886. Letters are preserved in the Ordway correspondence file, MOLLUS collection, US Army Heritage and Education Center, Carlisle, PA.

35. William A. Gladstone, "Civil War Photo Maps," *Military Images*, September and October 1982, pp. 16–19.

36. Miller, *Photographic History*, 8:23.

37. OR, Series 1, vol. 17, part 2, p. 286.

38. OR, Series 3, vol. 3, part 1, p. 1136; OR, Series 1, vol. 36, part 1, p. 235.

39. Gladstone, "Civil War Photo Maps," p. 16; OR, Series 1, vol. 43, part 2, pp. 947–948.

40. "Government Photography," *The Philadelphia Photographer*, July 1866, p. 214.

41. John A. Martini, "Search and Destroy," *American Heritage*, November 1992, p. 98.

42. Ibid., 98–103; OR, Series 1, vol. 50, part 2, pp. 925, 929.

43. OR, Series 1, vol. 46, part 2, pp. 59–60.

44. NARA RG 153, Records of the Judge Advocate Generals' Office (Army), entry 15, Court-Martial Case File II847. Statistics compiled by the Index Project, Inc., which has indexed all 75,962 cases. Contact civilwarjustice@ aol.com.

45. NARA RG 153, entry 15, Case file KK461.

46. NARA RG 153, entry 15, Case file OO1302.

47. Ibid.

48. OR, Series 1, vol. 33, part 1, pp. 178–179.

49. Ibid., 180.

50. Stephen W. Sears, "The Dahlgren Papers Revisited," *Columbiad*, Winter 1999, accessible online in 2005 at http://www.thehistorynet.com/acw/bldahlgrenpapersrevisited/.

CHAPTER 10. THE END FINALLY COMES

1. Long and Long, *Day by Day*, pp. 598, 603, 607, 610–612.

2. See LC-B811-2635, 2636, 2637, 2639, 2640 at http://lcweb2.loc.gov/pp/cwpquery.html.

3. Coonley, "Photographic Reminiscences," pp. 311–312, and "Veteran's Note-Book," pp. 105–108.

4. Keith Davis, "A Terrible Distinctness," pp. 164–165.

5. Anthony, "Catalogue of Card Photographs," was issued to the public and offered photographs by mail. *Cartes de visite* were 25 cents each; four-by-six-inch "extra size" card photographs were 50 cents each.

6. Anthony, "Catalogue of Card Photographs," 1864 edition (New York: E. & H. T. Anthony & Co., December 1864), p. 20.

7. Davis, *Barnard*, pp. 88–90; Coonley, "Veteran's Note-Book," p. 107; Frassanito, *Grant and Lee*, p. 21; Letter of 6 April 1865 from E. & H. T. Anthony & Co. to M.C. Meigs, "Photography" subfile, RG 92, Box 815, NARA; Anthony, "New Catalogue of Stereoscopes and Views."

8. Cobb, "Brady's Photographic Gallery," p. 29.

9. "Brady & Co.'s Catalogue of Photographs and Stereoscopes of Lt. Gen. Grant's Late Campaign, June 1864," filed at E 468.7 in the stacks of the Prints and Photographs Reading Room, LC. The catalogue offered 81 large format images at $1.50 each; 54 medium format photos at $1.00 each; and, at 50 cents each, 84 stereo views and four card photographs; Cobb, "Brady's Photographic Gallery," p. 29.

10. Ross J. Kelbaugh, *Directory of Civil War Photographers*, 3 vols. (Baltimore, MD: Historic Graphics, 1990), compiled from license records. The fee was $10 for photographers with annual receipts less than $500; $15 for receipts of $500 to $1,000, and $25 for more than $1,000. For more on the Civil War "sun tax," visit Bruce Baryla's "The Civil War Sun Picture Tax" Web site accessible in 2005 at http://www.pipeline.com/~ciociola/baryla/civilwar.htm. Sun tax revenue stamps are common and have little value, but their presence (or evidence of their former presence) on the backs of *cartes de visites* and stereo views definitively date the images to 1866 or earlier.

11. "Current Literature," *The Nation*, 17 August 1865, pp. 219–200.

12. A. J. Russell, "Photographic Reminiscences of the Late War," *Anthony's Photographic Bulletin*, July 1882, pp. 212–213.

13. Frassanito, *Grant and Lee*, p. 343.

14. Ibid., 345–364. Negatives are LC-B811-3175 through LC-B811-3191.

15. A number of original Gardner stereographs are dated 5 April 1865; "Views of Richmond," *Richmond Whig*, 7 April 1865 (at Mike Gorman's Civil War Richmond website accessible in 2005 at http://www.mdgorman.com).

16. "War Time Pictures," *Chicago Evening Post*, 11 February 1893; Townsend, "Still Taking Pictures," p. 26.

17. Coonley, "Veteran's Note-Book," p. 107.

18. Child, *Letters*, pp. 117, 139, 235, 265.

19. Ibid., pp. 339–342.

20. Based on review of Hamilton and Ostendorf, *Lincoln in Photographs*.

21. OR, Series I, vol. 46, part 2, p. 1319.

22. Ibid., Series I, vol. 46, part 3, p. 965.

23. Ibid.

24. Ibid., pp. 965–966.

25. Ibid.

26. "Gurney and Our Dead President," *Humphrey's Journal*, 15 May 1865, pp. 29–30.

27. Katz, *Witness to an Era: Gardner*, pp. 160–162.

28. Ibid., 162, 171.

29. Ibid., 164–171. Existing negatives are LC-B817-7769, 7770, 7772–7775, 7777–7781, 7783, 7784, 7786–7789, 7792, 7793.

30. Coonley, "Veteran's Note-Book," p. 107.

31. Katz, *Witness to an Era: Gardner*, pp. 177–179.

32. Ibid., 180.

33. Surviving negatives from the series, including four views taken before the hanging, are LC-B815-1287, LC-B817-7757–7760, 7795–7798.

34. Ibid., 197–201.

35. OR, Series II, vol. 8, part 1, pp. 339–340.

CHAPTER 11. THE YEARS AFTER THE WAR

1. *American Journal of Photography*, 15 April 1865, p. 479.

2. NARA RG 153, Records of the Judge Advocate Generals' Office (Army), entry 15, Court-Martial Case File MM 2040; Henry Kyd Douglas, *I Rode with Stonewall* (Chapel Hill, NC: University of North Carolina Press), pp. 336–337.

3. Douglas, *I Rode with Stonewall*, p. 339; Court-Martial Case File MM 2040 Trial Record.

4. Douglas, *I Rode with Stonewall*, pp. 348–349.

5. Cook Account Book, 1863–1864, Cook Collection, LC.

6. Ibid.

7. Ramsay, *Photographer*, pp. 72, 74; Long and Long, *Day by Day*, p. 640.

8. See card catalog and vertical files of Confederate notables in Cook Papers, Valentine; ca. 1880s gallery card of Anderson is part of the collection.

9. Ibid.

10. Cook's house on the battery appears shuttered but undamaged in an Anthony stereograph and other images taken in Charleston in April 1865; Ramsay, *Photographer*, pp. 78–79; Cook Account Book, 12 August 1865–11 January 1866, Cook Papers, Valentine.

11. Ibid.

12. *The Philadelphia Photographer*, June 1865; William A. Frassanito letter to the author, 19 February 2005.

13. *The Nation*, 6 July 1865, p. 31, 3 August 1865, p. 146,

and other 1865 issues; "New Catalogue of Stereoscopes and Views" (New York: E. & H. T. Anthony & Co., 1869), pp. 28–37. Brady, Gardner, and others successfully lobbied to have the stamp tax repealed in mid-1866.

14. A review of wartime and early postwar Civil War stereo views available on 2 March 2005 at the Web site of leading dealer, Jeffrey Kraus Photographic Antiques, showed sixty-two yellow-mount war views, fifty-eight orange-mount war views, thirteen Gardner's Gallery views, and nine views of other origins. See http://www.antiquephotographics.com/civilwarst.htm.

15. Based on review of Anthony stereo catalogs, 1865–1869, and one undated edition. Several Anthony stereo catalogs are on file at the Oliver Wendell Holmes Stereoscopic Research Library, 3665 Erie Ave., Cincinnati, Ohio 45208; John Waldsmith, *Stereo Views: An Illustrated History and Price Guide* (Radnor, PA: Wallace–Homestead Book Company, 1991), p. 155.

16. "Gardner's Photographs," *American Journal of Photography*, 15 July 1865, p. 33.

17. Alexander Gardner, *Gardner's Photographic Sketch Book of the Civil War* (Washington, DC: Philp & Solomons, 1866); soft-cover, half-tone reprint by Dover Publications, New York, NY, 1959.

18. Ibid.

19. Katz, *Witness to an Era: Gardner*, p. 276 (see reproduction of Ordway advertisement); "Photography" sub-file, Office of the Quartermaster General Consolidated Correspondence File 1794–1915, NARA RG 92, contains *Sketch Book* prospectus with newspaper reviews as well as Meigs transaction. The earliest review is from January 1866, but Philp & Solomons apparently published different editions, one dated 1865 and the other dated 1866. The first version was bound with a red leather cover, and each photographic page carried an "Incidents of the War" imprint and an 1865 copyright line. The second edition, in blue leather, used a different style for the photographic pages, each of which carried an 1866 copyright line.

20. Davis, *Barnard*, pp. 94–104.

21. Ibid.

22. Ibid.

23. Teal, *Partners with the Sun*, p. 119. Of the twenty-three apparent postwar images in Gardner's *Sketch Book*, eleven are dated in April 1865, eight in May, one in June, and three are undated.

24. "The Auction Block," Military Images, July–August 1999, p. 16, reported these prices, with buyer's premiums, for Civil War photography masterworks in a 12 May 1999 auction at Christie's East in New York: Barnard's *Photographic Views*, $43,700; Gardner's *Sketch Book*, $85,000; Russell's *U.S. Military Railroad Photograph Album*, with 117 albumen prints, $178,500. Civil War photography prices have continued to rise since then.

25. Horan, *Timothy O'Sullivan*, pp. 159, 161, 196–199; Katz, *Witness to an Era: Gardner*, pp. 235–255; "Andrew J. Russell Collection," Oakland Museum of California online exhibit accessible at http://www.museumca.org/global/history/collections_russell.html. John Carbutt was the first of the leading Civil War photographers to go West, photographing a Union Pacific Railway excursion in 1866. T. C. Roche photographed the railroad and Yosemite Valley in 1870–1871.

26. Davis, *Barnard*, p. 180; Teal, *Partners with the Sun*, pp. 116, 130, 134; Davis, *Barnard*, pp. 180–203.

27. Ramsay, *Photographer*, pp. 103–113.

28. Cobb, "Brady's Photographic Gallery," pp. 35–43.

29. Marder and Marder, *Anthony*, pp. 198, 199, 214, 155–161.

30. Horan, *Timothy O'Sullivan*, pp. 313–318; Katz, *Witness to an Era: Gardner*, pp. 264–265.

31. Marder and Marder, *Anthony*, pp. 261, 266–267, 291–298, 300. In 1901 the Anthony Company merged with the Scovill and Adams Co. (Scovill was the country's leading daguerreotype plate maker in the 1850s) and six years later reorganized as Ansco. Eventually, Ansco became a brand name for cameras and film for the GAF Corporation. The last link was broken when GAF surrendered to Kodak by dropping out of the photography business in 1977.

32. Panzer, *Brady and the Image of History*, pp. 21, 20; Cobb, "Brady's Photographic Gallery," p. 43; Davis, *Barnard*, p. 202; Ramsay, *Photographer*, p. 116.

CHAPTER 12. THE JOURNEY OF THE NEGATIVES

1. A. W. Greeley, "Introduction," *List of the Photographs and Photographic Negatives Relating to the War for the Union, Now in the War Department Library* (Washington, DC: Government Printing Office, 1897), p. 5; Katz, *Witness to an Era: Gardner*, p. 260.

2. Katz, *Witness to an Era: Gardner*, p. 259.

3. Foley, "Recollecting the Past," pp. 191–193.

4. Ibid.; Greeley, "Introduction," p. 8.

5. Francis Trevelyan Miller, "Martyrs on the Altar of Civilization," in *Original Photographs Taken on the Battlefield during the Civil War of the United States* (Hartford, CT: Edward B. Eaton, 1907), p. 9.

6. Ibid.; Marder and Marder, *Anthony*, p. 179; D. Mark Katz, "Albert Ordway: Our First Collector," *Incidents of the War*, vol. 2, no. 2 (Summer 1987): 24.

7. The date 1882 is printed on the title page of the first several volumes of the MOLLUS Massachusetts commandery collection, housed at the Army Heritage and Education Center (AHEC) in Carlisle, PA.

8. Letter of 28 November 1885 from W. F. Porter to Ordway, Ordway letter files, AHEC.

9. Letter of 4 May 1886 from George G. Meade to Ordway, AHEC.

10. Letter of 31 January 1886 from W. F. Hopkins to

Ordway, AHEC; James E. Taylor scrapbooks, Huntington Library, San Marino, CA.

11. Letter of 30 October 1885 from James E. Taylor to Ordway, AHEC.

12. "Memorial of Arnold A. Rand and Albert Ordway relative to a collection of photographic negatives illustrating the war of the rebellion," Misc. Document No. 19, U.S. Senate, 48th Congress, 2nd Session, 18 December 1884 (copy available at AHEC Library, E 468.7 R15).

13. "War Memories," *Catalogue of Original Photographic War Views* (Hartford, CT: Taylor and Huntington, 1890). Copy available at LC, Prints and Photographs Reading Room stacks, E 468.7 T24.

14. Waldsmith, *Stereo Views*, p. 155. Even though the stereoscopic era of American home entertainment did not reach its peak until the first decade of the twentieth century, the Taylor and Huntington series marked the first and only reissue of Civil War stereo views.

15. Williams, *Memorial War Book*, p. 3; Miller, "Martyrs on the Altar," p. 13.

16. Donald W. Smith, "West Hartford Man Owns Rare Camera Record of Civil War, Brady's 7000 Glass Negatives Originally Discovered in Attic," *Hartford Courant*, 11 February 1934, part 5, p. 1; Foley, "Recollecting the Past," *Brady and the Image of History*, Panzer, ed., p. 199; accession orders for purchase of the negatives on file in the Civil War photography subject files, Prints and Photographs Reading Room, LC.

17. Based on review by author of archival sleeves formerly used for negatives at LC.

18. Davis, *Image of War*, 1:9.

19. Numbers are based on a comprehensive review of all LC photographs available at http://lcweb2.loc.gov/pp/cwpquery.html. No wartime listings exist for groups of negatives preserved by NARA, so they cannot be audited as readily as the Gardner and Anthony "The War for the Union" images.

20. For more information on the Brady-Handy Collection and to review the images, visit LC Web site http://lcweb2.loc.gov/pp/brhcquery.html.

21. Letter of 22 January 1956 from Alton H. Keller, Chief, Exchange and Gift Division, to Roy Meredith, Brady-Handy Collection files, Prints and Photographs Reading Room, LC.

22. Ronald Rietveld, "Discovering the Last Lincoln Photograph," in *A Day with Mr. Lincoln: Essays in Honor of the Lincoln Exhibit at the Huntington Library* (Redondo Beach, CA: Rank and File Publications, 1994). Also available online in 2005 at http://showcase.netins.net/web/creative/lincoln/news/rietveld.htm. Rietveld went on to become one of the leading Lincoln scholars of our time and is professor emeritus of history at California State University–Fullerton.

23. Frassanito, *Early Photography*, p. vii.

24. Author's interviews with William A. Frassanito, 2 March and 9 March 2005; Gardner, *Sketch Book*.

INDEX

About the Author

BOB ZELLER is author of *The Civil War in Depth*, Volumes One and Two, groundbreaking stereoscopic photo histories of the Civil War. He is founder and president of The Center for Civil War Photography, Inc., a non-profit organization dedicated to the study, presentation, and preservation of all aspects of Civil War photography.